WESTERN BIRD HUNTING

The trademark Safari Press ® is registered with the U.S. Patent and Trademark Office and in other countries.

Mathewson, Worth.

Second edition

Safari Press Inc.

2000, Long Beach, California

ISBN 1-57157-209-0

Library of Congress Catalog Card Number: 00-100614

10 9 8 7 6 5 4 3 2 1

Readers wishing to receive the Safari Press catalog, featuring many fine books on big-game hunting, wingshooting, and sporting firearms, should write to Safari Press Inc., P.O. Box 3095, Long Beach, CA 90803, USA. Tel: (714) 894-9080 or visit our Web site at www.safaripress.com.

ACKNOWLEDGMENTS

The interest and aid of many people in forming *Western Bird Hunting* is greatly appreciated. Thanks are due Mr. Byron W. Dalrymple, Mr. Charles F. Waterman, Mrs. Ellen Trueblood, Mr. Bob Brister, and Ms. Caylee Richardson.

The chapter "Salt Marshes and Estuaries" was taken from the book *Window on the Sea* by Herbert L. Minshall with permission of the author and publisher, Copley Books, La Jolla, California.

"Ring Necked Pheasant", "Mountain Quail", and "Dusky Grouse" were taken from the book *Upland Game Shooting*, copyright 1944 by H. L. Betten. Permission granted by Alfred A. Knopf, Inc.

And thanks to Ms. Anne Poole, Editorial Administrator, *Field & Stream*, for her aid with author research regarding articles previously published in that magazine.

Art By:
Sherry Chadwell

CONTENTS

INTRODUCTION

On the evening of October 17th, 1805, at a point along the Snake River approximately seven miles from where it enters the mighty Columbia, Captain William Clark returned to camp followed by twenty Indians in three canoes. The fruits of his day's excursion were recorded in the Expedition's log: fish from the Indians in exchange for ribbons; several ducks of an unrecorded species that he had shot; and "several grouse". It was also noted that he: "also killed a prairie-cock, an animal of the pheasant kind, but about the size of a small turkey".

The "prairie-cock" was of course the sage grouse, which was recorded by the Expedition as being "found on the plains of the Columbia in great abundance". It was also noted that "the flesh of the cock of the plains is dark, and only tolerable in point of flavor, being not so palatable as that of either the pheasant or grouse."

The "pheasants" of Lewis and Clark journals were recorded as three: "the large black and white pheasant, the small speckled pheasant, and the small brown pheasant". The first two were really the same species, the Franklin's spruce grouse, only male and female. The "small" brown pheasant was the ruffed grouse.

The birds that Clark actually called grouse were *Tympanuchus phasianellus columbianus*, the Columbian sharp-tailed grouse. This western-most, pale-plumage race of sharp-tailed was a new bird to science prior to Clark's shots with his fowling piece on that October 17th. And like the prairie-cock, the bird was found in huge numbers on the plains of the Columbia down to a point that is now the city of The Dalles, Oregon.

At the time of the Lewis and Clark Expedition wildlife populations along the Eastern seaboard were beginning to feel the weight of increased human population. The bison and elk, which once roamed the mountains of states such as North Carolina, were gone, or very nearly so. The heath hen was starting to disappear from some of its native range in Massachusetts, New York, and New Jersey. The eastern-most flocks of passenger pigeons were falling in greater numbers to guns and nets. Even then, serious inroads were beginning to be made on the wild turkey in the Northeast.

Wildlife in the western U.S. wouldn't be subjected to such pressures until decades later, and in the case of some waterfowl and upland species, practically never. The grave mistakes perpetrated in the East served as lessons. The laws passed to correct the mistakes brought protection to western birds at a time when they too could have suffered gravely.

Obviously some did. Lewis and Clark's Columbian sharptail is now the most drastically reduced game bird in the West. Only a few token populations are left in Washington, Idaho, and western Montana. Also the band-tailed pigeon was shot to a dangerously low point at the turn of the century. And as in the rest of the nation there was a market hunting industry in the West. Perhaps the most intense was based around the California quail from San Francisco southward. The first Spanish settlers at San Diego noted that several tribes of Indians—the Miwok, Pomo, Maidu, and Patwin—were professional quail hunters. These tribes actively traded their catch with other tribes for acorns and other meat.

The Miwok tribe was especially known for the innovative "quail fences" that they laboriously built. Some were a half mile long. These fences were built by driving stakes into the ground, then interweaving brush to form a solid barrier about three feet high. There were small openings left, spaced about five feet apart, and at each of these was a snare made from the Indians' hair. Sometimes during a year as many as fifty quail a day were taken.

Commencing in the late 1860's and reaching its zenith in the late 1880's, the California quail was pursued also by white market hunters. In a roughly twenty year period hundreds of thousands of quail were sent to market in Los Angeles and San Francisco, selling for fifty cents to $1.75 per dozen. Many were also shipped live to the markets in the East. In 1901 a law was passed to end this market killing of quail.

Waterfowl too were hunted for market. Again, most hunting took place in California—at such places as Tule Lake, and along the coastal estuaries. The principal market was the hotels and shops in San Francisco. Here residents could buy almost any species, or be selective as was Jack London. For a portion of his life he made a habit of eating a *raw* duck daily, but specified that it must be a canvasback.

But speaking generally, the western waterfowl and upland species were not dealt as heavy pressure as their eastern counterparts. In part this was due to the fact that the real influx of settlers into the West didn't commence until the 1880s. Then roughly twenty years later laws were passed to protect wildlife. Another reason lies in the wealth of big game species found in the western states. Westerners became big game hunters on the whole. This is evident to this day. The large sportsman shows based largely around deer and elk draw huge crowds each year. However a promoter wouldn't give a second thought to staging something similar based on bird hunting.

Lastly, the West encompasses a huge land area, a lot of it still with a low human population. When viewing the awesome, and disheartening, urban sprawl in a state such as North Carolina, it is indeed a morale boost to return to Oregon where you are assured that with some species like the chukar you will be one of the very few to hunt in some areas that season. Or perhaps the *only* hunter for that year!

If one defines West as everything from the Rocky Mountains to the surf of the Pacific, there is a rather staggering number of species to be considered. Among North American upland and shore birds, only the woodcock and greater pinnated grouse are absent. The pigeons and doves are all here—bandtail, white-winged dove, mourning dove. The quail are complete: mountain, Mearn's, California, bobwhite, Gambel's, and scaled. The grouse include: ruffed, spruce, blue, sharptail, sage, lesser pinnated, and the ptarmigan—white-tailed (and in Alaska rock and willow).

There are native Merriam's wild turkey as well as the introduced Rio Grande race. Lesser sandhill cranes can be hunted in several states. Snipe are gratifyingly abundant in certain locations as breeding birds and fall migrants. Sora and Virginia rails are legal in some states, but the western clapper rail (unlike its eastern kin) is a rare and protected bird.

The introduced birds include the ring-necked pheasant, gray partridge, chukar, snow partridge, and red-legged partridge. And Hawaii offers yet another opportunity to bag exotics.

There are no black ducks, but the waterfowl are nearly complete, and there are a few species such as the cinnamon teal found only in the West. In the past we have had some unique species included in the bags. As the bobolink was once prized as a game bird in areas along the Atlantic seaboard, or the robin and meadowlark in the deep South, the white-faced ibis was once avidly pursued by western hunters, and called a "giant curlew".

Because of the previously mentioned enthusiasm over big game, and other factors, one species deemed the King over all in the East—the ruffed grouse—hardly draws attention in the West. This fact is puzzling because in some regions of Idaho, Washington, and Oregon this outstanding game bird can be amazingly abundant during high cycle years. The lone exception regarding this grouse could be found on Vancouver Island, British Columbia. There the waterfowling was limited almost entirely to black brant, and only two upland birds were native, the blue and ruffed grouse. This island was largely settled by English stock, of whom many had been bird hunters in their native land. Vancouver Island holds good populations of ruffed grouse, and there developed a ruffed grouse hunting fraternity along the lines associated with the eastern states.

The islanders call the species "willow grouse", and keenly pursue it during the fall months. Roderick L. Haig-Brown, while best known as an angler, also hunted grouse for a period of his life. He used black Labs for his grouse dogs. Mr. Skate Hames, one of Haig-Brown's hunting partners, once recounted past hunts during an interview. According to Hames, one of Haig-Brown's Labs proved to be an excellent grouse dog in terms of finding birds in thick cover and flushing them. But unfortunately the dog also developed a taste for birds.

"We would drop a bird, and Rod would have to run like hell to beat the dog to it," Hames recalled smiling.

In comparison to the East the western region produced very few personalities noted for bird hunting. In fact, when one considers eastern writers and hunters such as Ray P. Holland, Burton L. Spiller, John C. Phillips, Nash Buckingham, Archibald Rutledge, Havilah Babcock, Corey Ford, and George Bird Evans along with an impressive list of others, the western writers seem scant indeed. But we had some, and they were excellent. H. L. Betten was perhaps foremost. Rather amazingly he hunted ring-necked pheasant on the first day of the first season held in the U.S. This was in Oregon's Willamette Valley near Albany, Oregon in the early 1890s. Then sixty years later he was still writing about western bird hunting.

Ted Trueblood, who was active in all outdoor pursuits—especially fishing, as he served for a period as FIELD & STREAM's Fishing Editor prior to A. J. McClane—was also a noted bird hunter. Certainly one of the most interesting articles he ever wrote encompassed his quail hunting in Idaho from the late 1920s into the 1970s. As a boy Trueblood hunted the introduced bobwhite in the farm lands around his parents' farm. This bird was common in the Boise Valley until after World War II when it declined, then disappeared. When he was older he hunted mountain quail in the foothills. These too declined a few years after the bobwhite. But starting in the 1950s Trueblood noticed a marked increase in California quail. This species spread into Idaho both by natural expansion of range and limited introduction. Thus, Trueblood's article proved to be an unique record of fifty years of quail hunting with three different species before the dog.

Frank Dufresne also began writing in the depression era. For many years he lived in Alaska, and some of the better accounts of hunting in that wilderness carried his by-line. He later moved to Washington, and covered a great deal of the West Coast.

Westerners are indeed proud that Charles F. Waterman has elected to live part of the year in Montana over the past several decades. Anyone familiar with Waterman's writing on bird hunting, the birds themselves, and the dogs, would likely agree that he is the best in the business, both viewed from his actual time spent in the field, and his superb accounts of these days.

While we don't have woodcock, nor do we have black ducks, we do frankly have a wealth of other species every bit as good. And we in the West have a rather boggling variety. For example, if one wishes, one can hunt himself to a standstill in a few short months. Using Oregon as a home base the field array could look something like this: the big blue grouse in late August in the huckleberry patches of the Cascade Mountains, quickly followed by Labor Day mourning dove hunting. Or perhaps a trip down to Arizona for whitewings. Then ruffed grouse in early September over on the Oregon-Idaho border. This would be followed by band-tailed pigeons and mountain quail in the coastal mountains in mid-September.

Then over to Montana around the first of October for sharptail and sage grouse along with gray partridge. Then back into Oregon for the mid-October chukar, pheasant, California quail and waterfowl opening. The last of October, all of November and December belong to ducks, geese, and snipe. Side trips during this time frame can be made down to New Mexico for lesser pinnated grouse, or into Wyoming for sandhill cranes. Alaska has ptarmigan for a trip, and brant season opens around Christmas. After the first of the year the chukar hunting can still be very good. Or if there is motivation left a trip down to Arizona can be made for Gambel's, scaled, and Mearn's quail. Finally there is spring gobbler season in April. And a few short months later it is time to do it all once again!

In selecting articles for this collection, I tried to seek out a blend. First, as many western species as possible. Then both historical and present day accounts of hunting the West. Finally, articles and book chapters written by those who best represent the talent western based. It is to be hoped that this effort will be met with approval. And it is hoped that the reader will deduce—we in the West are fortunate!

Worth Mathewson
Salem, Oregon 1989

Ring-Necked Pheasant
by H. L. Betten

    H. L. Betten was active in the field beginning in the late 1800s. This book chapter is the recount of the first legal day in the U.S. for ring-necked pheasant. He was hunting within sight of the location where the first birds were released, Peterson Butte, near Lebanon, Oregon. The year was 1892.

He gets up with a rush—lets loose a couple of cackling curses and heads off in any old direction that will lead him to safety, long tail streaming back like a meteor, head proudly erect.

That's the ring-necked pheasant. He was brought here from Asia by way of Oregon on the Pacific Coast and from England by way of Long Island on the Atlantic Coast. Of course he's a foreigner, but he is the noblest, most enduring, most sportsmanlike imported game bird that America ever saw or our sportsmen ever crumpled in the field.

My first experience with ring-necks goes back to 1892 and that is only ten years later than the date when Judge Owen N. Denny, American Consul General at Shanghai, ordered the release of the first Chinese pheasants on the old Denny Estate almost within the shadow of Peterson's Butte in Oregon.

Since then I have hunted them in many states and have learned to admire their high sporting qualities as well as respect their unusual table qualities.

Today ring-necks are being hunted in a great many states in the Union and they have done extremely well except in certain parts of the deep South.

And, it is an odd thing that the ring-necks of basic Chinese pheasant stock which spread across the United States from the Pacific Coast have more readily been acclimated that the older type of the English pheasant which was brought here from Europe.

No matter where you go, whether it be along the irrigation ditches of the Northwest, or among the swales of the Dakotas, or the hills of New Jersey and New York, this stately brilliantly hued bird that may run as high as four to five and a half pounds in weight has come to enjoy the companionship of man and bask in the soft rays of the sun of civilization. In other words, the ring-necked pheasant is a semi-domesticated creature. He will approach to within a few yards of the ranch house. He will fight with the chickens and will enjoy leading the average untrained dog a wild chase—just for the fun of it.

There is very little difference between the ring-neck hunting of today and the sport I enjoyed nearly a half century ago. The birds haven't changed their habits; methods of the chase are identical. On that trip of a long time past, we pulled into the pretty little Willamette town of Albany very early on a September morning. We had been routed out of our warm berths by a unfeeling porter and were left standing on the station platform with our luggage while the train hissed away from us into the distance. Except for a couple of shadowy railway employees, the station was deserted. There was to have been a wagon and a driver waiting, but the rig was completely absent.

2

"That's strange," said my companion, Uncle John. "Charlie Loud's letter stated plainly enough that he would have the outfit here; wonder what's wrong?"

"Maybe he was expecting us on the afternoon train," I offered. Then I added, "Seems to me this is a crazy hour to arrive in a strange land for a wedding or a funeral or a shooting expedition. Why, dawn hasn't broken yet; sure you didn't mistake the directions?"

That made Uncle John mad. It was a mean crack and stung him like a whiplash.

"Thunderation, no!" he flung back at me heatedly—his snow white mustache bristling. "I can still read plain English, can't I? If there's any mistake, son, it's not on my shoulders."

So to relieve his soul, he began pacing up and down the platform muttering under his breath.

Well, it wasn't long before we heard the rattle of wheels in the distance and a farm wagon tooled leisurely up to the station. The driver complacently got down from the seat and ambled over to us.

"You be the gents that Charlie Loud sent after?" he drawled in a slow Missourian sort of way. "I thought so; I'd a been here a little sooner but my woman was a mite late in rousin' me this mawnin'; and I had a few chores to look after too. But they's plenty time. Don't resh—that's what I always say. Don't resh. Take it easy like and you'll get jest as far in the end. Them's my motto and she's a good one. Well, hop in gents and we'll mosey along."

We rolled down the road as the light began to crack in the east and after a while in leisurely Oregon fashion the autumnal sun climbed over the ramparts of the Cascades to usher in a new, and, for us, a perfect day. The sorrel team, full of ginger and life on the homeward trek, tugged at the reins and we swept along in a tremendous cloud of dust. For mind you, this was long before the days of the improved roads, and in the late summer of the Pacific Coast there was dust on the highways, and then some.

Great level expanses of grain and pasture, the Willamette River winding between dark-hued wooded banks, like a silver artery, the meadow streams lined with willows veining the dun wheat stubble, the great patches of irrepressible reddish maroon goat-weed on the knolls and in the distance hemming in this broad, beautiful valley, the mighty Cascade Range and his sister the Coast Range, rising from the foothills, ridge upon ridge of green and timbered up to the snow line. Then the crest of ghost-like snow-covered peaks with an alpine contour.

In short, my brothers of the open ways, that early morning scenery was tremendous.

Uncle John and I drank in and breathed in the glory of the picture and as the light grew stronger and objects started to stand out, we began to pick up details of the terrain. Remember that this was back in those distant days when the ring-necked pheasant was something new. Each of us wanted to catch our first glimpse of this remarkable blazing creature which within a generation was to write new history in wildlife. John had shot the familiar English pheasant on the other side of the water. This is the less colorful bird which for centuries, I suppose, had been a common sight on English and Irish estates. The Chinese pheasant was something new to both of us.

The driver of our rig had been telling us plenty about the rapid increase of the ring-necks in the Willamette Valley and revealed that although the birds had been under protection of the state, native residents were not above knocking a few of them off now and then for table use.

"They ain't no law kin stop a man protectin' his crops," he explained. "So, when my woman wants a morsel and they ain't no beef or venison hanging in the wood shed, why I get out my old 44 Winchester and snaps the head offen a couple of 'Chinks.' Naturally I hates to waste ketridges on sich small fry, but it's cheaper at that 'en choppin' off the head of a rooster."

Then he hesitated and pointed off to the side of the road. "Look yander. See those kinder pickets stickin' up in the stubble field that a way? Them's 'Chinks.' This year's hatch most likely. D'you wanter take a crack at 'em?"

John and I wanted to pile out of the wagon right then and there, but the chap who was handling the reins was wiser than we and knew more about pheasants than we did.

"Keep your shirts on," he said. "Jes' you get your guns ready while I drive on a piece and let you off behind that bunch of brush up there. If you got offen here every last one of them birds would beat to the thickets. The thing is to fool 'em. Keep behind cover and work around behind 'em betwixt them and the woods."

We started to work that strategy, but they were smart and maybe we were a bit careless. At any rate, before we could head off the pheasants they took alarm, flushed and flew to a brushy hollow off to the side. All except one big cock bird which had remained behind. He flushed when we drew near to him and he sailed off into the thick stuff after the rest of the tribe. In his lonesome flight he was glorious, thrilling. We spread out a bit and headed for the swale, our nerves tense. John was a marvelously quick shot, about the best all-around shot I ever met, but he was high-strung when he was in the field.

4

Suddenly, off to one side I saw John wheel and a handsome cock rose swiftly. In the still morning air I heard the initial flutter, then the whirring of wings as the big fellow rocketed from the weeds, and almost simultaneously an unearthly cackling. Just as he reached the crown of his rise and before he leveled off John nailed him. He crumpled at the sharp crack of the Schultze powder, which was a novelty in that era; he fell loosely and hit the sod with a thump.

The report of the shotgun roused two more birds. A long-tailed fellow rattled out of cover at my very feet and rose with pounding wing beats in a desperate effort to get away. To me it has always seemed that the shock of a flushing ring-neck is similar to the startled reaction when you get too close to a buzzing rattlesnake. It seems to put a mental hang-fire on my brain machinery. I was paralyzed—victim of some nightmare and unable to pull the trigger. But I came to my senses in the nick of time and my right barrel spoke spitefully with a nitric acid accent. The Asiatic bird folded up in a mist of feathers and came crashing down. He was still spasmodically strumming his wings when I grabbed him, held him aloft and shouted, "I've got my first 'Chink'!"

Don't forget that this was a prelude, an unscheduled performance to the big doings of a great day; a little scene enacted in the early morn before we had reached our destination. Also remember that this was back in 1892, the initial open season on pheasants in America.

Our hunting trip along the Willamette that year lasted three days and, if I recall rightly, we killed sixty-seven pheasants between us. I have a very distinct recollection of bagging twenty-nine birds with thirty-eight shells. John was really a great shot and his average was better.

I am mentioning these things because I want to bring out the point that ring-necked pheasants had been released only a decade before and yet in that comparatively short span the introduced birds had multiplied so rapidly that they were prevalent—almost pestilent.

I also want to bring this out—we used two and three-quarter drams of Schultze powder and seven-eighths of an ounce of No. 7 chilled shot in 16-gauge guns. Today thousands of pheasant hunters are shooting super-guns and loads with shot as large as No. 4.

A super-load is all right, but the average trained gunner is going to kill his birds cleaner with a charge of No. 7 shot than No. 4 shot. I don't care whether you are using No. 4, 5 or 6 shot with an extra dose of powder and a long shell, you are not going to bring down a ring-neck unless that bird is within range. I don't know of any bird that can carry away so much lead fired at long range as the pheasant.

The greatest pheasant hunters are the men who will blast the bird at close range and who will aim at the head. These are the boys who have learned the art of leading a ring-neck and the moment that the muzzle of the gun blots out the showy head of the ascending rocket, press the trigger. Which means that the charge is concentrated in the vital spot—the head and neck, and the kill is quick and merciful.

Within recent months, students of conservation of the Pennsylvania State College made a survey of pheasant shooting. They discovered that inexperienced sportsmen recovered only sixty-five per cent of the birds they hit, while the more skillful shooters got eighty-five per cent. That's just the difference between the dub who will fire a couple of charges after a ring-neck that obviously is out of range and the chap who knows and refuses to waste ammunition or needlessly wound a noble game bird.

You and I who go ring-neck shooting understand that it is a big bird, almost the size of a large chicken. Even at fifty yards it is a big target and a tempting one, but I have seen men shoot at the target at seventy yards; I have seen feathers knocked out. I have seen the bird continue in its flight.

It may sound absurd, but I've come to believe that pheasant hunters should be compelled to use dogs. Preferably the dog should be a competent pheasant dog, adept at the business. But at his worst he should be a good retriever, capable of finding a winged bird even though it runs off a long distance, or another bird mortally wounded but with sufficient strength to crawl into some hiding place and die.

On that trip to the Loud home, we reached the ranch house about eight o'clock and there met a neighboring farmer, Elmer Raemer, who had planned to put in the day hunting with us. We were introduced also to a pair of beautiful Llewellyn setters of the old type, strong in the blood of Druid, Count Noble, Gladstone and other outstanding field dogs. Belva and Nellie splendidly upheld their high lineage.

Our hunting ground that first day was in the basin of Soap Creek about ten miles west of Albany and approximately the same distance north of Corvallis. It isn't any wonder that the ring-necks took to that country so readily and multiplied so rapidly. As we know it today, it held everything that the ideal pheasant country needs. There were damp swales, there were thickets, there were weedy fields, plenty of wheat stubble, and here and there patches of woods.

We were on the hunting ground by eleven o'clock, John and I raring to go.

"There's no need to rush it," said Charlie Loud. "You native sons will get a bellyful before the day is done, and besides, in this section we get our best shooting during the middle of the day and in the afternoon.

6

In the early morning hours, those old roosters are fresh and lively and they have their running shoes on. Their feet are itchy and they can run like blazes unless there is a wise and a fast bird dog to head them off.

"Along about noon," he continued, "the birds begin to get tired, or maybe just plain lazy. They take to the cool, damp spots and seek thick cover; they hate like the devil to move out of these comfortable hiding places. They stick so doggone close that you need a keen-nosed dog to muzzle them out. Actually at times I've had to lift a close lying 'Chink' with my boot to make him get up. Along about three-thirty in the afternoon the birds begin to stir about; they are intent upon feeding. When we come across them on a feeding ground they'll squat and hide instead of running away. The air is cool and the scent hangs at just the right height for the dogs to do their best work."

Elmer Raemer confirmed this and added that prior to the open season the farmers in the district had slipped out now and then to get a mess of pheasants. At that time it was legal to kill hen pheasants as well as the cock birds, but despite this the tribe increased rapidly. In these modern days, the hen pheasants are protected in nearly all states although there is a strong tendency in many sections of the country to permit the shooting of an equal number of male or female ring-necks.

Pheasant hunting is more than a knack. You must know how to hunt them and you must study their habits. I have known men with such an uncanny sense that they have been able to walk into a field and go straight to where pheasants were hiding. That wasn't an accident. The men were real hunters.

Same thing with dogs. Charlie Loud had advised us not to bring our own bird dogs along on the trip. His two setters, Belva and Nellie, had been "brought up" on ring-necks and knew how to handle them.

Any man who is an experienced pheasant hunter is familiar with the habit of this bird to run long distances through stubble, brushy fields or low woods in order to evade the gunner. Your pheasant hunter also knows that birds may be running ahead of him and they will not take flight until they come to a break in the field. This may be a piece of plowed ground, or it may be only a road (by no means infallibly), but when that bird reaches the end of the thick stuff instead of dashing across the open space he is likely to take to his wings.

A good dog knows this too, and the best trained pheasant dogs are those which will head off the running pheasants.

Charlie Loud's setters figuratively tied those foxy ring-necks into knots. They were fast, wide and stylish, ranging in perfect form. For the first time in my life, I that day came to understand that the real pheasant dog is in a class by himself. I knew that my own dogs would have bungled the job. Charlie Loud's Llewellyns nailed the ring-necks almost infallibly; were staunch on the point and were steady in backing up. They often drew a hundred yards or more on game in the stubble and in the grassy swales.

It was a remarkable sight to watch those setters trailing a running bird. One of the setters would circle, race down on a side line and almost in a flash head off the rapidly moving ring-neck—hang an anchor around the bird, so to speak.

Maybe "Honest" John Davidson would have called this business of heading off ring-necks "blinking." At any rate he called Count Noble a blinker when that grand setter pulled the same trick on running prairie chickens. "Honest" John Davidson was a top-notch sportsman but with a vein of prejudice, I'm afraid. Or possibly, like many other old timers, he may have known only the dog that was trained to close lying birds like the quail, or the woodcock, although I doubt that.

In my estimation, it was prejudice that made him refer to this habit of Count Noble's as "blinking." For my part, I'd never criticize or penalize any dog if he broke point in order to corner sprinting birds. Why? Simply because the dog that can do that is exercising his brain, displaying strategy and giving an exhibition of high class performance. The years have come and gone and now the sportsmen who once looked only for appearance and style in a setter or pointer or a springer have broadened their viewpoint and come to the fundamental, for, after all, the crucial test of a field dog is whether he can competently find birds, hold birds, retrieve birds. They can rant all they please about ring-necks being the ruination of good bird dogs, but I contend that it has been the ring-neck that has helped to develop the highest type of the American hunting dog, setters, pointers and spaniels. And, as one proof of this, I refer to the fact that the greatest springers in the world are now coming out of districts where ring-necks are plentiful and smart. Because it takes a mighty intelligent bird dog to pin down a cute, wily old pheasant.

I recall one swale along a creek in the Willamette Valley which was a veritable nest for pheasants. There was a swampy corner covered with rushes which later had been broken down into a tangled mass by cattle or other stock. Long, coarse slough grass, rose briers and little clumps of stunted willows, together with alder, provided a combination of cover that fairly reeked with game.

It was a caution the way those well-trained setter dogs raced for that particular spot. And it was a thrilling sight to watch them as they made short side casts to try out the wind and, approaching from different directions, came to simultaneous points.

8

"This is sure enough town hall," Charlie Loud warned us. "There's likely to be a wad of 'Chinks' sticking in there. Get between the dogs and the heavy stuff yonder. You two fellows put up the birds and Elmer and me'll scatter out behind and cut 'em off from the brush if they come out toward us."

John and I walked in cautiously about ten yards apart. The dogs hadn't budged an inch, they were frozen like statues, a sure sign that the birds were tight among the rushes. We shuffled up gently. I kept feeling for sound footing in the damp ground, my eyes glued ahead. We reached the dense cover and started to kick and stamp, but nothing moved. I pushed ahead into the rushes.

Then the whole reed patch seemed to sway and weave and there was a mighty explosion, a roar of wings and out poured a stream of ringnecks—not in one solid mass but a straggling trail, for all the world like a string of firecrackers popping off in staccato rapidity. Actually the air was full of whirling forms.

It's a wonder we didn't go berserk and blast away in helter-skelter fashion. In order to cool down, I did pass up a couple of easy shots but two cock birds and a hen pheasant rocketed up in a trio so close together that you could have thrown a blanket over them. I smacked down the first rooster and he fell like a clod. Then just as his side kick companion was shifting into high gear, my Lancaster cracked again and the shot reached out and toppled him over.

In a number of central and eastern states, those two male birds brought down within the space of seconds would have constituted the day's limit, but don't forget that this was back in 1892 and the limit was plenty more than a brace of birds.

Had I been wise in that volcanic center, I would have followed the advice of Uncle John who used to say, "Listen; after firing both shells in your gun, grab a fresh shell and hold it in your right hand as you flip out the empties; that's the exact moment when many a bird will stage a getaway."

Well, I flipped out the shell and I went through the useless gesture of blowing smoke out of the barrels, and at that very instant the biggest and longest tailed cock pheasant of my limited experience roared up from my very feet and with a joyous mocking jibe put a lot of air between him and me before you could say Jack Robinson. In that small area, Uncle John had hammered down two birds in short order. A few minutes later he got another cock bird as it curved around a patch of screening willows.

By one-thirty in the afternoon we were pretty well pegged out. It had grown warm and we were weighted down with those big birds. The

9

pace had been a fast one, stimulated as it was by the novelty of a new sport and the thrill of excitement. There was no violent protest on our part when Charlie Loud proposed that we rest awhile in the grateful shade of a convenient grove of alders and willows.

The air was unusually clear that historic afternoon, so clear that from where we sat several butte formations stood out prominently to the southwest. Pointing to the nearest one, Charlie Loud said: "That mountain over yonder is known as Peterson's Butte. It was there that Judge Denny turned loose the first batch of ring-necked pheasants that were to inaugurate a new sport." History relates that there were forty-seven Chinese pheasants in the batch released. A prior shipment had died but Judge Denny refused to become discouraged and sent the second lot across the Pacific. I have been told that it was about 1885 that the sportsmen were convinced that the ring-necks had taken hold in America. By 1887 they had spread the whole length and width of the Willamette Valley and had overflowed into several smaller valleys to the south. Then they crossed the Columbia and went marching into Washington.

The original forty-seven birds have increased into the millions today, and the gunners can thank former Consul General Denny for giving them one of the finest game birds in the world.

When the afternoon shadows had lengthened and the air began to turn chill, we swung back to the wagon by a circuitous route. We were tired, but we had had a marvelous day. Just as we were approaching the rig, one of the dogs caught scent of game in a thicket nearby and quickly went on a point. Charlie Loud and I went in and flushed the birds with the blessing of Uncle John who said, "Boys, I'm all bogged down. I pass. You have my proxy to whale whatever's in there. Go to it."

So Charlie and I flushed three young ruffed grouse and got them. Somehow, they were not very impressive. They were much smaller than the ring-necks and they lacked the brilliant color of the imported bird. We laid them beside the resplendent Chinese pheasants and then and there for the first time I caught a vision of what pheasant shooting meant to me and to future generations.

For just as truly as the sun rises in the morning, the ring-necked pheasant has risen to fill the hunter's sky with dazzling color and to save that noble native, the grouse.

East and west, north and south, wherever the grouse was to be found, it was being hunted almost to the point of extinction. Along the Atlantic Coast as far south as North Carolina, your ruffed grouse was so reduced in numbers that in self defense protective laws had to be thrown around it. In the Mississippi Valley, men had hunted the pinnated grouse—prairie chicken—so hard that only scattering specimens were left. In New Jersey, Long Island and Massachusetts, the heath hen, close cousin to the pinnated grouse, was passing out; today it is completely exterminated. The sharp-tailed grouse, the sage hen and the blue grouse were being terribly reduced in the foothills of the Rocky Mountains.

It seems almost providential that at this particular time a bird native to Asia and possessing high sporting qualities should be planted successfully in the United States, not only on the Pacific Coast, but in Montana, Idaho, Wyoming, the Dakotas, and straight across the continent to the very shores of the Atlantic.

As a sporting proposition, the ring-neck is a great game bird and supplies nearly all the thrills that a grouse can give. It is a larger bird than the grouse, with a delicious, slightly less gamey, flavor. It can be raised on game farms and brought up in nurseries by the tens of thousands; protected for a couple of years it will take root and if the hens are guarded from game hogs, and a reasonable bag limit is set up, it will provide wonderful sport for our army of hunters. The ring-necked pheasant has taken the pressure off the grouse and now the grouse itself is holding its own in favored lands with the prairie chicken displaying a great comeback.

It is in the fall of the year that our forests become glittering, radiant, iridescent, throbbing masses of color, and they match the splashes that set apart the ring-necked pheasant. You have the soft gold, the deep maroons, the burning crimson, the delicate shades of green, the flashes of white, the touches of blue, and even the spots of black—as vivid as any autumnal woodland scene you ever gazed upon.

The same districts where the ring-necks were originally introduced continue to support them in numbers. In New York State, places where experiments were made with ring-necks and which were successful are notable pheasant hunting districts today. Pennsylvania released its first ring-necks within sight of the City Hall tower of Philadelphia, and in that same district today more than a hundred thousand male birds are shot during the brief open season. All through the Pacific Northwest their range is extending. We found them on countless islands on the beautiful inland passage in British Columbia and in the Puget Sound region, on Vancouver Island, and along the Maritime mainlands.

The delta of the great Fraser River and the country around Ladner, British Columbia, are now providing wonderful pheasant shooting.

Ring-necks were so plentiful on some of the fine oat lands not far from Ladner that at the mere clapping of hands the birds would thunder out of the stubble by the scores, sometimes hundreds of them being in the air at once. It was in that Canadian section that "Judge" Macdonnell, Harry Rolston, Charley Cocking, Baron Tiedemann, Tom Williams, and many other fine and famous Canuck sportsmen enjoyed hunting. Also the British aristocrats and the remittance men, and the chaps who had been sent into western Canada to take them away from the temptations of wine and women, added a sprinkling of romance to the ring-neck hunting as variegated as the colors of the birds themselves.

Wonderful birds, wonderful hunting country, wonderful men. Once upon a time J. M. Avent, the great handler of bird dogs and famous as a breeder, confessed to me, "This ring-necked pheasant is a high class game bird and next to the prairie chicken it provides a more thorough test of a gun dog's natural qualities than any other game." That was a fair and accurate statement.

At one of the gun dog trials up in the pheasant country of the Northwest there was a native who was so proud of one animal he owned that he absolutely refused to see anything good in the actual contestants.

"They don't know what it's all about," he confided. "I only wish I had my old Napoleon dog here. He'd run these four-legged bums ragged. He was a dog, mister! He was a dog that knew how to handle pheasants. Yes sir, my old Napoleon dog, he just runs 'em around in circles, and he keeps runnin' 'em around until they get dizzy and fall over, and then he holds them down with his foot until I get there, and if they try to squeeze loose or I'm too long in coming up, why he just naturally sits down on 'em. I never saw such a dog. Thanks—I don't care if I do."

This was the same chap who had a remarkable gun that also became historic.

"That gun of mine; she's an Iver Johnston and I had her made to order—she's just got one barrel, and she's a single shot, and she's got a boundin' lock. She can shoot to hell and gone. There was two old Chinese pheasants riz up behind me once and they was seventy yards away before I ever could see 'em. That shows how fast they were. They only had about five yards to go to reach the brush. Well, gentlemen, I turned around and I swang on them two birds like lightning. Yes sir, I swang on them two birds with my old single-shot. Bang! bang! Just like that. Those two shots came so fast that they just sounded like one, and so help me, I knocked both them pheasants deader'n bent door nails. Gentlemen, I'm tellin' you, she's a *gun.*"

Well, pheasants were plentiful up in those parts at that time—still are. But just how that gent got those two loads through the lone barrel of that single-shot gun remains a mystery.

Even in that great country, and even in some of the great ring-neck country of the Dakotas and other states, there come days when you don't get very good shooting. I was with Tom Johnson of Winnipeg on a trip and I was anxious to show him some worthwhile shooting in order to repay that good sportsman for a stop-over he had made. But it was one of those days when things didn't break right. For more than an hour we tramped and worked and the dogs ranged over every likely spot and we drew a blank except for one old bird that flushed wild. Finally, Tom got mad and he began to cuss, and he wanted to know what kind of blankety-blank bloody game this was anyhow.

"You call these blankety-blank things game birds? Why they're nothing but long tailed buzzards! Let's quit!"

I never wanted to put up pheasants before in my life as much as I did that day. We were about ready to stop when we came to a low spot overgrown with blackberry vines, rose briers, willows, and weeds.

"There must be some birds in this place," I said. "Let's hunt this swale, and if it doesn't pan out, you can wait at the crossroad while I hike back and bring the car around to you."

We came up to the thicket and there stood one of the dogs, stiff as a poker on a beautiful point at the edge of the briers. As quick as Tom could amble over I placed him in a strategic position and then put the boot to the cover. It was a very good imitation of a raid on a gambling joint. Those citizens piled out of doors, windows and everything in one wild rush. The air was full of cackling pheasants. Tom brushed two of them down with as neat a double as I've ever seen; missed his third bird clean with both barrels; caught a fourth bird squarely.

On his return to Winnipeg, Tom sent me a letter in which he wrote, "I had those roosters served to me and they were done to the King's taste."

Ring-necks are increasing in every part of the United States. As I said before, they are being raised on state and private game farms by machine methods; that is, incubators and patented brooders. They can be turned out almost as rapidly as day-old chicks. Seth Gordon of Pennsylvania, who really knows his business, in a recent monograph gives us an idea of the way in which this magnificent imported game bird has taken root in the land.

"Approximately five million pheasants are bagged annually in the United States. South Dakota tops the list with a million to a million and a half cock pheasants annually. Next comes Minnesota with a million male birds. Nebraska, North Dakota, Iowa, Wisconsin and Illinois trail along not far behind. In the East, Pennsylvania tops the list with a quarter of a million male birds bagged annually; New York, 185,000, New Jersey, 100,000, Connecticut, 50,000, Massachusetts almost 40,000."

The ring-necked pheasant has many remarkable characteristics but there is none more so than its ability to hide where cover is scant. It has the uncanny faculty also of picking the most absurd and unlikely spots imaginable for cover. I have seen pheasants secrete themselves on a plowed field and other almost bare ground. Maybe your dog starts across this barren ground and you whistle to him and curse him for the fool he is, and order him back, and then suddenly you see that dog go into a point, and there in an apparently open spot, Mr. Ring-neck is waiting for you to flush him out. It is an actual fact that nine-tenths of all the ring-necks shot are flushed in comparatively open areas. The fields may be brushy, but the brush is not high. It is not very often that ring-necks are found in thick woods. The ring-necked pheasant is prolific and elastic. It has few bad faults and is a table delicacy second to none. It may be naturalized, but it surely is a good citizen.

The Mongolian Pheasant in Oregon
by Thomas G. Farrell

This article was published in 1898. It is interesting to read that mountain quail were then found on the floor of the Willamette Valley. This species is now only encountered in the foothills surrounding the valley, or much higher in the mountain regions.

To hear an Oregon Sportsman explain how his dog had trailed something across a field, and how at a certain point two "Chinamen" had broken cover only to be bowled over with a right and left, the uninitiated might think that murder had been done, but "Chinaman" is the sporting term for the pheasant, and in the western part of Oregon, where the picturesque Willamette threads its hundred miles or so through the beautiful and prolific valley of that name, they have pheasants. Not the partridge of our grandfathers (the ruffed grouse), but true members of the first families of the Orient.

From Mongolia, a province of China, came the forefathers of the pheasants of Oregon, and when one tries to dissect a very old and well-developed cock he will, perhaps, think some of the pioneers yet exist.

Many doubtless know of the existence of these birds in Oregon, and of the manner of their introduction, but for those to whom the facts are unknown I shall offer a few words of explanation.

Some twelve or fifteen years ago Judge Denny, a loyal citizen of Oregon, was United States Consul at the port of Shanghai, China.

The thought suggested itself to the Judge that, inasmuch as the climate of that section of China differed but little from that of Oregon and pheasants could be had in large numbers, it would be a capital idea to send some over to the Western world and liberate them on his fine wheat farm in Linn county. This idea was, at quite an expense and lots of trouble, eventually carried out. The Legislature kindly extended to the immigrants protection for a number of years, and now throughout the length and breadth of the Willamette valley there are thousands of these fine game birds.

Although several varieties were imported, but one, the ring-necked, increased to any great extent, and none but this variety are met with in the field.

Since then hundreds, perhaps thousands, of these birds have been captured and sent to different parts for the purpose of propagation.

Providing food be obtainable, they are able to endure very low temperature, and I think I am safe in saying that the day is not far distant when ring-necked pheasant shooting may be had in many of these United States.

The ring-necked pheasant is distinctively a bird of the open fields, of the stubble and short cover.

It is true that when too persistently hunted he often seeks shelter in the semi-open woods and thickets, but his home is the wheat stubble, the orchard, the truck patch, and the fern cover.

Early in the open season the birds lie very well to the dogs, but, gaining experience with age, they soon learn to use their legs and powers of secretion, as well as their wings, in eluding the sportsmen.

The first day of September marks the beginning of the open season on pheasants, grouse, and quail in Oregon, and for two and a half months the birds do not lack for attention.

There is perhaps no portion of the Union where, in proportion to the existing population, so much gunning is indulged in as the western part of Oregon.

Grouse, quail, pigeons, pheasants and wild fowl have for years swarmed in this region, and nearly every farmer's boy is a Nimrod.

Despite this seemingly unequal chance the imported pheasant holds its own, although the blue and ruffed grouse become scarcer each year, and ducks are by no means as plentiful as they once were.

One day last September the mail brought me a note from my friend Hal, at Salem, who wrote that everything had been arranged toward my enjoying a little shoot, and that he would meet me on a certain train.

Speeding through the valley on the California express that night we passed through a vision of loveliness. Not a breath of air rustled the leaves of the fully clothed trees or ruffled the bosom of the river, and the harvest moon bathed everything in its effulgence. Even the ricks of weather-beaten cordwood beside the track were metamorphosed into bars of silver, and the limpid, placid Willamette gleamed through the trees, a river of light.

At the Salem depot I was promptly met by Hal, and after being introduced to Mr. Knight, who was to be one of our party, I turned in.

The hotel clerk was faithful to his promise that I should not oversleep, and in the glare of Salem's electric lights I made my way to the rendezvous with gun, camera and ammunition in arms.

Breakfast was shortly disposed of, and we were on the road. Hal and Glenn were mounted on their wheels, while Knight and the writer fought with two lusty dogs for our share of a buggy.

Driving through the wide and level streets of Salem, we met two more wheelmen also in quest of a little shooting. My companions explained that several of the local sportsmen made a practice of frequently riding out for a couple of hours in the morning, and that they seldom returned without several fine birds. The country about Salem is very level and the roads are good.

As we drove north the influence of the approaching sun's rays was causing the mists to rise in graceful lines against the oak and fir thickets. The fresh, cool air was laden with the fragrance of crushed weeds and shrubs, each in themselves perhaps not pleasant, but, commingled, a perfume.

We soon arrived at Knight's farm, which is situated on the shore of

Lake Labish. Lake Labish I soon learned to be a lake in name only, for the waters have long been drained, and the lake bed is now divided up into the most productive of farms.

We were soon afield. Glen and his black pointer strayed off to our left, and suddenly we heard the whir of a pheasant frantically cleaving the mist, quickly followed by a couple of hasty reports from Charlie's gun.

In answer to our question, Glenn shouted that they were "too far."

Knight, with his white setter puppy, worked off into the haze at our right, while Hal and I followed a drain across the low land.

We had not proceeded far before Beau Brummel, the prize dog of my friend's kennel, plainly indicated the proximity of birds. It was apparent that the pheasants were running, and we hastened on after the well-broken and thoroughly posted dog.

Many a pheasant has Beau hypnotized with his staring eyes, and many are the birds he has seen wilt in mid air at the crack of his master's weapon.

We worked through some fern, thistle, and heavy corn, and on to a piece of wheat stubble. Suddenly Beau straightened out with head slightly to the right on a staunch point, and soon a bird broke cover only to be grassed by a quick shot from the writer. This proved to be a full-grown hen pheasant.

Our rapid-working and businesslike four-footed companion was not slow in locating more game in this same piece of stubble.

The next bird was doubtless one of the local sprinters, for we were led a merry chase through stubble, a weed patch, up a shallow drain and down another. The bird flushed wild and at some distance from dog or gunners. My companion was in the lead, and at his second shot the race came to an abrupt end.

"Are they not a great bird?" inquired my companion as he mopped his brow and reloaded. "I tell you, the uncertainty as to what a Mongolian will do when discovered, and as to how he will break cover, are to me not the least of the many charms of a day afield."

He affirmed that he had in his day killed hundreds of bob-whites, pinnated, sharp-tailed, ruffed, and blue grouse, Oregon and California quails, but that, for cunning and ability to outwit the dog and his master, there were none of them "in it" with the beauty from the land of the Mandarin.

Soon falling in with Glenn and Knight we crossed over to another field that was used as a pasture. While sitting idly on the fence we descried two pheasants making their way along the ground and toward some short cover.

When they became lost to view in the weeds we went over to do some harvesting. We misjudged the distance, however, and sent the dogs into the wrong cover. In crossing the pasture, the writer doubtless passed within a few feet of the hiding birds, but, thanks to their ability to escape detection, they were undiscovered.

When I was safely out of gauge, the old cock jumped up and made off for the timber. Glenn and the black pointer located the other bird, and a requiem was shortly sounded. Charlie concluded that he would work off toward the fir timber while we made our way up the lake and in the direction of a large corn patch.

Crossing through a pumpkin patch and a field of volunteer barley (ideal cover for the birds), we were disappointed in not meeting with a feather. Skirting a large cornfield, the neighborhood of which is generally the trysting place for a few birds, the dogs located a covey, which became frightened and took wing.

I was loafing along in the rear as usual, more intent on studying the beauties of the landscape than on searching for pheasants, and as a result I did not get an opportunity to scatter any shot. My companions, however, grassed a brace of plump birds.

Down at this end of the "lake" the drainage was not perfect, and we soon reached some very good snipe ground minus the snipe. Crossing a piece of high land, we again entered a stubble field in which Beau declared game was to be found. Cautiously trailing the old dog, we shortly saw a small bird fly into the neighboring field.

Beau moved on, and as we crossed the rail fence and entered a brushy pasture we found ourselves nearly jumping into a frightened flock of quail.

"Bang!" went Knight's rain-maker and "crack!" "crack!" from the other guns.

The Oregon mountain quail is a plump little beauty, somewhat larger than bob-white, quick as a shooting star, and seldom found outside of the brush. As we made our way between the hazel thickets and scrub evergreens the birds continued to break cover, and we found quite a hot corner for a minute. As two of the blue beauties flushed near Hal and the writer, one of the little fellows was unfortunate enough to catch a fair shot from each gun, and at the close range he was Hamburgered.

Our friend Knight, who is not so young as he used to be, finds these little birds a trifle hasty for his aim. Two or three times, as the birds made a plunge for the green, did I see his trusty gun go to his shoulder only to be lowered in disappointment and disgust. I have a habit, often an unfortunate one, of being very quick on the trigger, and at this point

19

I made a shot the memory of which yet causes me to puff up.

He was searching for a bird that had dropped into a brush heap, and I was standing at "parade rest" on the other side of the fence. Suddenly with whir of wings a straggler came out of the hazels, and as he went into the air Knight put a charge of lead in that direction.

This but accelerated the bird's speed, and like a batted ball it passed directly over my head. But a second only it took, still in that brief interval I had thrown my gun up, raised the hammer, turned around and let go at the vanishing blue sphere, and it came down, too.

"They're too quick for me, boys, too quick for me," quoth Knight. "John can get his Chinaman once in a while, but these blue racers are just a little too rapid."

Over in the heavy timber we found the air delightfully cool, and we enjoyed a quiet stroll and conversation. An early frost had crimsoned some of the vines and deciduous trees, and the vistas between the great trunks of the firs were marvels of rustic beauty. Here and there the poison oak stretched its now gaudy foliage far up the trunk of a forest monarch. Treacherous indeed is this plant, for, at all times of beautiful foliage, the colors taken on in autumn doubly invite the unwary to handle the poisonous tendrils.

The dogwood, vine maple, blackberry, and other shrubs and vines were taking on the russet and crimson and adding not a little to the beauty of the forest. Lake Labish was, before the husbandman coveted the rich deposits of decomposed vegetation that formed its bed, a famous resort for wild fowl. Knight entertained us with tales of many a day's sport with the whistling widgeon and noisy goose.

Once again descending into the marshland we took our way in the direction of the barn. Moving up through a large pasture where the grass grew long, Hal and his dog took one side of a drain, while Knight, the writer and the white puppy looked after matters on the other side of the drain.

At our left grew the nearest timber, and we knew that any birds which might flush would take that direction.

"Say, John, what a joke it would be on Hal if he was to get up a couple of old cocks, miss 'em both, and they were to come over to us. If we downed them what a laugh we would have on the old man."

A few minutes later and Beau began to get uneasy. We noticed Hal quicken his pace and closely follow the dog, which, after many a twist and turn, "froze" on the edge of the ditch.

As his master walked up a fine young cock jumped into the air and flew directly toward us. Involuntarily I dropped to the ground, but Hal, fearing that he might hit us, did not fire on the instant. As a result of the

20

delay the bird was soon at long range from where he stood, and although he put two charges in pursuit they did not kill. My companion next put in a shot, and then I had my turn at the rapidly vanishing cock. It had by this time simply pulled the throttle wide open, but my second shot did the work, and then I yelled.

Knight also yelled, and then we yelled and whooped in chorus.

"Just what we were talking about," we shouted; "how we did wipe your eye! Oh, it's a good thing you've got us over here to pick 'em up after you've scared 'em nearly into a fit."

Thus we chaffed Hal, who said little, but thought considerable, and, as results proved, plotted vengeance. At the barn we learned that Glenn had preceded us, and that he had "cached" several birds in the buggy. These, with our bag, made the number of slain nineteen, and, as it was yet hardly 11 A. M. and we had hunted leisurely, we voted the sport very fair.

Glenn soon strolled up, and, in answer to our interrogations, said that he had killed one bird since visiting the barn, and he walked over to the buggy, into which he hastily tossed something.

Lunch disposed of, we took the birds out to photograph them, and then learned the cause of Glenn's stealthy actions. The last bird deposited by him in the buggy was about the size of a robin, and then what a shout went up at its appearance!

"Why, Charlie! what's this?" said Hal. "Did you take it from a nest, or did you scare it to death?"

Charlie excused himself with the statement that the bird jumped up in the thick brush, giving him but a snap shot, and that he thought it larger until the shot left the gun.

We crossed the road into an orchard and stubble field, which, after beating unsuccessfully, we deserted for a pasture filled with high fern and stumps.

The sun was now setting, the quiet air a-quiver, and at such times the Mongolian pheasant seeks the cool ferns and heavy corn.

While threading the mazes of a hazel thicket I jumped a young cock, which I missed with the first, but dropped with the second barrel.

Glenn and Knight were beating the other end of the field, and we frequently heard their guns.

Upon again falling in with them we learned that Glenn had killed six or seven pheasants and a quail in as many minutes, and his companion had secured a pheasant and two quails.

Chukars
by H. L. Betten

Although there had been a few other scattered writings regarding the chukar, this 1937 article by Betten was really the first insight into the species read by North American sportsmen. Thirty years later the chukar was well known indeed. It can be argued that it is the best game bird of the West.

L ike some motion-picture star who steps from obscurity to fame almost overnight, the chukar partridge looms as an introductive possibility in American covers. This bird is a native of China, India, Afghanistan and adjacent countries. It is essentially a resident of wild hill lands, more particularly of the Himalayas, at elevations of from 2,000 to 9,000 feet. Its scientific name is *Alectoris graeca meisner*, and the family embraces several sub-species.

Prominent among these sub-species is *Alectoris graeca chukar*, which is the variety now quite commonly bred by game breeders in the United States. This bird is rather closely related to the red-legged partridge of Europe and is a more distant relative of the European gray partridge, commonly known as the Hungarian partridge. However, the chukar partridge differs materially from European partridges in its habits.

In general appearance the chukar resembles the European gray or Hungarian partridge, for its predominating color is almost gray, while in conformation and apparent size the difference is not great. Put the two species together in the same pen when the light is dull, and it is hard to tell them apart at first glance. In bright sunlight, however, the prominent vertical bars along the sides and the black band at each side of the head, much like the markings of the killdeer, readily distinguish the chukar. Also, this broad-chested fellow is a much heavier bird, with an average weight of about 22 ounces as against 15 ounces for the gray partridge, or Hun.

When reviewing the important matter of game introduction in America, we find that initiative in this field can rarely be traced to state conservation departments. Almost invariably it is some public-spirited citizen or a group of sportsmen who starts the ball rolling. Judge Owen N. Denny's generous donations of Chinese pheasants paved the way to very wide distribution of the ringneck in this country. Likewise, Clay Fruit, unheralded donor of Hungarian partridges to the state of Washington, pioneered successful acclimatization of the great little gray bird in America. And now it seems certain that because of the unflagging interest of Frank E. Booth of San Francisco in the chukar partridge over a long period of years, this fine species will be added to the list of American game birds.

Referring to game-breeding experiments in his large private aviary, Mr. Booth states in a letter: "I think perhaps I was the first one in California to properly value the chukar and to release this game in the state; this was done some ten years ago in Marin County. However, the birds did not thrive because of uncongenial conditions.

"Some of my chukars were presented to August Bade, in charge of the California State Game Farm, who afterwards supplemented this

23

breeding stock with imported chukars.

"Friends of mine in whom I have every confidence hunted chukar partridges in India and in China; they stated these birds lie well to a dog, are very fast fliers and afford the acme of upland gunning. They are said to live at elevations from practically sea-level up to eight thousand feet. They are a most excellent table fowl—that I know from experience. As to reproductivity, I know that Mr. J. Leroy Nickel of Menlo Park, California, from thirteen pair raised 440 chukars to maturity in one year."

While it was the wide knowledge of its possibilities and infectious enthusiasm of Mr. Booth which first interested California sportsmen and game breeders in the chukar partridge, August Bade was responsible for its practical development. A former agriculturist and a game breeder, Bade played a large part in the successful introduction of both the Hungarian partridge and the pheasant in eastern Washington and Oregon. His fame as a successful game breeder having spread, he was commissioned by the California Fish and Game Commission to establish the ring-necked pheasant in California.

That heavy task was undertaken less than a decade ago. In the face of much criticism and skepticism, Bade buckled down to the job and put the ringneck over in a big way. Now, with three successful open seasons behind them, the sportsmen of California, and the Commission as well, acclaim Bade as a genius.

Once the pheasant was thoroughly established in California, Bade turned his thoughts to those millions of acres of semi-arid land untenanted by either the prolific ringneck or by native partridges. After a careful survey of this territory and a thorough analysis of the qualifications of various exotic game birds, he decided the chukar partridge was the logical candidate for naturalization experiments. However, in this connection, it was desirable first to enlist the interest and support of the sportsmen and the Commission.

The hearty endorsement of the Associated Sportsmen of California and of its energetic president, C. R. Danielson, was readily obtained. In fact, Danielson traveled all over the state and spoke before approximately one hundred member clubs of the organization, and many civic clubs as well, in behalf of Bade's program. As a result, acclimatization of the chukar in the Golden State is already far along the road to success.

Although additional heavy plantings over a period of four or five years may still be required to fortify earlier releases, it may safely be stated that the chukar is close to final naturalization in America. But let me quote from statements of August Bade to Mr. Danielson and me during a recent visit to the state game farm at Yountville, California:

"The chukar partridge, perhaps the most important of several important exotic game birds not acclimatized in America, has practically all the qualities essential to successful introduction in California," declared Bade. "The chukar is finding a large place in the minds of sportsmen and game breeders everywhere. However, like all other species, it demands suitable climatic conditions and habitat. Mind you, it is not a miracle bird which can succeed in any and all environments. I wish to make this plain, so that sportsmen and others will analyze its possibilities and exercise sound judgment when making releases. Otherwise many will duplicate the unfortunate and unwarranted failures which resulted from planting Hungarian partridges and pheasants on unsuitable grounds.

"Today, the stocking of covers requires, first of all, a game bird that is smart. By smartness I mean the ability not only to survive but to thrive under tough conditions.

"In many states besides California are millions of acres of waste land, unfit for cultivation, of little value for grazing and of practically no value to sportsmen because of the almost total absence of game. Strangely enough, it is in this type of country the chukar partridge finds a congenial home and where he is making a real showing in a wild state in California.

"In native haunts the chukars are found mostly between 2,000 feet and 5,000 feet elevation, but certain varieties thrive from sea-level to altitudes as high as 10,000 feet. In this state we have a tremendous acreage of semi-arid and desert lands which lie out of the range of the native quail and the introduced pheasant. Most of this is rolling and rocky land which might be termed third-class sheep pasture. Vegetation is scanty, consisting mainly of a short, thin growth of grass and scrawny weeds and low brush. Such are the native haunts of the chukar, for he is known as the bird which lives on nothing and he hides successfully in the scantiest cover.

"Like most of the partridge family, chukars provide fine sport with dog and gun. Coveys usually run from twelve to twenty birds, and, as with Hungarian partridges, the young are regularly under the control of the parents until they mate in the spring. This insured a large percentage of matured birds, for the young benefit by the cunning and sagacity of their elders.

"Chukars compare favorably in a sporting sense with any game you can name. Not only do they hold well to a dog, but they flush with a great roar of wings and fly faster, I believe, than Huns or quail; I have reached this conclusion after liberating thousands of the three species. When a covey of chukars is flushed, the birds scatter wide in all directions, each bird for himself—in this respect they differ materially from Hungarian partridges. Scattered birds sit very tight, even in scanty cover or on bare ground. In the last instance their dove-gray and slate-gray colors blend so perfectly with ground colors that it is almost impossible to see them before they take wing."

At the present time Bade has approximately one thousand chukars on the state game farms for breeding purposes this spring. He has already planted 4,500 birds on some eighty areas in thirty-two counties. Careful selection of breeding stock in the past now insures an average lay of seventy eggs per hen, while that of the exceptional individual runs well above one hundred eggs. Last season the queen of the farm, an undersized chukar hen, laid 136 eggs, which doubtless is a world's record.

The fertility of chukar eggs runs very high. And it is a remarkable fact that the chicks require only one-fifth as much water as young pheasants and can withstand extreme drought and heat; they are, besides, very hardy and resistant to disease. Ordinarily chukars are monogamous, but are easily paired off. In all other respects they are as easy to propagate and rear in confinement as pheasants.

The chukar has remarkably steady nerves and plenty of brains as well. Being hardy, wary and adaptive, it seems suitable for many sections of America. However, successful acclimatization of a new or alien species depends primarily on its ability to reproduce and thrive in a wild state. Nevertheless, artificial propagation, if easily accomplished, provides not only abundant seed but heavy additional plantings with which to fortify stocks of wild game. Such qualities have proved invaluable in connection with the ringneck and presage a successful future in America for the chukar partridge as well.

While it is true that the chukar can be reared in confinement almost anywhere, its practical value to sportsmen is the primary consideration. Therefore, let us discount extravagant claims put forth by a few commercial game breeders and properly appraise the introductive possibilities. The important question is, where will the species multiply and thrive in the wild state?

It is the opinion of Bade and other authorities who have known the chukar on native heaths that it is best adapted to thrive among the grassy foot-hills and wild grazing lands of hot and semi-arid regions—even on the desert. This indicates these birds will not succeed where humidity runs high and rainfall is heavy. Doubtless it is best suited to grazing and other primitive lands west of the Continental Divide where precipitation is light and possibly to semi-arid sections of the Dakotas, Kansas, Oklahoma, New Mexico and western Texas.

Considerable literature which bears on chukar shooting in India and China may be found in the *Field, Asia* and other publications dealing with sport in the British possessions. It is unfortunate, however, that many accounts deal with gunning in a haphazard way and do not afford the information which American sportsmen desire. For instance, we would like to know how the chukar compares in the field with such splendid game birds as bob-white, prairie chicken, Hungarian partridge and California valley quail.

The following brief description, while it does not involve all the questions, provides an accurate outline of the sport. It was given by an English sportsman of quite wide experience, who stated:

"I must say I enjoyed partridge shooting in the Northwest (Alberta). Quite different from the driven game at home; more difficult, I believe. I also tried California quail in two instances. It was very dry, the game was not plentiful where we were and the dogs wild; so I cannot say much for or about the sport. Still, it did remind me a bit of partridge shooting in Nepal and Afghanistan. That is to say, the grounds were quite the same—rather dry and barren—and when a covey flushed, the quail flew wide of each other and lit in cover, far apart, as chukars do.

"How do I rate the chukar? A very excellent bird indeed. Next to our red grouse at home it is my favorite; it has some similar characteristics. I shot quite extensively in the rolling grass country along the Himalaya foot-hills below timber-line—they never go to forests or thickets. You find them along the dried-up watercourses and among extensive rock outcroppings; in stunted brush at the head of ravines and on the grassy slopes, but seldom on cultivated areas. They are quite as fast as our gray partridge and grouse on the wing.

"Chukars are very clever at hiding. The smallest tuft of grass answers, and they often crawl between rocks and into clefts where few dogs seem able to smell them. Quite often a covey when flushed scatters out over a wide expanse of grass or bare ground. But look as you will, you rarely see a squatting bird; usually it waits until you pass, and when your back is turned it buzzes away. The natives believe this game can change color to match the surroundings, but that is not true. It does, however, seem to arrange its plumage to that end.

"Yes, chukars do run badly at times and bewilder a dog. But so do other game birds; I have seen grouse, partridges and pheasants do the same back home. With chukars, however, it is often the fault of the gun, who fails to flail the covey on the rise. You must shoot into them regardless of distance, for then the birds are inclined to sit firmly. A dog must be well conditioned to handle these hill partridges properly, when they present no greater difficulties than other game. Not many such were to be found in the back country, yet I saw some excellent work at times.

"On the approach of cool weather chukars congregate like the prairie hens in Canada, in packs of one hundred or more—I have seen all of two hundred birds in such a flock. After autumn rains and heavy frost they become wild and are then most inclined to run. A broadside on the rise, no matter the distance, is a good remedy, however; it often makes them hold like leeches. Then the dog must do his part, or it's up to you to 'rackle them oot,' as the Scotch say, with a pair of brogans.

"How this game would behave when heavily shot I do not know. Where we hunted, chukars were so prolific and plentiful there was no occasion for that. Really, I can think of no finer or more sporting game for your dry Western country than this Himalayan partridge, if it can be introduced in America."

In a practical sense the value of exotic game to the sportsmen is in ration to its ability to thrive in a wild state under modern conditions. The chukar partridge seems to possess every essential requirement; it is hardy, wary and very prolific and is well adapted to thrive on a tremendous acreage of primitive and waste lands in western America in particular. In this last connection it has a decided advantage over both the pheasant and the Hungarian partridge, which rely more or less on agriculture for a living. Apparently, drought areas are made to order for "the bird which lives on nothing," and it is able to wring sustenance from the most barren hills. Thus, if successfully established, it will not infringe on the habitats of other American game species and will be free to expand tremendously over a limitless field all its own.

As to the courage and resourcefulness of the chukar hen in a wild state, August Bade recites this instance: "In one of our refuges in southern California, King's Cañon, to be exact, C. H. Edmondson, the refuge patrolman, discovered a nest. The chukar hen had laid ten eggs and hatched every one of them by August 13, according to Edmondson's report.

"For three days after the young were hatched Edmondson could find no trace of the mother or her brood. On the fourth day he found her, but in a very dilapidated condition so far as looks were concerned. Her tail was gone and her head was badly scratched up. But she still had eight of her original family of ten. Just what happened will never be

28

known. Whatever took place didn't have the least effect on her morale. It was just a part of the day's work in bringing up a family, and she was ready to do battle again to protect the remaining chicks."

The foregoing sounds as if the chukar partridge, the female of the species in particular, might have what it takes to succeed under tough conditions in an alien land. Chukars will be heartily welcomed by American sportsmen.

Buzz-Bomb of the Rimrocks

by Frank McCulloch

The two premier chukar states are Nevada and Oregon. As far as which is number one, take your pick. Both have a lot of birds. As H. L. Betten's 1937 article "Chukars" was among the first written on the species in North America, this 1950 McCulloch article was one of the first accounts of actually hunting them. Then, as now, in order to bag chukars you climb. And then climb some more.

We were sitting cross-legged in a ragweed duck blind, surveying the horizon. "There's no doubt about it," Old Sidekick observed judiciously, "he's the greatest game bird alive."

He had inexplicably missed a good shot at a quartering widgeon just a few minutes before; so I was a little confused. Old Sidekick liked his ducks, including widgeon, but not that well. He apparently sensed my confusion. "The chukar," he explained, "not that widgeon."

I sat and basked in the slow realization that I was in the process of scoring a great personal triumph. "You're stubborn," I told him. "For two years I've been trying to convince you of that. And you finally make your mind up to it sitting in a duck blind, twenty miles from the nearest chukar."

He solemnly admitted he'd come to his conclusion about the chukar ten days before, but just hated to admit it.

Old Sidekick was practically teethed on the ruffed grouse of his native Maine, and there was an understandably large soft spot in his heart for the gallant drummer of the New England thickets. He had been living in Nevada for forty-five of his sixty-five productive years, but it was hard for him to forget the grouse hunting of his boyhood.

So it wasn't until the three-day season of 1948 that I had managed to talk him into a whirl at Nevada's newest game bird, the chukar partridge. He had sniffed at the experimental one-day season of 1947 as "a waste of time, no matter how you look at it." A year later, however, he found out what "a waste of time" the chukar is, under any conditions.

It was back in the early '30s that this hell-for-leather speedster from the great plateaus of the Himalaya Mountains came to Nevada. His introduction was in the form of a hesitant, half-hearted, experimental planting at the western edge of the state.

What the chukar found in the very wide open stretches of this Great Basin state he apparently liked, for he has thrived mightily and beyond all expectations. So far, of course, he's virtually unknown to the majority of the nation's upland bird hunters, for the simple reason that he has rocketed up before only a relatively few guns. But in Nevada he is already becoming a legend, and should the seven red gods of fate allow him to spread and multiply in other areas the chances are good that he will continue to increase so rapidly that he will eventually provide sport for thousands of hunters.

The chukar is even physically constructed to be gamey. He's trim but solid. There's no fluff to him as there is to a dove or a quail. Like a well-knit football half-back, he's built both for speed and durability.

31

The average bird is about 14 inches in length from bill to tail, and he'll weigh anywhere from 15 ounces up to two pounds, rough-dressed. We heard of a number of males being killed during the 1949 season, each of which went 2 1/2 pounds, though neither I nor Old Sidekick saw them. Give or take a few ounces, that's quite a bird—as big, for instance, as a young pullet or fryer.

Though he's predominantly gray in color, the chukar is a long way from being drab. Both his bill and his feet are almost brick-red when the bird is in good condition. And on his flanks a series of alternating vertical black-and-white stripes dress him up beautifully.

The chukar mates and nests anywhere between the first of March and the end of May, depending largely on the weather. The hen may build her nest almost anywhere, but seems to prefer it up among the rim-rocks. She may drag together a real nest of twigs, grass and other material, or she may simply nestle down in the most convenient cover.

Size of the brood varies, but the bird, on the whole, is a prodigious reproducer. Hens have been seen with as many as twenty-four chicks, but game biologists believe those were cases of the mother bird taking over a brood of orphans after another hen had been killed. An average family probably would run between eight and fourteen chicks, of which an amazingly high number reach maturity.

The chicks are pretty well able to take care of themselves from the first week on, demonstrating the same rugged adaptability which characterizes their parents.

Unlike the pheasant or the quail, which, of course, thrive best in cultivated areas, the chukar likes it where things are rugged. Original plants of the birds in or near Nevada agricultural areas were never as successful as those made in the hill country. Whether the birds died or simply moved off to more remote desert areas has never been definitely established. In any event, they didn't increase as had been hoped on farm-land.

In some areas—Nevada's Nye County particularly—the chukar is found in considerable numbers on cultivated land. But in those cases the desert hills of which he is so fond aren't far away. A peculiar thing about the bird is that, while he is next to impossible for a dog to handle out in the hills or up in the rim-rock, he holds beautifully when he's found in an alfalfa or wild hay-field. Hunters who were lucky enough to locate him in such country during Nevada's 1948 and 1949 seasons were wildly enthusiastic after shooting their limits over dogs.

The chukar is a voracious feeder, tackling almost anything that any other bird will eat. But one of the main items in his diet seems to be the seed of broncho grass (*Bromus techtorum*). That, incidentally, may partially account for his success in Nevada. Not even sage-brush or grease-wood is more widely found in the state than broncho grass.

Because the chukar originally came from the Himalaya Mountains, Nevada's hard winters don't bother him much. As a matter of fact, they serve to demonstrate again the bird's versatility.

Once the snow has fallen, he has sense enough to range on the hilltops, where the wind probably will have blown off most or all of the snow. If the drifts are too deep, he still isn't troubled. Field personnel of the Nevada Fish and Game Commission say it's an amazing sight to see a covey of chukars alight on a snowbank, decide there's feed beneath—and go after it. They beat their wings so rapidly that the human eye sees only a blur, and as they work the snow flies in all directions. The bird resembles nothing more than a tiny, highly efficient rotary snow-plow in action.

This trick serves him in good stead in more ways than one. In the first place, he won't starve to death. In the second, it provides him with a warm, protective cover when the blizzards are howling.

The chukar can be reared successfully in captivity, but he does much better in the natural state if conditions are right. A considerable number are now being raised on the Nevada state game farm, and other planting programs are carried on simply by trapping the birds in areas where they are thickly populated and moving them to another region where they aren't.

It is interesting to note that almost none of these transplantings have failed in Nevada. In each case the bird has taken hold and thrived in his new location, and he now ranges in each of the state's seventeen big counties.

Chukars pair off for mating, and there is some indication that the pairing may be lifelong. In any event, they are definitely monogamous during the mating and nesting seasons. And they don't like anyone else to pick their mates for them, game biologists found out.

When the birds were first raised at the Nevada state game farm, workers there paired off hens and males when the mating season rolled around. The next morning they found all but a few of the hens dead— killed by the males. They tried it again with essentially the same results.

An amateur psychologist in the crowd mulled things over and came up with the solution. He suggested that a large number of males and females be placed together in one pen. Sure enough, it worked. The next morning the birds were happily paired off, and mating began on a normal basis.

The chukar has been experimented with at one time or another in each of the eleven Western States. All met nothing but discouragement until recently, when success was attained with the bird in eastern Washington, where conditions are much like those found in Nevada. The hills are rough, steep and hard to get to.

Elsewhere fish and game commissions are stubbornly, though not too hopefully, experimenting. They had seen what the chukar can become to a state's sportsmen, and they liked what they saw. Perhaps transplants of Nevada wild stock may be the answer. Only time will tell.

The chukar was even introduced in a number of Eastern and mid-Western states early in the 1930's and quite a fanfare surrounded the plantings. The bird thrived briefly and then disappeared. It would appear that he requires more in the way of wide open spaces than the East has to offer.

All this may have been going through the mind of Old Sidekick as he sat there in the blind. It was a clear, still afternoon and the ducks weren't working; so there was plenty of time to think. And I knew my partner well enough to be sure that if he rated the chukar as highly as he said he did he'd take the trouble to find out all he could about the bird.

He must have read my thoughts. "The greatest game bird flying today," he said again. He grinned. "I'll never forget that first hunt."

I had called for him at about 4 A.M. on opening day. When I went around to the back door, he was gathering up his coat, shells and old pump gun on the back porch. As I opened the door he muttered something about the fool who would get up in the dead of night and go off looking for some kind of bird that probably didn't even exist.

It was only forty-two miles, or 50 minutes, from Reno to the mouth of White Horse Canyon, in the Olinghouse Range northeast of Reno. As I stopped the car Old Sidekick wanted to know how I knew there were any chukar out here. I told him I had seen them on a scouting expedition three weeks before.

He grunted. "Never were any birds like that when I was buckarooing in this country," he said.

"That was a hundred years ago," I told him. "They've only been in here since 1941."

While he was wriggling into his hunting coat I pulled my field-glasses from out of the glove compartment and hung the case around my neck.

His eyes bugged. "I thought we were going bird hunting. What are those for?"

I told him to wait; that it would be easier to show him later in the day than to try to explain.

We got away from the car as soon as we could see the bronze sights at the end of the barrels, and we hadn't walked a hundred feet when Old Sidekick found a mule-deer track. It was so fresh that it looked as though our arrival in the car might have scared the animal out.

"Look at the size of that!" he breathed. He looked back toward the car. "Did you bring a rifle?"

I told him I hadn't. "Look up the canyon there, near that first patch of wild peach." Five or six indistinct shapes were hustling off into the nearest cover. They moved so fast that they were gone almost before I saw them, and I didn't know whether they had been running, flying, or both.

We sidled easily up toward the spot and half-way to it we heard a bird call up on the side of the hill, off to our left and above us. Another answered from the canyon wall to the right. Others called from farther up the canyon. It was a sharp, almost querulous call.

Old Sidekick stopped and looked cautiously around him. "Gives me the feeling the damn things have seen us and are yelling back and forth about it," he said.

I assured him that he was probably a good deal more right than he thought.

We moved on up to the clump of wild peach. Nothing happened. We relaxed, and the O.S. looked at me scornfully.

Suddenly there was a thunder of wings, and I could have sworn I heard twigs snapping in the wild peach, as though deer were running through it. The six chukars came out, headed in six different directions.

I froze to the spot and to my shotgun. Finally I brought it to my shoulder in time to snap a silly, desperation shot after the bird heading up the canyon. He swerved abruptly to the left, dipped and then plunged into the canyon wall in a puff of feathers and dust. I swear to this day that it must have been a heart attack which dropped him.

I ran to the spot in case he was only wounded and might try to run, but he was a thoroughly dead bird. A handsome young cock, the zebra stripings on his flanks were bright in the early morning light. He weighed, I guessed, about 18 ounces. As I tucked him into the back of my coat I noticed Old Sidekick picking up a bird on the other side of the canyon.

My spirits soared. In 1947 I had hunted all day with two partners, and we had bagged one bird among us. And here we were with two in the first five minutes.

I walked over to Old Sidekick. "What do you think of it now?" I asked.

He hefted the bird in his hand and grinned. "But this is no sport," he suddenly said. "A five-year-old could fill a limit of these birds in fifteen minutes."

I didn't answer.

We swung back to the bottom of the canyon and worked the remaining cover without results. Then Old Sidekick saw them—twenty, maybe twenty-five of them, strung out in single file and sliding snakily along a path about seventy-five yards above us.

They didn't look too badly frightened; so we took off after them. By the time we reached the rocks in which we'd last seen them, they were out of sight. Out of breath, we labored to the top of the first little hill above us, our hearts galloping in the expectation that we'd jump them again just over the top. We gained the crest, moved cautiously forward a few steps—and there was the covey, weaving its way, still single file, up the next little knoll.

During the next two hours we repeated that process time after time, along one wall of the canyon, until both of us had long since lost all count of the number of small summits we had topped. After the first hour I joined the O.S. in roundly cursing the chukar and all his ancestors, and promising never again to be fool enough to hunt him.

It was a glimpse of the head of the canyon that gave us heart again. There was the last big rim-rock, and there, we figured, they might stop gliding ahead of us long enough for another shot. The plump weight of the birds in our coats added luster to the prospect.

We all but loped up the last few hundred feet to the base of the rim-rock. The chukars were nowhere in sight. Then they exploded right at our feet, as they had before. They came boiling out from the brush and rocks ahead of us. But did they sail away over the summit, out of range, out of sight? Not on your life. Up they rocketed, and then they doubled back—right over our heads.

There was plenty of shooting for about forty-five seconds. There would have been plenty of birds in the bag, too, if either of us could have swung a shotgun fast enough to come anywhere near one of those feathered bullets. They weren't dodging in and out of cover like a grouse; they were out in the wide, wide open. But their speed was so incredible as they whirled back over us that we both were shooting yards behind them. The last bird went out of the rocks just beyond range, and we watched the covey barreling it down the canyon.

"What in the name of Hannah!" Old Sidekick exploded.

Five hundred yards below, the hurtling chukars were folding back their wings, exactly like hunting falcons in a dive, and plummeting straight down to the far canyon wall. In comparison with this power dive, their speed on the take-off was nothing. It didn't seem possible

36

that they could pull out in time.

But if they didn't, they must have bounced well. A few minutes later we heard a call, then another, float up from the canyon. The covey was reassembling. Old Sidekick and I? We had nothing but our first two birds—and a lot of empty shells at our feet.

It was a good spot for a dramatic act; so I dragged the field-glasses out of their case. O.S. snorted as I began to inspect the rim-rock above us. So I handed him the glasses and told him to train them on the needle rock to the south of the biggest rim-rock. He did, and reported some kind of small hawk perched there.

I told him to have another look, remembering that the chukars had looked like falcons when they folded their wings back for that dive to the canyon floor.

"By golly, it is a chukar," he finally decided. He looked through the glasses again. "And he's sitting up there watching us and everything else moving within a hundred miles," he added.

We decided that we might get a shot by swinging far to the right, picking our way through the rim-rock and coming in behind the bird.

After what had happened, we considered it as nothing short of a miracle when we flushed the single and I folded him up with a shot from the full-choke barrel of the little 20-gauge. He was another young male, and when he'd been tucked beside my first my coat was beginning to bulge comfortably.

The day sped on from that point. We climbed in and out of innumerable canyons. We saw literally hundreds of chukar, thanks to those handy glasses. We heard what seemed to be thousands more. We got a few shots, and we were thrilled once more when a covey zoomed back over us again at the head of another canyon.

It was on that covey that Old Sidekick made as nice a recovery and shot as I've ever seen. He whirled one way when the covey broke, but found he couldn't pick up a target over the end of the pump in time to shoot. So he whirled back and caught the last bird going out just as she started to plunge for the far wall of the canyon.

The bird was traveling so fast when the shot caught her that the wind was whistling through her pinions as loudly as it does through the wings of several pintails wheeling into a set of decoys. She plunged at least fifty feet more through the air before she hit the ground.

Old Sidekick's hand was trembling a little as he picked her up. "Tired," he explained. But I don't believe he had ever made another shot that thrilled him more.

We reached the car two hours later, having seen a lot more birds on the way but agreeing that we were too tired to chase them. Maybe we'll bring the dogs next year, though those who have tried them say the results are about the same, at least out here in the hills.

We had pushed the unloaded guns into the back seat and were making ready to toss the bird-heavy coats back there when Old Sidekick looked up. He swallowed once before he said it. "They'll push a ruffed grouse hard as a game bird," he admitted.

The sun was just going down behind the last high rim-rock where we had flushed the covey the second time early that morning. The autumn chill was already settling fast over the desert country. Suddenly a chukar called, not more than two hundred yards up there in the canyon. Both our heads went up. We stood tense for a moment, and then looked at each other and grinned.

"You're a chukar hunter from here henceforth," I said, and he nodded.

Greying Hunters Hunting Greys
by Charles F. Waterman

Waterman is our senior statesman of western upland bird hunting. He has been afield for decades, in many states, and has hunted almost all the species. His writings are correctly viewed by most as the final word. So when he suggests that—of them all—the gray partridge is the West's best, take heed. It *is* a fine bird, and Waterman isn't prone to making off-hand statements regarding such matters.

"**G**rey partridge" is a better name but I've always called them "Huns," from *Hungarian*. I prefer not to think of them as *Hunkies*.

They came to America from Central Europe, largely from Hungary, I understand. An exotic gamebird in conservative dress, settling quietly in a new hemisphere and adapting to new conditions.

Back in Europe the beaters drive them to aristocratic gunners, and there have been times when I needed a few beaters myself. When some American biologists were doing a study on them a few years back (a long-neglected project and badly needed) I approached a project leader for the latest dope. The personnel and scientific gadgets were ready for use, he said.

"Now if we can just catch some of the damned things!" he snapped.

By devious methods I obtained a copy of a biologist's report which covered the attempts at catching adult Huns for scientific purposes. In straight-faced biologist's language it was hilarious, especially the part about the Oriental mist net (a fine-stranded net supposed to be unnoticed by birds until they flew into it). The Huns went under, over and around the net, even when it was trolled by speeding jeeps.

The relocation of the Hun to the United States is a mystery story, so vaguely documented that I have even resorted to some of my own works of past years. It seems that the earliest serious attempts to establish the bird in this hemisphere were made around 1900 in Washington, Oregon and Alberta; but Americans being what they are, I suppose a few birds had been uncrated almost anywhere there was a faint chance of survival.

Early attempts in the eastern farmlands weren't particularly successful, although a distribution map will show pockets of them all across the northern states. It appears that the best foothold was gained in Alberta—and those birds (we think) have populated our northwestern states, where they live around grainfields as well as on high grasslands and mountain slopes that Huns aren't supposed to like but sometimes do.

I like a quote from Dan Holland, who wrote *The Upland Game Hunter's Bible*, a paperback of 1961 which deserves more attention than it gets. Holland says:

"Apparently these birds [of a 1906 planting in Washington wheatfields east of the Cascades] didn't know they had ever left home. They filled their crops with grain, settled down to a life of ease and plenty, raised healthy children and discussed plans for thwarting the Hungarian beaters which they expected during the coming autumn drives."

Ben Williams of Montana may be America's leading Hun hunter.

But don't get excited, Ben. You don't have much competition because the Hun has no tradition, glamour or press agent—except me, and I don't work at it full time.

Ben, a sort of boondock track star, once followed a covey of Huns through nine successive flushes. Or was it 11? Anyway, that kind of Hun hunting is athletic. Ben has a constant hunting companion, an eager beaver named Dr. John Cey. The idea is that these guys hunt in some of Montana's high grassland with a corps of Brittanys. They keep chasing the birds, either seeing them land after a flush or guessing where they'll be. After Huns land they tend to run. I am not referring to bobwhite trotting. I mean *run*. Getting a lot of flushes from the same covey doesn't necessarily mean a lot of birds. On some days, especially windy and snowy ones, they tend to get up wild, and several flushes don't necessarily mean that many shots, or even any shots at all.

The most flushes I got from a single covey before it broke apart was five, and the fifth was from exactly the same spot I jumped them the first time. A well-organized bunch is likely to follow a fairly rigid flush-and-land schedule, using the same spots and ending up where they started. They don't always. Often the last lap is done on foot, up to several hundred yards. If your pointer comes in and looks up at you with a harried expression, be sympathetic. After all, a dog can feel insecure when pointing is measured by the mile.

Since the European birds were primarily grain-eaters and since wheat, rye, barley and the like are preferred habitat in this country, there are gunners who call in their dogs when they run out of cereals. But in a good year the Huns scatter to chukar habitat. I have found sassy coveys at 8,000 feet on a rocky slope where I was panting after mule deer in the patchy snow. There was no grain near that spot. Like the chukar, the Hun can be comfortable in cheat grass.

Some of Ben Williams' most reliable hunting is high pasture country he has worked for some 15 years, and those birds don't have grain. I have one place of my own, a series of rocky sagebrush knobs with water nearby (urgent requirement) where I have found birds for a decade. The productive area is only a half mile across, mostly up and down, and the birds buzz around those knobs as long as you will chase them, although they will get harder and harder to locate as the day wears on and the coveys scatter. Some years back Ed Gray was up there, and as we were getting ready to leave he looked off across a hundred square miles of such knobs and marvelled at the number of Huns there must be. Forget it, Ed. I wore out a set of Vibram soles on those other hills. The birds are on those three little humps.

A man told me of coming upon a covey of Huns playing on a hillside. The snow was just right, and he said they were taking turns going down a slide on their rumps. I don't think I believe that.

One November I was hunting a steep slope with only a single patch of snow about 20 feet across. A large and fat covey of Huns was sitting in that snow and the patch was trampled and splotched with droppings, indicating they had been living there while there was plenty of sun-warmed grass over the rest of the hill. I asked some biologists about this but they immediately clammed up, looked suspicious and wouldn't even explain the things they *did* understand, so I don't say much about the snow-patch Huns.

They're especially hard to hunt in snow, generally being pretty wild and unwilling to hold for a dog. When they feed in the snow their heads appear briefly as tiny black dots as they peer around before going back to the foraging for seeds. Marcus Crosby, an addicted Hun watcher, sat on a ridge last fall with binoculars and pointed out Hun coveys to me— little dark areas that kept changing shapes far down there on the white field. As they plowed about in the snow the birds were sometimes completely concealed.

Good eyes, and I mean really good eyes, are a great help with the high-country Huns, the ones that live on the sweeping flats and the brushy draws just below the rimrock. I am about 20 years past the efficiency point in that business.

The dog points and moves and points a few more times and I puff along behind him, knowing that when the birds go they will probably be pretty well out. If he'd been steady the first time he stopped, there might have been one of those treasured moments when the birds hold like bobwhite quail and go cheeping up around your ears. But if they're running, there's no telling. My version of scientific accounting has shown the average rise from which a bird is killed to be about 15 yards— which translates into a 35-yard shot most of the time, unless you're the fastest gun in the West.

When they go up, whether I get a shot or not, I try to mark them down. It looks easy at first but they tend to sweep in a great curve, alternately silhouetted against the sky and unseen against the grey sagebrush and the brown grass of late fall. Then things get a little confused and the cluster of dots somehow merges with the little dark specks permanently installed in my retinas (the doctor calls them "floaters"). Generally they just fly out of sight unless I can get my binoculars on them. The latter is not as easy as it sounds if I've shot a bird and tried to mark it down, or have missed and paused to swear or scream at the dog. Half the time I am so spooked I forget my glasses anyway. I simply trudge off in the general direction they flew.

Despite the morbid thoughts of classic bird-dog men who say no dog can handle mature Huns, much of my pleasure and agony is in association with long-time canine Hun hunters. Most are perpetually confused and surprised at where the birds really are. A few become schemers and conspirators who eye you like owl-hooters planning a bank job when they get a sniff of Hun. I have known a couple who grinned from ear to ear and began to tippy-toe at the slightest whiff of grey partridge.

If there is such a thing as a typical Hun debacle, I guess it happened last fall on the knobs where my old Brittany, Tex, an individual noted for enthusiasm if not staunchness or style, froze with his stub tail vibrating and his breath coming jerkily. It was a miniature swale on a steep hillside that dropped off into a draw with near vertical sides. I had first found Huns in that spot during the Johnson administration. I walked in from the side so old Tex could see me and wouldn't get worried. Walked in well ahead of him so I'd be that much closer to the birds that would go up 15 yards from his nose. But there was no spatter of wings or avian squeals of dismay. It's common enough for a cautious Hun dog to point when the birds are too far off so I walked cautiously in the direction Tex was headed. I'd gone too far, I decided, and turned back toward Tex, now locked in a hypnotic stare as if the birds were under his nose. As I started to walk back toward him the Huns went up behind me, a full-fledged clatter-and-squeak flush—still a good way off but within satisfactory range. Twenty yards?

Aha! I pivoted with my gun coming up as smoothly as a gun can come up for me when it is to be pointed in the direction I've just come from. Flash of grey-and-tan birds roaring down toward the draw proper and time to shoot. That was when the other birds went up back under Tex's nose where I'd walked past them.

With the cool logic I display at such times I concluded it would be easier to shoot the birds near Tex so I abandoned my gesture toward the others and stabbed at the four headed over the ridge. I fired so efficiently my shots almost rolled together in a single report, as they used to say of the Western gunfighters. Not even a feather fell and with an empty gun I watched the things go squeaking and buzzing over the rocky top. I have no recollection of where my muzzle was pointed.

Then, for the first time in our long association, Tex really forgot himself. He stood and barked at me. The stinking potlicker.

The most humiliating thing about Huns as targets is their wide range of speeds. When a big covey takes off at close range it may go pretty well up before choosing a direction, or they might flap out like so many

43

overweight bantams. Take a nice, open twenty gauge and poke at them. Blap! Blap! Fetch!

The next time they buzz instead of flap, leave from 25 yards away and have broken the sound barrier before they're five feet in the air. It is too late to go back for the full-choke duck gun. But if you had it, you would probably have one of those shirt-button rises where you can feel the wind on your face.

Ben Williams uses an over-under twenty, improved and modified. Cey uses a side-by-side, same boring. Since Huns are in the open, why not always use a tightly bored gun? No reason except that there's some kind of mental hazard, I think. Seven-and-a-half shot is about right unless you are a full-choke pointer, when sixes might be a good choice.

They say Huns can ruin a good dog. My white setter Danny wasn't getting any full-page stories in *The American Field* to begin with, but I believe he really became a degenerate the evening we hunted those draws above Tom Lane's wheatfields. It was early season and for some reason the Huns were holding a picnic at the edge of some stubble. As nearly as I can figure there were seven covies there and they flew in all directions. Danny pointed in all directions, the Hun scent evidently hanging in the September air like warm smog. When I picked up Danny and several Huns he had a funny look in his eyes. It was a month before he pointed again.

These Hun gatherings are not unusual, but I don't understand them. The typical complete Hun covey of early season is a family group with a dozen to 16 birds. This covey has its own escape plan. When it joins other birds to make up a big flock it keeps its strategy on file. Flush the big bunch in a single, ragged uprising and each covey will head for its own hideout. That's what Ben Williams says. I had supposed they just split up at random but I can see it now.

I know where Huns rest at midday. They want enough vegetation for concealment but they want it open enough to run in and to take off from without too much wing battering. They also want to watch you as you slink up the draw. Only a very young, tired or confused Hun dives into really thick brush.

There are some Hun rules, and while frequently suspended, they give you a good start. Like the quail expert who marked a scattered bunch of bobwhites into a hollow and then showed me he could kick up four to my one without a dog, there are Hun hunters who have a feeling for where the birds go and stop.

There's the business about walking over a hill. When a covey alights on the near side of a rise the chances are they'll walk out of sight over the top before settling down. Follow them over the crest and then get your finger next to the safety.

But it's the reversal that keeps me from getting cocky. I have watched a full covey sail into an arroyo from a field of sage and followed them confidently, only to find the dog acting a little retarded instead of pointing where I was sure they should be. Then, walking back the way I'd come, I've found they'd actually hiked back past me, my hunting buddy and the dog and were back where they'd started, although somewhat scattered. I considered giving the dog a nasal spray.

Certain conditions make them fly faster. I have never understood why Huns fly faster when they're in rocky canyons, but some of the rimrock whistlers have cost me considerable ammunition. There have been occasions when the same birds got a little confused and passed me several times. Of course, standing on a near vertical canyon wall is not conducive to the best marksmanship and provides a ready-made alibi. However, if I were standing on flat concrete with my gun mounted and could yell, "Pull," I'd still miss most of them. Chukars, bonefish and Huns suspend my mental machinery.

The best Hun dogs are likely to display various tactics. Although some of the good ones run hard and stop quick in the time-honored style admired by quail hunters, there are days when Huns won't freeze but will take off while the dog is still legging it, certain he isn't yet close enough to point.

I confess that the best Hun dog I have ever seen was what I call cautious and what dog experts call piddling. He became a gumshoer at the first whiff of Hun, made most of his points from considerable distance and generally moved the last 30 yards on tiptoe. This has obvious advantages when you're hunting wild flushers because you can hurry up and be with the dog as he closes in. Not exactly classic form, but a hell of a good way to kill a Hun or two.

I would like to get poetic about Huns for nobody else has. I like them in Oregon dry country when they flush from the edge of a giant erosion and swerve with the air currents caused by a ribbon of river far below. It is wonderful in Alberta when they leave the stubble and go against a backdrop of blue sky and a bright orange grain elevator. In Montana they flush from the abandoned homestead where they and their ancestors have lived half a century.

I love to look for them in the edges of the golden stubble, but perhaps the high-grassland Huns are best of all. The country is wilder and more lonely. Small European gamebirds making a home where the summers are dry and the winters are cold.

Scatter the covey and look fruitlessly for it as night comes on, your

45

dog confused by occasional shreds of scent, finding nothing. Bone-tired, unload your gun and start back toward the truck as true night closes in. There's an occasional bullbat when the first stars show and a little wind in the grass. Then you hear the faint, reedy sound somewhere on the shadowy slope. A lonely Hun asking about his friends.

Dove of the Desert
by Byron Dalrymple

Dalrymple wrote this in the late 1940s. At the time white-winged doves were still very abundant in sections of Arizona. Today there are still populations, but actually only tokens of those now passed. Vast, complete nesting habitat destruction was almost the sole cause for the species' decline. This amounts to a real heart-wrencher because as Dalrymple pointed out, the swift, high flying whitewing of the late afternoon is one of the champions in all of wing shooting.

I will never forget my first trip into the Southwest, and I will never
remember it without immediately associating with it one of the
grandest and most unusual game birds it is our privilege to hunt in
the United States. Having been born in the Great Lakes country, I
looked forward to my first sight of Arizona in particular with much
excitement. I was not disappointed.

One of my first interests was in the many species of cactus. People
kept telling me that I should be sure to visit the organ pipe forest—
which has since become a fully protected area set up as the Organ Pipe
National Monument—because there was nothing like it to be found
anywhere else. The strange clumps of this cactus are restricted in the
U.S. to a rather small area in the vicinity of the little town of Ajo, in the
southwestern part of the state, and run from there on down and across
the Mexican border.

As it happened, the day I planned to visit the section the dove season
opened. Once I began to see doves whisking over mesquite and
paloverde thickets as swiftly as our car was slicing along the ribbon of
road across the desert, you could have wrapped up the organ pipes and
pitched them all down across the border. However, the doves and the
cactus together were that day to play an important part in my gunning
education.

My companion and guide was a man who had lived in the Southwest
for many years. He had the patience of the desert itself, and he needed
it, I'm sure, where I was concerned. From the moment the sun knocked
the top off a yonder mountain and came blasting like a rocket across the
gray desert just after our early departure, I was wanting to stop and get
on with the shooting. For with the race of dawn over the desert, here
came innumerable mourning doves right on Old Sol's tail, making him
hump to keep ahead of them as they headed for water and feed.

When we had got well on down toward Ajo, I could stand it no
longer. "Now dammit, Doc," I said. "Pull over here somewhere. This
foolishness has gone far enough."

He chuckled. "You northerners are always in such a cussed rush.
You can't kill all the doves in this country, anyway. Why don't you just
relax till we get where we're goin', then you can shoot yourself blue on
both shoulders."

"Just one shot," I pleaded. "Just to blood me."

At that he pulled the car over, making a great pretense of effort with
his patience. He didn't unlimber his gun, but squatted in the shade of
the car, flat crown cocked over one eye, rolling a cigarette and watching
me as I stalked off into the desert a little way to wait for a shot at one of
those gray sizzlers.

48

I did little waiting. Here came a bird, rather high, and, it seemed to me at a distance, merely coasting along. The flight appeared not labored but of a slower, more deliberate and lumbering fashion than I mentally matched to the mourning doves I knew. And the bird appeared exceptionally large. I had heard that the western mourning dove is a bit larger as a rule than our easterners, and, since I naturally didn't want Doc ribbing me about my barn-door shooting after I'd made him stop, I decided it might be advantageous for me to swing on this slow bird. Only when it had got within range and I started swinging, I suddenly realized that here was a fooler for sure. Slow? That bird knew where it was headed and it wasn't kidding!

I remember feeling strangely puzzled, because there was something about this bird in flight that didn't click off "mourning dove" in my mind. Then it was swerving—it seemed to me it acted far less bold in its approach than the dove—and I was frantically trying to hang a proper lead out in front of it. And then I had done it, prettily as if I had really known what I was doing. It came hurtling down into a head-high patch of furry looking, every-which-way cholla, spiking itself belly down and fully spread-winged on its countless thorns.

Before I had reached out to retrieve my bird I knew that here was the most peculiar mourning dove I had ever seen, if indeed it was a mourning dove at all. The tail was squared, its center feathers dull brownish gray on top, but those to either side lighter gray for two-thirds of their length, followed by a dull black band, and with their long tips white. The upper side of the spread wings showed a wide band of white running from edge to edge across their center portion. The bird was definitely heavier and larger than any mourning dove; the bill had a noticeably more downward curve.

"Now what," I said to Doc when I had walked back and held the bird out to him, "have I got here?" At that time, aside from my tyro's knowledge of the mourning dove and my Oregon experience with the bandtail, I knew nothing much of our dove species except that we had once counted passenger pigeons by the billions.

Doc answered me briefly in his best below-the-border manner: "*Paloma de pitahaya.*"

"Indeed!" I said scornfully. "Now tell me in Yankee."

"Well," Doc said, "that means doves of the cactus, or cactus doves. Since you've gone to college, you'd probably call it a white-winged dove. Or you might, like some old-timers, call it a white-winged pigeon. To us here in Arizona—and in Texas—it's simply a whitewing. I've always felt, like most hunters who've had experience with 'em, both on the wing and on the table, that they're a better customer than the mourning dove from both angles. Matter of opinion. They're different, anyhow. And there's such a little bit of territory where you can find 'em in the U.S. that they've always excited me. Now get in the car and let's go. I want to show you something more than those organ pipes."

What Doc had in mind, as I was soon to learn, was to show me whitewings and organ pipes together. In the section that is now the National Monument, and where shooting is now prohibited, the organ cactus grows in great clumps, the numerous shoots of each clump upwards of eight inches thick and anywhere from five to twenty feet tall, and the plants scattered so profusely that they form a veritable forest, a weird and unusual landscape indeed. Oddly, this species almost never grows anywhere except on the southwest exposures of fairly low mountains and benches, up to about 3,500 feet elevation. Their blooms, the petals of which shade from brownish green to greenish white, to purple and maroon, appear during May and June, which means that the fruits mature late in summer.

The red, fleshy fruits, or cactus apples as they're sometimes called, are not bad eating. In fact, Papago Indians regularly harvest them in large quantities. Out in the Growler Mountains west of Ajo we found the apples in abundance, and from here on around to the south of Ajo, where several springs—now inside the Monument—are located in this exotic forest, they continued so. But the important part of the picture is this: everywhere you looked there were *innumerable* whitewings, perching in the cactus and the brush, flying high, flying low, trading constantly from place to place seemingly without plan or direction, all of them intent upon gorging themselves with the ripe fruit.

Doc pointed out to me the blood-red droppings of the birds, colored from their cactus-fruit diet, and later on, near a spring where we did some shooting, he called my attention to the ground. For several hundred yards around the spring it was littered with shotgun shell cases of all sizes and vintages. How many years some of them had lain there no one could tell. But it was obvious that here was—and long had been—a favorite shooting ground for those who knew the whitewing. And it was obvious, too, that the organ pipe and the whitewing enjoyed a close relationship in nature, one undoubtedly of value to each. In fact, it has since been fairly well substantiated that the late-fruiting organ pipe is often responsible for stretching the rather short nesting season of the whitewing in Arizona for it provides food at times when other natural foods may be lacking. And no doubt the doves are responsible for furthering the interests of the cactus, too, by dropping its seeds in new ground.

This day with Doc is one I'll never forget, especially since, as I was to learn later, we were very lucky in finding the birds so abundant. I've never seen that many at any other time. And the season now, of course, is not altogether advantageous to the gunner. The whitewing concentrations don't stay long after nesting, and they have such a short distance to move into Mexico that you're lucky to catch the big flights even with the season opening as early as September first.

This bird, you see, is really a foreigner. Although it appears by the thousands each summer in U.S. territory, we are in the position, so to speak, of borrowing them from Mexico. Our southern boundaries lop off just a wee bit of the northernmost portion of whitewing range. And, as the bird is essentially a desert species, only a few small areas along the border form suitable whitewing habitat. It thrives on torrid temperatures and arid tropical environments. Undoubtedly this is what eliminates much of the high mountainous terrain along our southern border as congenial territory for him.

Beginning in California, along the western side of the lower Colorado, you find a few birds. I believe this is a fact not generally known among sportsmen. This situation comes about because California makes no distinction between whitewings and mourning doves so far as game laws are concerned. Therefore, whenever California's game laws are studied by non-residents, or even by residents living outside the Imperial Valley and the lower Colorado River region, they miss the inference that either dove may be shot during the special season set for that section. The regular mourning-dove season farther north opens at a different date. As a rule, when the Imperial Valley season opens, a limit may consist of either mourning doves or whitewings, or both, but, if both, the limit must apply to the aggregate. Whitewings are never found in unusual abundance west of the Colorado, but at times fair shooting with them may be discovered.

When you cross the Colorado and enter southwestern Arizona, however, you enter one of the two special domains of the whitewing in the U.S. If you drew a straight line from west to east, beginning at the Colorado and ending in Prescott, about a third of the way across Arizona, then continued the line from here on a straight southeastern tangent, down across the Tonto National Forest and the San Carlos Indian Reservation, until you bumped up against the border of New Mexico, you would box in for all practical purposes the nesting range of the whitewing in Arizona. In this area, the main summer distribution centers in the following locations: 1) a wide region surrounding Phoenix and running from there in two directions, the one northwestward up and around the rim of the Harquahala Desert and on to the

Colorado River, the other southwestward and down the Gila River Valley to the Colorado near Yuma; 2) a solid concentration to the west of Tucson, and a larger one from Tucson south to the Mexican border. There are, of course, other good whitewing sections in our boxed-in portion of the state, but these areas, with perhaps one more added near Sonoyta, on the border far to the southwest of Tucson, are the main ones.

Eastward, into New Mexico, the bird is nowhere abundant enough to make shooting feasible. All of the border country is too high, most of it above 3,000 feet, to intrigue summer whitewings from out of Old Mexico, and though it might seem blistering hot to a human, it's too cool for these cactus-fed customers. But Texas, in the vicinity of the Rio Grande Valley, is a different story. Here the whitewing flourishes in the mesquite and blackbrush—or did, and would, except for the inroads of agriculture and gunning, which have made it necessary drastically to restrict shooting at present.

That ties up the U.S. gunning possibilities with this wonderful desert exotic. Not much territory, to be sure, as far as the majority of our hunters are concerned, but well worth a thousand miles of travel each way for even as little as a three-day shoot. Or so I choose to believe, and there are many enthusiasts who do just that every year, for whitewing shooting is of a different cut in many ways from regulation dove shooting. Not necessarily *better*, but, as Doc said, "different anyhow."

As this is written, the season in Texas allows three days only— September 17, 19, and 21—and on those days shooting only from 4:00 P.M. until sunset, which gives the birds a chance to eat and drink on the morning flight, and by staggering the days keeps them from being immediately driven below the border. This season at present applies only in the following counties: Cameron, Hidalgo, Starr, Zapata, Webb, Maverick, Kinney, Dimmit, La Salle, Jim Hogg, Brooks, Kennedy, Willacy, Val Verde, Terrell, Brewster, Presidio, Jeff Davis, Culberson, Hudspeth, and El Paso. The remainder of the state is closed. In most of these open counties, the mourning-dove season is open on the three whitewing days, to avoid the snarl of doves illegally killed in error. But the main mourning-dove season in these counties does not open until later, when the whitewings are long gone into Mexico. This is an excellent conservation measure. The same effect is gained in Arizona by opening the whitewing and mourning-dove seasons together on September first. The whitewing season then runs for only fifteen days, but the mourning-dove season continues. However, since by September fifteenth almost every whitewing has migrated, the possibilities for illegally taking whitewings mistaken for doves is almost entirely eliminated.

For those who may be interested, the scientific name of the whitewing is *Melopelia asiatica*, and the species is arbitrarily divided into two subspecies, eastern and western, the birds of Texas being supposedly of the eastern subspecies and those of Arizona and California of the western. For all practical purposes, no gunner need make any distinction between them. The whitewing has a wide range below our borders, covering most of Mexico and on down to Panama. It is abundant in parts of Cuba, Haiti, Jamaica, and the Bahamas. It also has been recorded as a straggler within our borders in Florida and Louisiana.

There is probably no other dove whose flights, even in the present day when the whitewing is in a somewhat precarious position, are so reminiscent of the passenger pigeon. And, oddly, the whitewing as well as the bandtail had its page of history that matches on a less violent scale the slaughter of the passenger pigeon. Strange it is that this sort of misfortune should have followed civilization's discovery of the passenger pigeon, the bandtail, and the whitewing, all the species that had restricted ranges, and yet have missed in good part the mourning dove, which is so much more widely distributed.

In early days along the Rio Grande and in Arizona, the whitewing was awesomely abundant. Without question there were millions and millions of birds in the race, which had over the centuries established itself in these sections now included in the U.S. We know now that whitewings born in one section will return to it for nesting. We know also by observation and logic that good feeding, nesting, and watering conditions were what drew them in the beginning. And it is important that we keep these facts in mind as we take a brief look now at the history and habits of the whitewing in the U.S.

Picture these tropical doves, long ago, wintering in southern Sonora, and from there on south throughout Central America. There are literally billions of them. With the coming of February and March, they begin to migrate northward. The birds that have wintered farthest north in what is now Sonora will undoubtedly move, many of them, to the northernmost limits of what they consider congenial territory. And probably every year a few adventuresome fellows will push on past the place where they were born. In what is today Arizona, for example, they found the great deserts stretching on and on to the vicinity of the present Phoenix, and so, over the centuries, an abundant race of whitewings became established upon them. Here and there were streams and springs. Nesting sites in the great mesquite and cactus forests were abundant. Food was bountifully existent. These birds—this race of them—were truly of this country, and the birds with which they may have consorted during the winter down in Mexico never did come up into this northern range.

Presently man's civilization began to discover this civilization of birds. Man followed the river valleys—the Salt, the Gila, the Santa Cruz—and it was along such bottom lands that the whitewings were concentrated. They seemed, therefore, to be even more fabulously abundant than they were. Where the old San Xavier Mission, built several centuries ago, now stands, a little way from Tucson—which itself is one of the earliest settlements in the U.S.—whitewings by tens of thousands were making their daily morning flights from their nesting colonies in the great mesquite forests in that section, out into the desert to feed and drink. These flights, usually high and swift, and seemingly endless as flock after flock passed overhead, were undoubtedly watched by rugged fathers and their followers who raised gleaming white San Xavier from out of the barren desert. And unquestionably thousands of them never returned to their nests, but were utilized as a staple item of food by these same pioneers.

By the time Arizona had collected an appreciable number of white men, the cactus dove had become not only a main entree on the summer bill of fare, but had made itself an enviable place on the list of birds of sport. In fact, early in this century, whitewing shooting was the main hot-weather diversion of Arizona's outdoor-minded population. Hundreds of citizens took their stands late every summer afternoon along the flyways, and it was the usual thing for each gunner, if he could shoot at all, to knock down anywhere from fifty to a hundred birds before he quit.

This had not gone on long before the word had spread. Wealthy sportsmen from the West Coast, and even from as far away as New York, where game laws were beginning to cramp the style of the big-bag enthusiasts, began to flock to Arizona during the summer months, to get in on the fantastic shooting. The San Xavier Crossing, still a famous flight lane near Tucson and still just as popular today with hunters each fall, saw well-equipped camps established and sports paying good prices to lads to retrieve their birds for them. As far north as the valleys of the Santa Maria and the Bill Williams River, the northwestern limits of whitewing range, the shooting was just as heavy. The Cave Creek and Wickenburg areas, still favorite spots in the central northern portion of the range, the big, solidly established whitewing colony in what is today called the New York Mesquite Thicket on the Santa Cruz River south of Phoenix—a colony still one of the largest in Arizona— were hot spots for the wealthy big-town sports and the native hunters. And, before the sport hunting had more than barely established itself, market hunters began to see possibilities. San Francisco and Los Angeles began to receive shipments of thousands of birds.

But all the time something else was happening which went unnoticed by those who said the whitewing would always be so abundant that shooting could no more than put a dent in its numbers. Agriculture was getting a start in Arizona. The portions of southern Arizona most advantageous for crop raising were obviously those which already supported the best vegetation, and this of course meant that land was swiftly cleared in places where the most water was likely to be. The great mesquite forests, always favorite nesting grounds, were slowly cut and burned away. River bottoms were cleared of brush; natural waters and springs were often diverted.

It has been established through painstaking research of wildlife biologists that the worst predator of the whitewing in the U.S. is man himself, not only because of his gunning, but because the whitewing is not the farmyard nesting bird that the mourning dove is. When cutting of wood in the mesquite thickets disturbs nesting colonies, they often fail to bring off their broods. In addition, the whitewing nesting season in our territory is extremely short as compared to that of the mourning dove. Contrary to popular opinion, the majority of cactus doves in our territory seldom raise more than one brood—sometimes two—of two squabs per season under normal conditions. Further, the whitewing is not the grain feeder on the whole that the mourning dove is. He is more wary and sticks closer to his desert foods.

Thus can we begin to see what happened to the fabulous whitewing population that the pioneer knew. Since it is only for nesting that these doves stay for a few weeks in our country, it is obvious that once the major portions of their traditional nesting sites were destroyed and disturbed, their watering places often taken over by man, and crops grown where once desert foods abounded, the entire routine of the U.S. tribe of whitewings was completely upset. They could not adjust swiftly, and especially they could not bring forth numerous young during such a short season under these new conditions.

That is not to say, of course, that the whitewing in the U.S. is doomed. Far from it. Birds are still reasonably abundant in both Texas and Arizona. In Texas, cutting of the blackbrush in the small area originally inhabited by whitewings and plowing up of fields almost drove them out for good, or rather almost brought that race to extinction. But now we are seeing something in Texas that augurs well for the future of the birds there. Whitewings are spreading out over a much wider area than they inhabited before the coming of the white man. Counties far from the southern tip of Texas, counties where the whitewing was always unknown, now report more and more birds every year. Holding down of the gunning season has allowed them to hang on while making adjustments from their traditional ways. They now swarm to the grain fields to feed avidly as they once blanketed the tangles of arid-country vegetation. And along the Arizona-Mexico border whitewings by thousands may often be seen in grain fields during the short migration season.

In Texas, not only did agriculture run the whitewings out of house and home, but, curiously, it brought a predator little known previously along the lower Rio Grande, the purple grackle. This bird, which followed the opening of the country by the plow, delights in a meal of doves' eggs, and, since the whitewing is more colonial in its nesting than the mourning dove—not from choice but because of the small suitable areas in its arid habitat—the grackles found it possible to wipe out many nesting attempts on single raids.

The whitewing has been a difficult problem for the Fish and Wildlife Service. First someone would claim that it was nearly extinct, a half truth, for millions still swarm below our borders. It was our tribe that was in trouble. Again, when the gunning seasons were held down, many sportsmen who happened to have good shooting cried "Non-sense!" at the study-project men. As I've said, the whitewing comes closest to the passenger pigeon in its awesome flights. It flies high and swiftly and in loose flocks, one following another, until you think when you watch a flight that it is never going to end. But during the time when hunters see these flocks, they sometimes forget that they are seeing practically all the whitewings in their area concentrated during a migration which begins abruptly and has a very short distance to travel.

The high flight of this dove annually saves it from much overgun-ning, and makes for some of the grandest shooting any American gunner will ever experience. Here again, the bird shows that it is a product of its environment. In arid country the distance between a water hole and a good roosting site, or between roost and feed, may be very great. Thus these doves habitually take their time about starting off in the morning. They know the flight will be a long one, and since they don't mind the heat as much as the mourning dove, you always see the mourning doves begin to fly out first, then half an hour later the whitewings begin to pass over. And, being lazy in their way like many another desert species, they stay at their feeding longer, so that the two species may use the same flight lanes but seldom will you see them flying together. And of course it is always the food and water problem of desert country that keeps whitewings in rather compact concentra-tion.

This last has a curious bearing on the history of whitewing hunting. Some years ago the season in Arizona was traditionally during summer. Gunners claimed that as soon as mid-summer rains came, the birds headed for Mexico. And they proved it by showing how birds would be swarming at a desert tank, then almost entirely absent after a heavy rain. What actually happens, of course, is that once heavy rains have left puddles where the birds can drink closer to their nesting sites, they temporarily scatter, abandoning the tanks to which they formerly swarmed. Nest counts in such areas during rainy seasons finally proved the point. The cessation of summer hunting was an excellent measure. Thousands of parentless squabs were left to perish from the summer shooting. And early and late shooting to avoid the severe heat was seriously upsetting the sex balance by taking a preponderance of males that had left their mates at the nests.

Primarily the cactus dove is for the pass shooter. And let me tell you it calls for a real knowledge of lead and swing! For when the flights begin, they are really *up*. No gun is too large, no charge too punchy, and the gunner's eye must be good to drop them consistently. The one prime rule is to choose a stand where the birds will come down in the open. Otherwise you lose many, for with a fast, high bird the fall is long, and you don't always get clean kills. One of the common criticisms you hear of whitewing shooting these days in Arizona particularly is that the flights are too high to reach. Often, however, this is the fault of the hunter who doesn't know his birds.

To wit, when you see a heavy flight of whitewings begin to pass over, you have a frantic urge to get under it no matter what and blaze away. It's sport, to be sure, and tremendously exciting. But quite often it is just as unproductive. The point to keep in mind is that your stand will always be more important, as far as your bag of birds is concerned, than the number of birds in the flight. When these birds are flying high they are not so inclined to follow land contours. They fly straight and fast, especially if going from water to roost late in the day, or from roost to feed in the morning. Thus, a stand on a rise or knoll, even if it has but few birds passing over, will usually pay off with the whiteings better than one under the main flight on level ground.

Traveling *toward* water, whitewings usually fly lower, especially if they must travel uphill. And very often if not too heavily shot at they will pause here and there to rest in the bushes. This is a good thing to know when you pick a stand, for the time of day will govern which way the flight will be going, and likewise your choice of stand. But no matter what flight or stand you choose, you always have to remember that the whitewing in the U.S. is a skittish little critter. A man hunkered down

57

at the edge of the brush will cause it to dive and swerve and flare, falling all over itself in its escape gyrations. However, a man going unconcernedly about in the open, walking, especially where men may be working in grain fields, will get little attention, and therefore quite often better shooting.

I can't say that I believe too strongly in shooting right at the tanks, although I know it is popular. A bird that flies upwards of twenty miles for a drink when temperatures are scorching ought to be allowed to have it. Besides, it has been well proved that sometimes all cactus doves from an area of almost a thousand square miles will concentrate at the single tank in their vicinity. Tank shooting may thus equal overgunning, and may conceivably tend to discourage the birds from using a great area.

On the other hand, shooting along any particular flight but at sporting distance from the tank, so that missed birds can drink in peace before going to roost, seems to me legitimate practice. Years ago there was a watering place in the Sand Tank Mountains southeast of Gila Bend, Arizona, where whitewings came by thousands. They nested in the area because of its good cover, and water. The place was—and the general locality still is—a hot spot for whitewing hunters. Now a man-made tank replaces the old watering hole, but I feel that such spots should be inviolate. You can often see several thousand birds in the vicinity during nesting. If we keep in mind that the water, primarily, is what holds them year after year and brings them to this entire area to nest, we may well reflect that by doing our shooting some distance away, under the high flights, we may make that pleasure last a lot longer.

We might also take a potent lesson from this very tank. Man-made watering places near good nesting sites in the large old mesquite thickets—which the birds like much better than second growth for that purpose—will unquestionably give us better whitewing hunting in years to come. The birds don't mind flying long distances to feed, if they feel secure about water. Besides, such tanks scattered over the desert are inexpensive, and invaluable to quail and all manner of game.

If you think you are going to "walk up" whitewings very often as can be done fairly consistently with mourning doves, you'd best forget it. Mexican whitewings may be tame enough to be hunted thus, but our birds have known concentrated barrages for too long. Our cactus doves just aren't walk-up birds. But you can get feeding-field and roost shooting if you happen to be located in the right places. The reason I hold that pass shooting is the major whitewing sport is that scattered feeding grounds that make long-distance flights necessary also make long-distance trips necessary for the average hunter. If you're lucky enough to get the birds at a grain field in either Texas or Arizona, however, during the peak of migration, you can partake of some of the craziest shooting I know anything about.

The whitewing appears slower in flight than the mourner. But it takes a big wing bite and is a fantastically wild flyer when you plug away at it as it skims in to its feeding ground. When cover is such that you can get right out into the middle of a field, well, your guess is as good as mine as to how to hit the birds. You try it. That's all I've ever done. You'll get your limit, without doubt, if the birds are plentiful. But you'll burn a lot of useless powder. You'll kill a bird that is burning its wing feathers doing six-sided loops through the low cover, and then along will come a single who appears to be just drifting by without concern. This easy one you'll miss cold, and then you'll be so exasperated you'll begin missing the tough ones you've just learned to hit.

Off some little distance from a roost edge, if there aren't too many hunters around, you can get wonderful late-afternoon shooting of a quite different sort. Here you can catch the birds letting down, coasting on set wings—a whitewing habit that differs radically from mourning-dove flight—coming in low and looking easy. These fellows won't flare, however, when you fire. If you miss, they'll dive. Again, you try to hit 'em. Don't ask me how. Then, if you want the superlative of wild shooting, get yourself right into a whitewing roost. You can get good cover for yourself in such a brushy spot, and whang away to your heart's content. Someday someone will write a whole book about this hunting. It's worth a whole book. And the author will tell you exactly how to hit these crazy birds from a roost stand. Be sure not to read the instructions, for you may be certain the author won't know what he's talking about! In all the wingshooting world I know of no bird flight to equal in calm determination and detachment the high, straight pass flights of the whitewing, nor do I know of one which can even compare with the fantastic frenzy of it when you catch the birds low and unaware.

Indeed, if you have never hunted this cactus dove, you have a surprise in store for you. There is no other American gunning like it. You can take a man who has hunted every other U.S. game bird and put him to shooting at whitewings, and he will tell you that he has never tried anything even remotely approaching this, or witnessed anything like this. I've seen that happen. It is without question one of the greatest shooting thrills still left in the U.S. today.

In Texas nowadays, of course, you get no morning shooting. To my mind, afternoon shooting is best anyway, although it's hot work, even when you sit quietly with your water jug and let the birds do the hardest part. But you have to make it a point always to be on time. Usually you find it necessary to get your birds in an hour or not at all. Sometimes, in fact, your shoot will last only twenty or thirty minutes. That few minutes, however, packs a wallop, that many a whole day at other wingshot work can't touch. We can keep this wonderful shooting, too, if we carefully watch our limits and our seasons, protect what is left of our ancient and traditional whitewing nesting areas, grow new ones for them, and see to it that watering places near these areas are furnished for the birds.

Among the Doves in California With A Shotgun

By T. S. Van Dyke

While the southern states are truly the classic mourning dove states, southern California deserves to be considered among the very best locations in the U.S. for the species. This 1900 article by Van Dyke depicts an early interest in dove shooting in the West. That interest certainly expanded in the years following!

G ame is no longer valued by the thump it makes on the ground; while those who return from shooting at the dove in flight to water, with the weight of the bag less than that of the cartridges with which they proudly started, are convinced that the proverbial innocence of the dove is all imaginary. Improvements in guns have developed in the bird such a surprising ability to take care of itself that scarcely anyone is to-day ashamed to hunt it. Some of the most difficult shooting to be found with the shotgun is on this bird when it leaves a tall tree, dipping downward as it goes; while to stand under a tree and make a double shot on a pair of them, catching one as it comes in to alight and the other as it goes out at the other side, is one of the finest bits of practice one can have.

In California, although we have plenty of other and larger game, the dove ranks high as one of the game birds, and probably there is no Eastern State where it makes as fine shooting as here. We do not go after doves among the stubbles or long weeds, seeking a rising shot, though they rise far enough and fly swiftly enough to make a double shot on a pair thus springing from the ground, a shot that no one need be ashamed of. Flight shooting is so much more difficult that rising shots seem child's play.

It is in the countries having a dry summer, with water-holes plenty enough, yet not too plentiful, and reasonably near good feeding grounds and sufficient shade, that the dove makes the best shooting. These three are the prime factors, and when well combined they often make an evening flight of doves such as is never dreamed of in any of the wet countries. And they have a velocity, a twist and a finish about their style of flight that are seen only in the land of dry summers when the birds are moving for water. And where these are well combined marvellous flights of doves are yet seen in many places, in spite of settlement that has long since driven out all other game.

At two o'clock one afternoon the Southern Pacific train landed seven of us at the station of San Fernando, and in a few minutes we were in one of the adjoining orchards. The valley of San Fernando contains about one hundred and fifty thousand acres, mostly covered with immense wheat fields, and girdled with rugged mountains. In some places, such as the tract around the old Mission where we stopped, several thousand acres are in orchard and vineyard. In the deep shade of the orange, lemon and olive, the birds were sitting by dozens enjoying the cool breeze that swept through the trees from the distant sea. Sometimes fifteen or twenty would be almost together under a tree like a flock of quails. Wherever there was a spot of water from the leakage of an irrigating hydrant, doves could be seen drinking along the edge, with some in flight to and from it. In the corral of the old Mission were dozens around the water-trough and the puddle its leakage made on the ground.

But this was not the shooting for which we had come, for the birds in flight were not yet numerous enough, and while a good rising shot could sometimes be had, it was rare. The birds were wild and rose out of shot, and though they came around the corrals and associated in a friendly way with the cattle and horses, they knew right well the sheen of a gun, and had a strong suspicion of everything with two legs. It was far better to await the flight to water in the evening, when a single hour was liable to call for all the cartridges one could comfortable carry. Therefore we spent an hour or so inspecting raisin-grapes and prunes, with pears, peaches and nectarines, that were in great abundance; and then about four o'clock some of the party took a stand near the irrigating hydrants that were at the head of every forty-acre field, while the rest spread out on San Fernando Creek, on which the water runs all summer for some distance above ground.

I went to an orchard of orange trees about three years old, just large enough to hide behind without stopping, while the well-cultivated ground was so free from weeds or grass that I would have no trouble in finding fallen birds, a very important point often overlooked in many kinds of shooting.

I could have gotten probably very much better shooting on the stubble and over the patches of sunflowers on the uncultivated ground, but without a good retriever one will have plenty of work, and lost time as well as lost birds, on such ground.

Orchards were round about me on every side and thousands of birds were in them. These places are the summer home of the dove, and the evergreen shades of the lemon, olive and orange they especially love. Here their cooing resounds from early spring, and here they breed in spite of all the civilization around them. Sometimes there are a dozen nests in a tree, and in early summer the young ones learning to fly whisk and flutter about the houses and yards on downy wings, too feeble to make the whistling sound of the older bird. These orchards they love as much as the live oaks of the hills or the sycamores and willows of the water-courses, which they also frequent in great numbers. But the gentle cooing of summer was gone, and the birds were now strong on whistling wing, and seemed to know that the time to look out for the man with the gun had come.

Scarcely was I in position when my first bird came in straight as a bullet. I was about a hundred yards from a hedgerow of eucalyptus tress some sixty feet high, the next best thing to a hill to get under the lee of, if you want hard instead of easy shots: Birds were so plentiful that we cared nothing for easy shots and rather avoided them. I was so much out of practice from shooting nothing but a rifle of late that almost any shooting would be hard, but I followed my usual rule and stood where they would dip and twist the best.

The first bird I shot at cleared the hedgerow and came downward with a lurch and a twist rather alarming, and as I raised the gun he flew away to the right with a dip of some fifteen degrees toward the ground from the line of his swift flight. The motion of a quail's wings often makes its flight seem swifter than it really is. On the other hand, the motion of a dove's wing is often so deliberate as to make its speed appear less than it actually is. I was not quick enough to catch the bird on the quarter, and its first twist would have left the shot above it if I had. Fully five feet ahead of it I held as it whistled past me, and had the luck, so common, of pulling just as it shot downward from its course. Through the haze of the smokeless powder I could see that not a feather quivered, and before I could turn the second barrel upon the dove, it went, in a whirl of gray, around an orange tree in the next row. I had made the common mistake of forgetting that I was somewhat out of practice and allowed the bird to get too nearly on a line with me. Such shots should be taken on the quarter; if for no other reason, to land the birds near to you. It is only when in good practice that one can allow them to pass that point with much assurance of getting more than a tail feather, as the distance necessary to hold ahead becomes surprisingly great.

Far and near other guns began to ring over the land; doves were spinning over the lines of trees and over the open fields as gayly as if winged with the wind, and here and there one or two went whirling over, while the rest shot ahead as if little alarmed. While I was watching them, s-s-s-s-t came a dove, scarcely a foot above the end of my gun, resting in the dense top of a young orange tree behind which I was standing out of sight. The quickness of early years seemed to come back with a rush as I wheeled and landed the bird almost in the top of a tree in the next row behind me.

The birds, in pairs, in threes and in small bunches, were scudding about and preparing for the evening flight for the water-holes. But I had little time to look, for over the row of tall eucalyptus trees came a pair of doves directly toward me and at a speed that left no time for play. Holding two feet or more ahead of the nearer one as it came in on the quarter I sent it whirling over with the first barrel; then as I turned the gun on the other one it was not there, but well past me speeding down the wind at a pace that left no hope of hitting it. Shooting almost entirely

64

with the rifle for a year or so, had made me wholly too slow with the shotgun on such game.

Bang, pop, rattle-te-bang went gun after gun around me. Here I could see a dove whirl out of its straight line of flight, and there a lot sheer at the report of a gun, or some one run to pick up something; and while I was watching them the whistling wings of a pair of doves right over my head made me turn around just about the time they were comfortably out of reach behind me. Three more followed them over the hedgerow, the first of which turned over in a cloud of feathers as it passed the quarter, while the other two dipped and twisted with a rush that I was too slow to catch, and away they went unshot at. Two more followed almost before I was fairly loaded, descending over the row of trees with still more of a dip and twist than the last; and again the first one went over as it passed the quarter, dropping almost upon the last fallen bird, while the other was again a trifle too quick for me, and at the report of my second barrel only a tail feather came fluttering down from its swift course.

Faster came the rattle of guns up and down the line, and faster streamed the doves in all directions across the land. As is usual in such cases, everyone seemed to have better shooting than I. But I had little cause for complaint, for hardly had I returned to my tree after picking up the last two birds than half a dozen rose over the row of trees ahead, shooting up as they came into sight, and dipping downward with a quick twist as they came over and settled down to their course. Over went the first as it reached the quarter, and bang went the second barrel at the last one of the others as it passed me on the other side. But again I was too slow with the gun, and away it went with the rest, darting upward, and speeding like the wind.

In this way I soon shot ten doves in succession with the first barrel, and missed ten in as quick succession with the second—a very peculiar record, and one that I had never before made. As I was not shooting for count, I concluded I would see what was the matter. If I could no longer hit anything that passed the quarter, it was time to know it. So, when the next ones came, I let them come alongside before firing. They came in great shape, dashing down over the row of eucalyptus, and whisking low over the tops of the orange trees. Six feet, as it seemed, ahead of the leader, I turned the gun and pulled the trigger. Do doves shoot down intentionally? They do it so often that it certainly seems so, and this time anyone would have sworn that it was with malice aforethought, for never did a bird shoot downward from the line of flight with a quicker twist at the exact moment I pulled the trigger. No mortal could have caught that bird, and scarcely anyone could have recovered in time from his surprise to do better than I did with the second barrel, namely, nothing.

Scarcely had I loaded when a couple more were on hand. They seemed flying slowly and easily, but what a delusion I found it as I raised the gun! They shot swiftly upward instead of downward, as so many do, and before I could resist the impulse I fired where I had first raised the gun. Not a feather floated on the air, and I was not at all consoled by catching one of them at a long shot with the second barrel as they wheeled. I found what I knew long before, but had forgotten, that one must be in the best of trim for these rapid flyers, and that playing too exclusively with the rifle on game will make one too slow for doves.

As the lofty hills of Simi were turning blue and the granite peaks of the Tejunga range began to glow under the sinking sun, the number of doves increased by the minute. The main line of flight was along San Fernando Creek, where four of our party were stationed. But the largest rush of birds was in the corral of the old Mission, and to the water in this inclosure they were pouring from all directions. Down out of the sky they came, with others apparently rising out of the horizon; around the corner of the old church they whirled with a velocity that gave you a crick in the neck to turn quickly enough to follow them, while others came, swift and straight as flights of arrows, from the fields and orchards. Along the creek, however, were birds enough to keep any gun hot, and there was the center of the uproar. Up and down this there was a steady whistle of wings until the shadows of the mountains stretched across the broad valley, while the constant rattle of guns sounded much like the fire-crackers on the eve of Chinese New Year's. When we had all the birds together, there were 236 for the seven guns, and on the same ground the next day there were apparently more birds than before.

When the Gray Birds Fly
by Edward C. Crossman

Crossman was a frequent writer of California hunting subjects at the turn of the century. This 1915 article is directed toward waterhole dove shooting, and somewhat oddly, the "contest" of sorts between a ten gauge and a twenty. At that time a lot of people still shot tens, and apparently even at doves.

I t was made to order for a dove flight. Also there was the evidence of those truthful ones who had been at this water-hole earlier in the season and who averred that they had shot the limit. We marveled at the number of birds there must have been. They got the limit, and the limit is twenty.

Castaic Creek, slinking bashfully along the low bluffs of the canyon, dropped into a hole in the ground miles farther up in the hills, then crawled doubtfully from its subterranean passage where we stood. A hundred yards farther down it again lost itself in a small crack in its channel and again left its storm water bed glaring, dry, and white.

This is the habit of California streams, saving the rivers, which would be creeks in the far East where water is not a curiosity. Did this Castaic stream stay above the ground most of the time, enough for a flume to gather up part of its flow without having its boards crack open during the absent spells, it would be a river, not a creek. A creek is a channel that in the dry season is damp in spots and in the wet season is receiver-general for floods that change its shape and alter its countenance and move small ranches to spots it considers more suitable.

Willows, low ones, but three feet higher in dignity than the seven-foot bushes that dotted the open space next to the low bank of the wash, fringed the wash and the thirty-yard shelf that bordered it. Beyond lay the white, rocky, glaring expanse of the creek bed, half a mile wide and nearly half a mile dry. The water lay in small pools below the three-foot bank.

Across the half-mile waste and beyond the orange trees that lined its farther bank lay the grain country and the weeds that furnished provender for the doves. More provisions for them lay behind the willows, east of us.

Presently two of the gray birds dropped quietly across the willows, flew past me as I loafed in the warm morning sun, ignoring the frantic grab I made for the 20, stirred up the Fat Man to a frenzy that didn't get off a shot, gazed down the muzzles of the ten-bore the Heathen had not been able to give away to anyone, grinned at the near-case hardening on the solid malleable-iron frame of the Trusting One's weapon, and then flew leisurely across the wash. Evidently they did not fancy that particular watering place, but were in no hurry. The angry volley that broke out at the range of 150 yards was very gratifying to the feelings of those they left behind them, but that was all.

Then we gathered by the streamlet and marveled, each one, as to the slowness and soporific disposition of the others. The gentleman with the ten-bore and the one with the 20 were later parted by the spectators after various remarks as to dove shooting at 150 yards, said remarks degenerating into slurs as to cannons and popguns. Then we again basked in the warm morning sun and waited for the dry seeds in the gizzards of various doves in the transwillow and wash regions to arouse a thirst within their breasts.

Three of them hissed over us from the orange groves beyond the wash, forty yards high and forty miles strong. Nitro powder roared and banged and thudded to mark their progress. Visibly gratified by the salute in their honor, the three continued on their way. The wash became alive with remarks, the sort of remarks women think about each other, but don't say—and that men say, but don't think.

One of us was observed to gaze with dark suspicion on a $20 gem he had accumulated from a former friend, which the friend had purchased on the strength of the remarkable things said about it in the catalog of the mail-order house. Said former friend hastily explained that it was a long-range goose gun, page 284 in the catalog, and that forty yards was too close for it. Then the Trusting One sat moodily glowering at the perfectly good one-dollar license. His lips moved, continually forming the word "goose." It seemed to have no pleasant sound to him; his bosom was rent with doubts.

We had hastily explained the reasons for our own misses, but he could not. The gun, he averred, was pointed as straight at the doves as ever gun could be pointed, nor did the muzzle move a hair when he pulled the trigger. Yet he had missed them!

Then a W.C.T.U. convention of doves burst across the low willows, seeking those little pools below the bank. They spouted from the tops of the low willows as though shot out of spring guns on the other side.

A larger tree marked the entering place for the horde that came within shot of my little bush in the clearing. For this they seemed to head for miles back.

A pair turned as they swept across the willow tops and flew past me, bound for the regions of the other hunters up the wash. Foolishly they got within the charge of the little 20, and both of them stopped to the one shot. Remarks as to the animal from which ham is obtained came from the next blind, fifty yards up the bar.

Then six singles dropped one after the other, as is the fashion of singles, shot across the bar, and then turned and followed along the low wash bank, forty yards away—six fair crossing shots at only intermediate dove speed, at forty yards, and six rank, never-touched-'em misses. The ranks of the small-bore shotgun lost an adherent for three whole minutes.

Up the bar the six, each in his turn, shot by the hunters with the quick, flickering, twisting flight of the shot-at dove, while mourning sounds came from the bushes. Two of them stopped at the end of the gauntlet, with the Fat Man and his long-barreled pump, four of them turned across the white expanse of the wash and became specks in the sky.

Two came whistling across the willows, flickered twice in the uncertain fashion of the alighting dove, then flopped down into the very low weeds of the bar, forty yards away from me, and yards away from any possible cover around which to dodge. I could see them walking about with the perky gait of the dove that is certain of himself.

I pushed off the safety and walked quickly toward them, figuring as I walked that two already dead and the two in front of me made four of the twenty limit. It seemed absolutely impossible to miss both of them. I got within fifteen yards before they decided to fly. One flew low and hard straight away, and I covered him. The other turned and flew at waist height half around me for the open wash, and the uncertain 20 changed from the first and chased him.

I would not have believed it, but the rest of them did—and said so joyously. Never do people in such cases miss seeing all there is to see. The one I chased and chased in vain fell to the cannon up the bar. The other is still going so far as I know.

Presently they stopped coming. The sun grew hotter and those that meant to sample the water before us had apparently done so. The time arrived when they roost comfortably in the cool spots in trees.

We set forth, prospecting, seeking a field where the birds still fed, that we might try the hard, walk-up game on late season, sophisticated birds. Presently we found them, in a field grown over with knee-high weeds. One whistled up with the never-failing whistle of the flushed dove. Then he flew straight away while an automatic safety blocked further performance on the part of the spectator. Presently it was persuaded to release its hold on the triggers, and the dove stopped, stopped dead, too, when the nines caught up.

Sixty-two yards it stepped, with a 20 bore. It was not fair to the dove; the figures all said he was safe, but then, he would probably have fallen off a limb somewhere and broken his neck; he was evidently predestined to die.

As they got out, they headed for a little shallow barranca across a fence, cutting diagonally across a weedy field, and leaving a little 300-yard strip of weeds, triangle shaped, along one side. It didn't look like dove country; the little affair was hardly thirty feet wide, not seven feet deep, and with a few near-trees growing along one side.

Yet the doves made for it when we walked them out of the field and didn't persuade them to stay with us. The man with the cannon sought the little triangle near the barranca, and immediately there began the sound of a Balkan engagement. The Fat Man broke down the fence and joined the fray.

Five hundred yards away we could hear the noise of the combat, five loud and vengeful bangs from the corn-sheller, then two heavy, ponderous thuds from the equally heavy, ponderous, ten-bore hammer affair. Later we discovered that you can't count the slain from the number of shots you hear—and that when you hear a man with a pump-gun shoot five equally spaced shots it does not mean five birds, but one bird going scot-free. Anyhow, those unfortunates get far more shooting for their money than the citizen with but two shots available at any given time.

We hurried over, certain that the limits of the two were near the lawful notch and wanting to deliver them from temptation.

Gray doves were rising in front of the pair, shooting across the little barranca, and then back toward us, or along before them, for a brushy expanse of uncultivated ground and circling back toward the creek and the hills. All of the doves we had missed, actually that many, seemed to have gathered in that weed-patch in sort of a veteran's reunion.

"How many ye got?" shrieked the Trusting One at the person with the pump, still one hundred yards away. No reply. A dove rose before him and flew around him in a long circle, with a strange ratchet-sounding flight, thus: "Bang-clatter! Bang-clatter! Bang-clatter!" and so on up to six times. The last sound of the peculiar phenomenon occurred while the bird was passing the 200-yard post.

We listened interestedly and yearned for a pump-gun. In our unhappy cases we would have been able to shoot but twice, two miserable, paltry shots at the bird, as compared with six separate and various thrills, and things to marvel at later on.

"How many ye got?" inquired the Trusting One again, not aware of the fact that etiquette prescribes no speech with a person who has missed six times—merely speech about him, which is different. No reply.

"How many ye got?" shrieked the curious one again.

The badgered one straightened up from a bush into which he was glaring.

"I got one, y' idjit, if I can find where it fell in this dambush," and set to peering once more into the mysteries of the dove concealer.

Just to make things interesting, the little 20 cleaned up two birds that flushed in front of it, downing one that circled to the right and the other as it crossed the bank of the barranca. The small bore again leaped into

71

place in my affections, especially when its six pounds snapped around on a circling dove, where a heavy twelve would not catch up in shooting time.

We held a council of war, once we had combed the weedy tresses of that triangle. Two of us had followed up the barranca into the wild land, beyond the fence, and had returned with a determined vaquero escorting them to the line fence. In view of his rudeness and the fact that his boss had been party to a very bloody gun fight in years gone by, we decided to boycott that wild land, to refuse to honor it further with our presence. Besides, they could see us with glasses from the ranch.

Naturally, after witnessing the performance, every dove we jumped made for that wild land. A few stayed with us, but their intentions were bad.

It seemed to be a loafing-place for the doves—that barranca. We would skirmish along it, one in the sandy bottom, and the rest strung out along the weeds, and each time we flushed doves, wild, twisting, scary doves. We became pained after a while to see them waste their young lives on that patch of sagebrush beyond the line fence.

Therefore we resorted to strategy. We put the Fat Man with the stutter-gun at the spot where the barranca crossed the dead line, with instructions not to let a dove pass him. Then we formed across the lower end of the gulch, 400 yards away. Daringly he sneaked up the gulch into the wild land, while waiting for us, and fired four shots at doves he jumped from places of fancied security, running out a horde of them from the brush, then sneaked back again to our side, under cover of the gulch.

He didn't feel a bit the worse for seeing an angry vaquero ride out in the hot sun and search the brush for the hunter whose shots he had heard.

Then the skirmish line started its march.

We had given the birds an hour's rest, so far as the patch and the barranca were concerned, and they were in again. The 20 and the 10 bore patrolled the gulch side, a fair test for the two on doves—3/4 ounce of 9's, and an ounce and a half; six pounds against eight and a half.

Where the break was even, the bird flushed where both could see it, the 20 almost invariably got off two barrels if the first missed, or two birds arose. The great ten rose ponderously to place, and when it killed its birds it killed them fifty yards away. This sounds lovely, but if the bird is a fast crosser and the brush is high, you have two difficulties to overcome—a lead that is double what the quicker 20 required at short range and a chance of losing the bird when it went down.

Never did the 10 get on a quick-flushing bird that flashed around the gunner after the habit of a badly frightened dove, and there were many such birds. I hate to say, being modest, which gun came out ahead, but truth compels me to state that the little gun with its 3/4 ounce of 9's fairly outshot the big 10 and the many-shot pump-gun. It is only fair to admit that this sort of work is where the 20 bore scintillates, and that at fifty yards on heavy sea ducks the story would be different.

At the head of the gulch the stutter-gun roared and clattered and roared again. A game warden, listening, would have begun mentally to compose his speech to the hunter on arresting him for breaking the bag law.

Before our march the birds whistled out of low weeds—the most thrilling sort of a shot, and darted from the limbs of the low trees by the side of the barranca. The big gun boomed away, dragging down birds that had begun to gaze around behind them to see what the fuss was about, while the 20 snapped down birds before they had hardly a fair start.

Occasionally we could see a bird perched on a dry twig by the side of the gulch. Then would begin the conjectures as to how close we could get before he flushed. Once a dove, thinking itself hidden, insisted on perching quietly and letting us walk past within twenty yards. A rock crashing through the brush undeceived it, and the big gun cut it down about the time it straightened out for a sober flight.

The airy contortions and twistings of the flushing dove were all lost on the sober-minded 10 bore. It calmly waited until the bird ceased to imagine itself a jack-snipe, then—provided it was still in view—it cut down the dove with the calm certainty of a fat man sitting on a newsboy.

Two of the birds turned at the fire of the very busy man with the pump-gun and came hustling back for us. We sank to the ground, and they didn't change their course an inch. There was an elegant chance for a double, but the fellow with the 20 was too anxious. With the first bird fifteen yards away the little gun snapped up and the charge met the dove face to face. A cloud of feathers and meat flew to the four winds at the range of twenty-five feet, while the second bird collapsed at sixty yards before the double handful of shot from the cannon. Not satisfied with being a 10 bore, I have the awful suspicion that the beast was cylinder bored into the bargain, and that it threw an eight-foot killing spread at game ranges.

We drove out the last skulkers, knocked down a pretty one that circled around us back along the gulch, and then found the guard at the dead-line busily gathering up his slain. He had experienced the time of his life, he averred, and declared himself heartily in favor of the

European game-driving system. Also we noted that he kept his hands away from the barrel of his gun, and that the wood of the action-slide handle seemed scorched.

He confessed later to an average of seven shells to the bird, and he's a good shot with a slower-talking gun. From the standpoint of the man who likes to burn up shells, he had the best of it.

The casualty list showed our bag pretty close to the plimsol mark. Therefore we withdrew the sentry and marched for home.

Clover Valley Bandtails

by Tom Burrier

The band-tailed pigeon is solely a western bird. Under the right conditions—such as a high fir-clad ridgetop—it can be unexcelled as a gamebird. And few hunters know just how well decoys work at times for this big pigeon. Burrier's 1947 article was among the first to point this out. He also managed to capture some of the Northwest flavor of pigeon hunting. Reading this makes one yearn for the month of September and the flocks trading over mountains on strong cool afternoon winds.

The maples were beginning their fall fashion show, and the last song birds of Indian summer were seriously considering a winter vacation farther south. Wheat stubble glistened in the pale September sun; stray gusts of wind sent acorns rattling through the naked branches of giant oaks. Autumn had come to the Puget Sound country of western Washington.

It was that in-between time for hunters. Too late for the spring-born cottontail rabbits, too early for the upland bird season; but the season on band-tailed pigeons would be open tomorrow.

At home all was gloom. Even Orvie, the black tom-cat, wore a downcast look. I had pulled in early that afternoon, eager with plans for a good shoot on the morrow. Mom had given me the bad news.

"A group of city hunters has rented most of Clover Valley," she said, "and they intend to shoot it tomorrow. Dad went out and talked with the farmers a few days ago, but it's all sewed up. Seems it was rented from the seed contractor. Pigeon season is only fifteen days, and you can hunt Chinks pretty soon."

It wasn't much consolation. Clover Valley closed! Why, that's pigeon headquarters—the only spot on the island where there is any shooting. It's a natural bowl some two miles square, located about six miles from Oak Harbor and criss-crossed with drainage ditches and tiny sump holes. The migrating bandtails come for the peas grown in that lush valley, seed peas that supply a good part of the world. Harvesting of the crop in August left a carpet of ripe seeds, burst from their pods during the picking. Perfecting the pigeon set-up, the valley was fringed with small fir trees, and a hundred tall, burnt-out snags were scattered through the area.

During past seasons the valley had been open to every one; but the building of the bridge had changed that. The new span across Deception Pass connected Whidby Island with the mainland for the first time. It was now accessible by auto.

"Where's Dad?" I asked.

"He went out to John Markham's place to see if you could hunt there." Mom felt as badly as I did. She had been counting on pigeon potpie for months.

Markham lived clear out of the valley, a mile or so to the south. He was on the island's West Beach. Dad must have been desperate.

I was morosely oiling my 12-gauge when he came in. It was late, and a gentle breeze was rippling the bay. Mom took his supper from the warming oven, and I joined them in the kitchen.

"Well, we've got a place to hunt tomorrow," he announced. "John said we could use his side-hill. I built a couple of blinds and fixed up the place. We might get some shooting. Not as good a spot as the valley, but it'll have to do this year."

"There's no use kidding, Pop," I said. "Markham's place is at least a mile from the valley. By the time the valley shooters get through raising the morning flight, those bandtails will be three hundred yards over us, heading for King County. We may as well stay in bed and forget it till Chink season opens."

"Well, we might give it a try. We don't want John to think we're not grateful. Besides, I worked out another idea, and it might pan out."

I wasn't hopeful, but the thought of missing opening day wasn't appealing, either. Dad and I had opened the bird season together for years, and I didn't feel like clipping it off now, even if we did nothing but sit listening to the barrage from the valley.

"Let's get out before daylight, then," I said. "Maybe there'll be some strays for a shot or two."

It was foggy next morning, and I wore an extra sweat shirt. Dad had on his shell vest for added warmth—quite a concession, as he dislikes them. In silence we drove along the familiar rutted road leading into the valley. I tried not to look as we passed our normal parking place and continued through the valley to Markham's place. It was quiet as we climbed from the car in the half-light of approaching dawn.

Dad knocked at the kitchen door of the farmhouse, and John Markham wished us luck. Then we plodded down the hill through ferns and second-growth fir until stopped by a rail fence. The light was growing, and fog swirled far down the valley below us. We could make out car lights moving along the road we had left, and stopping where we had parked in former years.

"The blinds are over here to the left," Dad whispered. "I built 'em about forty yards apart, and put the decoys in those three trees behind."

"Decoys! For pigeons?" I sputtered.

"I don't see why it won't work," Dad said. "You know how they take to those snags in the valley. If there's only one pigeon in a tree, a whole flock will head directly for it. Why won't decoys work here?"

Maybe they would. Besides, we had nothing to lose. The valley was lost to us this year. And Pop might have a winner.

"What did you make them from," I asked, "and how did you get them fixed in those little trees?"

"They're cardboard cut-outs. I cut them in the workshop and mounted them on plywood strips. Little Danny Markham climbed the trees yesterday and put them in place. They look real, don't they?"

I gazed intently toward the clump of little firs he pointed out. There were twenty or more pigeon silhouettes outlined in the branches. Even as I watched there was a flapping of wings—half the decoys flew away!

"They must have roosted there," Dad exclaimed. "Let's get into the blinds before those fellows in the valley open up. It's shooting time."

It was daylight now, and the fog was lifting rapidly. I scrambled hastily into the first blind, and Dad went down the fence line to the second. The blinds were built with the careless skill of fifty years' hunting experience. I knew their cornstalk-and-fern exteriors would reveal little to even the wisest of pigeons. If only the decoys would work!

There was a burst of firing from the valley, then scattered shots in the first volley of the season. Far below, a cloud of birds rose from the peafields and scattered toward the valley edges. The main flock came directly toward us, gaining altitude with every wing-beat. They passed overhead—about three hundred yards overhead. I rose and stared after them as they vanished toward the salt water.

Two quick shots—and I spun around. Dad was lowering his double, and over the stubble field before us two gray forms were plunging earthward.

"Part of the stragglers," Dad grinned. "They came in low, behind that big flock. I thought you saw them. I think they wanted to sit with our decoys. They're still hungry, and none of 'em will go far from these peafields."

He climbed the fence and came back with the pigeons. They were beautiful full-grown birds; their sleek heads were dark gray, with the color lightening toward the breast into a light pearl shade. Their trim fan-tails were irregularly marked with the black-barred splotches from which they gained their name.

"Let's get back under cover," I suggested. "Maybe there'll be a few more strays."

"There's a pair with several friends." Dad pointed down the valley with his gun barrels.

Another flock of pigeons was boring into the valley. They were clearly heading for the peafields, circling lower and lower as their leader selected the landing spot. We crawled into the blinds and peered through the rail fence.

As we watched, figures rose from the ditch-blinds in the valley, and the delayed sound of shotguns was relayed seconds later. The pigeon flock beat frantically for altitude, then straightened out for our side of the hill.

"Watch it," Dad called cautiously. "They haven't fed this morning, remember, and they're wanting another chance to go down. Maybe they'll come into the decoys."

The flock quartered toward us, sighted our decoys, and were gliding in. I held my breath. There were thirty or forty pigeons in the flock. I couldn't miss, or so I thought. My first target zoomed overhead, and I missed; but with the recoil of the second shot the bird hesitated, then tailspinned to earth. I swung quickly to a second gray blur. He must have realized he was under fire, for he swung into high gear and vanished over the firs.

"You've got to lead 'em a little more," Dad called. "Those birds are as fast as teal when they're sailing in like that."

"How did you do on that bunch?" I called back, pushing fresh shells into the magazine.

Dad hedged. "I—uh—think I had 4's in the gun. I must have held too close."

Smiling to myself, I retrieved the bird. It's a rare occasion when Dad misses two shots, especially at that range. But, then, pigeons are different, and this was opening day.

"Mark!"

I didn't stop to look; I flopped in the ferns. There was one shot, the bark of Dad's twenty.

"That's better," he was saying in a satisfied tone. "I was beginning to think your mother was right; that I should see about glasses. But now I won't have to worry for a while. That bird was sixty yards!"

It was all of sixty yards. He stepped it off from the fence line, and was smiling as he walked back to the blind.

There were more scattered shots from the valley. The great flocks had broken up now, and singles, twos and threes were flying aimlessly about, trying to settle in ungunned portions of the peafields. Some were roosting safely in the tall charred snags overlooking the fields. They were safe there.

The sun had crept high from the ocean, and its warm rays slanted on the golden wheat stubble. It dispelled the last of the ground fogs and threw the entire valley into sharp relief. I settled back in the blind, idly following a small group of birds milling over a ditch to our right. I didn't hear the bunch come in. There was a sudden wingflapping and then silence again. I craned my neck cautiously.

"Turn around and take 'em!" Pop shouted.

I whirled, and the air came alive with birds. They had sailed in behind us and headed for our decoys in the firs! I felt better as the automatic reached out and pulled down the second bird of my double as it disappeared over a brush clump. I heard Dad's twenty bark; he also scored a double.

"Things are looking up," he called, "and the sun is getting warm.

Now I can take off this shell vest. It binds my shoulders."

There was continued fire from the valley. Singles and doubles drifted our way or sneaked in from the bay and glided into the decoys. Our bag grew as the morning lengthened. The decoy set-up was fine!

Dad stood up and stretched finally. "About ready to go? I'm getting hungry again. We'll get in another day this week."

We packed our pigeons carefully in the game bag and climbed the hill to Markham's farmyard. Mrs. Markham waved a cheery greeting from the porch, and exclaimed over the bag. Would we save the rest of the breast feathers for her? With those from the five birds we left for their supper, she could complete a down comforter. We would.

Dad drove carefully down the valley road. With a contented expression on his face, he pointed out more pigeon flocks. Midway through the valley a hunter stood in the road, hailing us. Dad slowed the car to a halt.

"Happen to have any 12-gauge shells? We're not getting many pigeons in spite of lots of shooting. I'm out of shells. Birds are too high for us; don't want to come down."

"I've got a box you can have," I said. He paid me for them and thanked me.

"Are you having any luck, or are you quitting in disgust?"

I looked at Dad. He grinned. Then I opened the rear door and unstrapped the game bag.

"Lord!" breathed the hunter. "How did you get those? Pot-shoot them?"

"Pot-shoot, nothing," Pop snorted. "We used decoys!"

The hunter stared at Dad. "Decoys! For pigeons? Who are you trying to kid?"

He was still laughing as he crawled back through the fence.

After the Band-Tails
by Edward C. Crossman

California has long been noted as the number one state for bandtails. While it has its own population of breeding birds, these are greatly augmented by migrating birds from British Columbia, Washington, and Oregon. Crossman's 1915 article was somewhat typical of pigeon hunting during past eras; as many were shot from trees as from the air. And he was incorrect regarding the bird's numbers. Two years prior to the publication of his article the bandtail population had been shot to a low point that saw a 21 year closed season on the species.

As the light grew stronger, there spread out before us the valley of the Santa Ynez, with its center of white stones, polished by the flood waters of the spring, and its border of gently sleeping, live-oak studded hills.

In these live-oaks, said the three veracious ones, lived the rare and shy band-tail pigeon, denizen of the mountains, expert in shotgun ranges, cat-like in its possession of nine lives, a morsel like a quinine pill to the unwise, a dish fit for the king to the man knowing the ways of the band-tail.

As a mark for the gun, the bird was new to me. It was old in the wondrous tales of B. L. and the Reformed Golfer.

A story there was of the crack shot, and the usual gathering at the country club, and the gentleman with unhappy experience trying to kill the birds. In the tale there appear the details of how the crack shot, unknown as a crack shot to the denizens of the country club, offered to bet money on his ability to stop so many birds with so many shots.

I quote no figures, and not quoting them, am safe from the fate of the nature faker.

Anyhow, much money suddenly leaped into sight on the rash pronouncement of the crack shot. He found himself with much money his if he could make good his words. Then they repaired to the Santa Ynez, seeking the mountain pigeon, the band-tail.

The figures were something like seventy-five birds killed with ninety shots, but I refuse to commit myself. Anyhow the crack shot won. With later experience of the same birds I am still wondering how big a gun the crack used to make his record. The tale went to show the pessimistic view of the Santa Barbara sportsman as to the possibility of making any wonderful record on these shy birds.

Our way led along the sides of the low hills that bordered the wide, white wash. Presently we edged off the road, into a green park-like opening, and halted. The hills from which we had come were just turning orange in the morning light. Wisps of fog lay along the little river a few hundred yards away.

We emerged from the trees a few moments later. As we stepped forth into the open, there came flying six very black looking birds from the farther side of the wash. At sight of them the three veracious ones capered and yelled and testified to their being possessed by extravagant joy. They declared with unseemly language that our fortunes were made, that the birds were still at that spot.

The six crossed below us, and I watched them curiously.

They flew with strong regular strokes like ducks bound somewhere. With their long tails and their peculiar flight, they reminded me strongly of sprigs really bound for some point beyond the horizon. The first impression they give in any light is their extreme blackness. They looked large, larger than the tame pigeon, larger by far than the ordinary dove.

Now came others into sight, crossing the wide wash with their steady, strong flight, like reduced versions of these dragon-fly monoplanes.

Then I became acquainted with one of the methods of the band-tail hunter. B. L. marked down with fiendish glare the lighting place of a dozen of the birds that had crossed below us. Then he proceeded to stalk them, giving an imitation of a man trying to show that he's not looking for anybody in particular, compounded with an Indian creeping up on his unsuspecting foe.

Gradually he approached the tall tree in which sat the birds. I looked about that time to see him yell or throw a stone or fire a wild shot, something to make them fly. Not the man really out to get band-tails and knowing the uncertainty of said getting.

He took deadly aim with his pump-gun, then it remarked hurriedly to the tree top, bang-bang-bang, with two more bangs to the flock of horrified pigeons that hustled from said tree.

Two dark objects came tumbling through the leaves; two thumps greeted our ears. Came a joyous war-whoop.

I looked to see him blasted where he stood. I expected to see the wrath of the Reformed Golfer and the Schuetzen Artist fall upon him then and there for shooting the birds on the sit. Not so, they merely looked envious.

Then I began to learn the nature of the band-tail, and as I learned I hankered more and more for one of those huge English eight bore guns, with a handful of BB's in each barrel, and a flock say of 500 birds just above me in some treetop. And ordinarily I am not a hog.

The Schuetzen Artist and I betook ourselves to the trees at the other side of the wash to see if we could not come upon some late-risers among the pigeons. Then we walked through the live-oaks, up the gentle slopes, and before us there rose the sharp snapping of fast-moving wings, with occasional glimpses of dark bodies darting down the open spaces. Not a shot did we fire. Shooting at such marks was equaled only by the feat of the man who stood inside the barn and hit marbles thrown across the open door. I yearn to see a well-picked ruffed grouse shark stop band-tails as they leave their roosts in the thick live-oaks.

As we stood watching by the edge of the wash, we noted that small flocks of the birds were seeking the top of a half-dozen tall sycamores growing halfway out across the white expanse of wash. The tops of the trees were black with them.

We separated and strolled casually toward the trees, 300 yards away. We endeavored to give by our actions the impression of two gentlemen out viewing the scenery. Closer we drew, and still the pigeons sat on their lofty perches and watched our approach. We began to think no small beer of ourselves as actors. We were deceiving those fool birds.

Then, just out of even the scratch range of 6's, they rose as one bird and sailed calmly away for the hills. I know now that if we had been loaded with 4's, they would have risen just out of the reach of scratch shots with 4's.

Over against the hill there sounded the irritated voice of a pumpgun, bang, bang, bang, bang, the ticking of a very loud clock for regularity. The clatter of the mechanism came to us between the shots. A bird tumbled out of the flock.

The Artist and I were rejoiced. Our desire for revenge on that flock rose above even our desire to get all the birds ourselves.

We sat down, craftily, at the foot of the sycamores among some shoots that grew there. Then, as is ever the case, the shooting of the other fellows became a lot better than our own. Over along the hills bordering the river there flew agitated flocks of the birds, but they were scandalously high, out of the range of any respectable shot from a 12 bore. Ever there rose the hopeful banging of the guns, futile but amusing to the gunners.

Presently we gazed up at the top of our tree. Six pigeons sat there sociably. Cautiously I raised my gun—raised it a few inches. Then six pigeons departed that place with celerity, nor did our indignant shots make any change in their numbers. We communed with ourselves as to the beauties of doing our sleeping only at night. We were pigeonless, and still scores of flocks hustled up and down the wash.

We departed for the hills where stood the machine and where the two gunners saluted each flock that flew leisurely by. Immediately our old stand became densely populated with band-tails. Ten of them flew from the hills and lighted in the tree we had so zealously guarded. We stood and hoped that some evil thing would come upon the ten. While we stood there a foolish and lone bird came sailing out from the hills. His estimate of range was poor, or perhaps he did not see us.

Two guns fired four hasty shots at him, and joy of joys, he came flopping down. He was a big, black looking bird, slaty blue and faint green in various spots on his somber colored body. He was bigger than a tame pigeon. He had a bill and claws, giving the suspicion that in days gone by there had been a scandal between his family and that of the hawk. The hooked beak did not testify to the vegetarian habits of the bird. His wings were long and powerful, his tail broad and stiff.

Apparently the band-tail is the nearest living relative to the extinct passenger pigeon that used to darken the sky with its flocks. Two of the California birds were taken to Cincinnati a year or two ago. The sportsman who took them alive to the eastern residence of the only living passenger pigeon stated that the birds are much alike. The western bird is larger, and the feet are different in color, otherwise the resemblance is marked.

Until the passage of Uncle Sam's migratory bird law, there was no closed season for the band-tails, and there was as much limit to the bag as there was closed season. And even now, I see no reason for a bag limit if the pot-hunters are forbidden to sell the birds in the market, and so are deprived of the inducement to sneak under the trees at night and pot the pigeons. Otherwise the birds seem amply able to preserve themselves and enough of them manage to live to perpetuate their race. All of which is putting the case mildly.

We found the other two gunners. B. L. had six and explained at length and violence how he shot each one on the fly. The Reformed Golfer had five, but he told the truth about his. I understood then. The man who could stalk and shoot the sitting pigeon could creep up and lay his hand on the shy deer. Shooting a band-tail on the sit is proof of craft that is nearly superhuman.

We arrived, in our search for a spot where the birds had less contempt for the earth and its denizens, at a little valley that ran down to the river. It was a cosy, comfortable little valley, with rounded sides all dotted with the live-oaks and with three hundred yards of level space in the bottom.

Across the 300-yard width there flew divers flocks at a height that was just low enough to arouse wild hopes and aid a starving ammunition trust. Also by some chance they invariably came from the direction to which we had our backs turned, nor did it matter which side of the valley we selected.

For an hour we banged away at them hopefully. Perhaps one shot in ten connected, and a bird came fluttering and fighting to the ground. Like the California quail, they fight to the last gasp. The helpless, soft, purposeless fluttering of the dove is not for them.

Once the Schuetzen Artist and I sat on the gentle slope, talking about a brand of shooting that had to do with paper targets and not with vexing band-tails. A dozen came over us from behind, and they were nearly by when we saw their shadows sliding across the ground before us. I cast a despairing shot at the flock, and a bird came out of it, turning and fluttering to the ground.

I walked out the fifty yards to pick it up, when it arose and started across the valley in helpless, fluttering, nearly all-gone fashion. I hot-footed after it angrily, not caring to waste a shell on a bird so obviously all in. Finally, not gaining an inch, I stopped and shot at it. It fell, and once more I walked up to bag it.

My hand was within two feet of it when it rose into the air and started back across the little valley for the Schuetzen Artist. I had reloaded, from force of habit, and I took deliberate aim at a range of ten feet. No results followed the shot. I slammed in the second barrel at a range of twenty feet. Also no results. Came across the little valley a most delighted howl, "Throw the gun at him."

Then, nearly 300 yards from where I stood, the S. A. cut down the heroic bird, the third charge that had hit it, and the fifth one that had been fired at it.

For two hours, during lunch time, the birds considerately refrained from disturbing us, while we enjoyed the feelings of an anaconda that had connected with a goat. Then all at once they began to fly again.

We arranged a deliberate campaign against a large flock that we saw alight in a big oak toward the river. We had an advance guard, cavalry screens, feint attack, real blow, and all.

We got within eighty yards of the tree when B. L. put the fat in the fire. He was detailed to deliver the feint, to keep the birds watching him, while we crept up on the other side. Perfidiously he opened up with his long pump gun. Six shots clattered from that awful gun, two birds tumbled out of the mass that erupted from the tree.

It was a long shot, seventy-five yards or more, but it had turned him into a nuisance of the first class. Nor had he any appreciative audience in those he had betrayed. He bragged about that gun when he was 300 yards from the nearest man. His roars of joy whenever he thought of it frightened away birds not yet in sight. He opened up at remote specks in the sky after that, and when said specks failed to fall he blamed the ammunition, never that gun. So arise the reputations of many guns that on paper targets pattern about in the sixth or gaspipe class.

For a half-hour I watched him, and watching learned the ethics of the pump-gun shooter. The program was about like this:

Flock heaves in sky, grows closer, gets within say eighty yards. Then the gun speaks. It speaks five times like the ticking of an agitated watch while the birds travel fifteen yards. Then, when as usual no bird responds to the cannonade, there rises a voice of infinite gladness, and pitched to carry three-quarters of a mile. It says "Well, I'll be ——— wotche know about that?"

And later, at the gathering of the clans he relates it thusly: "It was eighty yards if it was a foot. I swings about twenty feet ahead of it, pulls, and down comes Mr. Pigeon. One shot? Sure, how many shots d'je think I need, huh?" And the tale varies not from one pump-gun man to another.

We wound up with about twenty birds to the four of us. Truth forbids me to say how they were apportioned in the record of the kills, because the truth is at times hard to tell.

Dusky Grouse
by H. L. Betten

Blue grouse are the big forest grouse of the West. At times they can be almost too foolish to afford good sport. At other times they can be superb. On his venture to British Columbia in the 1930s Betten apparently found them at their best. And that can really be very good.

From the eastern slopes of the Rocky Mountains across almost to the Pacific Ocean and from the Mogollons of New Mexico far up into the Yukon Country, there is a grouse that is a thoroughbred. No matter whether he fits into ranges that sweep to twelve thousand feet, or whether you find him down on the edge of the wheat fields, or whether you run across him in thick timber, the dusky grouse BELONGS.

Members of the clan are elastic in their choice of habitat, and for this reason have come to be known under several names, the most common being the blue grouse; then, the sooty grouse, the Sierra, and Richardson's.

They are at their finest in alpine regions where the strum of mighty wings harmonizes with the boom of mountain cataracts and sturdy, graceful bodies in flight are limned sharp and dark against snowy, glacial backgrounds. There, in a setting surcharged with beauty and romance, a feathered mammoth roars aloft as the hunter approaches his rigid dog. It is with supreme exaltation that the gunner catches a glimpse of his fleeting mark; it crumples in a mist of feathers and he hears the hollow thump of a heavy body; listens to the beating wings among the fallen leaves as a gallant bird taps out a threnody in its death throes.

For the dusky grouse is the largest member of the North American family next to the great sage hen, and in appearance he is far more impressive than that grouse.

I aim to take nothing from a fine lowlander, the ruffed grouse, but I insist that in identical environments the old fan-tail must play a second fiddle to his huskier relative, the dusky grouse.

You can get all sorts of discussions and arguments as to which of these two birds is the smarter. I don't pretend to answer that question, but I really believe that the dusky or blue grouse has just a few less tricks in his bag. I can't overlook the fact that the ruffed grouse in all parts of the United States has been hunted harder than its big western cousin but has managed to endure after taking fierce punishment over more than a hundred years.

Many gunners will tell you that in the early days of the West the unsophisticated dusky grouse qualified to the name of "fool hen," and a covey of young birds could be picked off one after the other from perches in the same tree.

But don't overlook this, that in Maine the ruffed grouse was the first member of the family to be given the name of "fool hen," and this epithet pursued the ruffed grouse through New York, through Michigan, and as far west as the bird located. Then the same name of "fool hen" was given to the sharp-tailed grouse of the Northwest and it is quite possible that ranchers in Colorado tacked the nickname onto the dusky grouse or, as they called it, the blue grouse.

You hunters with experience on various members of the grouse family know that the birds have absolutely no fear of man at first contact and it is only after a number of years of hard shooting that a native instinct is developed to protect them.

And it is still possible to find dumb grouse of all species in the remote backwoods. The proportion of feathered suckers among these tribes, however, is dwindling rapidly as civilization pushes deeper into the forests, the mountains, and the distant and little travelled pioneer areas.

In order to make satisfactory bags of either ruffed or blue grouse today, different tactics must be employed than formerly. Of course, there are residenters with superior local knowledge who can get by without leaning upon a competent grouse dog, but the most of us are not so fortunate.

A dog is almost a necessity in grouse hunting in any section of our land and under present conditions. My own experience with grouse dates back many years and to a time when market hunters were the principal men in the field, together with a sprinkling of real city sportsmen and a motley assortment of rural loafers who enjoyed the sport. At that time rifles accounted for many of the game birds killed. To kill a grouse with a rifle means that the bird is mostly roosting in the branch of a tree. There are places in the United States and in an exceedingly large number of spots in Canada where you can get both ruffed and blue grouse with either rifle or revolver.

After all, it is merely a matter of experience and a repetition of fear piled upon fear, alarm surmounting alarm, that brings about the change in the grouse today and makes him a timid creature, difficult to find and nearly as difficult to flush. Hence, the larger need for a truly good grouse dog.

Looking back through the corridor of time and making due allowance for the glamor of years long passed, I realize the shortcomings of the grouse dogs which were then commonly used, deficiencies which I hold were due to defective training. The dogs covered little ground, were extremely slow and cautious, and the racket made by the hunter enabled cunning birds to run swiftly ahead or to dart aside and later take wing silently. In this way, no end of grouse were missed, and it was only a great abundance of the game that made large kills possible even in that era of plenty. Many market hunters didn't employ dogs at all, depending upon an intimate knowledge of woodcraft and the habits of grouse to fill the bag.

Yes, a great majority of the dusky grouse are still being killed in the hit-or-miss manner without dogs; being tramped up in haphazard fashion. Well, there is no law against that, but there are few gunners more arrantly foolish than the greenhorn who believes his own dull wits qualify him to hunt difficult game in difficult fields without the strong aid of a good grouse dog.

When a dog is used there is no member of the grouse family that affords a higher quality of sport than the dusky grouse.

Off in the humid Pacific Northwest, I had a typical hunt on the birds with "Judge" Macdonell of Vancouver, B. C., and his team-mate, a versatile pointer, Champion Spots Rip Rap—actual star of the adventure.

I had a rendezvous with the spare, angular, intensely active barrister in Canada very early one fall morning.

"Everything's arranged," the Judge declared when he met me at the depot. "We'll have a bit of breakfast and be quickly on our way. Spot? Oh, he's in the car yonder; yes, yes, the old rascal's feeling fine, but not too fine, I hope. You know how it goes with him when he feels his oats. Ran him three hours yesterday to take off the wire edge. Maybe that will hold him. But you know Spot. The beggar's a problem."

Did I know Spot? I certainly did; an unpredictable black and white rascal; a master mechanic and an unbeatable virtuoso at his trade of hunting birds—that is, when he was in the mood. A wilful, rascally so-and-so when he went on a bust or a rampage. All genius is like that, and Spot was a genius among gun dogs.

Cunning, keen-nosed, super-capable, a nonpareil at field trials when he felt like cooperating, and at his devilish worst, a grinning little rascal who ran wild and nigh broke his owner's heart on ill-starred occasions.

We were off to the grouse country, a matter of thirty miles away. First through the flatlands and wooded foothills, all scarred and looted by ax and fire, where an occasional small orchard or cultivated field relieved the monotony of stumps or squalid second-growth. After that, along a sizeable river which rolled through a wooded ravine; then over a winding muddy road down on one side of the stream, again on the other, as we crossed numerous bridges. All the while, the hills became steeper, the trees grew taller and the whole aspect greener. Aromatic firs and cedars, dense groves of feathery hemlock displaced the acrid willow and alder: low hanging branches of giant red cedars were caught in the river's flood.

The jouncing car chugged and coughed and climbed mostly in second gear, finally going into low as the ascent became steeper. At length we topped the ridge crest and slid into a boggy vale where the car slithered crazily and threatened to reverse ends.

"We've got to put on chains," the driver told us. "Don't think we can muddle through the blasted clay. It's too thick."

"Stop right now and put 'em on before you break our necks," insisted the Judge. "And while you're at it, my man, throw away that infernal cigarette. I don't like tobacco smoke around my dogs."

You just naturally couldn't convince the Judge that a pipe or a cigar or cigarette wasn't detrimental to the dog's nose and injurious to its scenting powers. He may have been partly right at that.

More bumping, more grinding, more sputtering, and at length we swung across a parklike meadow to the very foot of a mountain. The Judge and I got rid of surplus baggage, including clothing, for a skyward climb, while our driver curled up in the car.

"How's your wind?" the Judge inquired. "We have a real pull ahead of us and the grade is deceptive. The blue grouse in this country are high up on the mountainside where lateral canyons join the crown of the main ridge. We're apt to find them feeding on the secondary ridges and well up toward the heads of swales and gulleys. There are some mountain meadows up there too, with bogs and brush-lined creeks to make them especially attractive to the grouse. At this time of the year, when there are still plenty of berries and wild fruits, most of the birds are feeding in comparatively open ground until about ten-thirty in the morning when they head for the marginal brush and timber.

"From then until about three o'clock in the afternoon they will probably be found among the 'sticks' or big timber. I am just telling you this as a general rule, but not as a certainty. Some of the birds may stay along the main ridge throughout the day, especially if there are springs near by."

Macdonell knew his grouse and he knew his grouse country. Of course, you will find the birds in all sorts of shooting grounds, depending upon local conditions. Now, logged-off flats and other exploited timber lands with their numerous charred stumps and logs and occasional stump craters, not to mention the second growth, and also the inevitable berry patches—these became ideal blue grouse hunting country.

Stump craters seem to have a peculiar fascination for both blue and ruffed grouse. Many a time my heart has pounded from the shock of an unexpected rise and even now I cannot approach a well-known stump pit without tense nerves and high expectancy. On the well-watered flats and adjoining slopes, you may find occasional clumps of thorn or crab apples, also huckleberry bushes, elderberry, snowberry, and numerous other wild fruits. If you are wise and know your grouse, you will remember that berries and grouse are almost synonymous.

Up the long steep incline, the wiry and tireless barrister led me toward the hunting grounds. Spot heeled us. Now and then we stopped to take a brief breather. The judge was right; the grade was stiff and it was a tough grind. During one of these stops, I said something about the tremendous scope of potential grouse country that lay below us. To this the Judge shrewdly replied, "All that glitters is not gold. The man who started out aimlessly in that immense basin down there would walk his legs off and blunder into mighty few grouse.

"It was years before I finally realized that grouse are very much like trout; they have definite ideas and preferences, nearly all of which are deadly practical. What we may think is one thing; what the grouse think is another, and they know their business. Ruffed grouse don't move around much. You will find them in the same thickets year after year, but the blue grouse are rovers—I wouldn't call them migratory.

"They are apt to range far both afoot and on the wing. My dogs have roaded them half a mile and more by the scent. I have seen unalarmed blue grouse take off from one side of a valley miles wide and continue flying until they diminish almost to pin-point size and finally disappear in the vast distance. Now and then, I have seen the reverse, watched the birds approach, and I never knew how long a flight they had made.

"I believe they are actually faster on the wing than the ruffed or 'willow' grouse, as we call them here. Both members of the family used to feed in a buckwheat patch on grounds where I conditioned my dogs. Occasionally, I would put up both kinds almost simultaneously from a dog's point. It was about two hundred yards to the nearest thicket, and the big blue grouse always beat the little fellows to heavy cover."

I told the Judge that I agreed with him and said, "That reminds me of the palmy days of Virginia City, Nevada. Uncle Billy Dormer imported some valley quail from California and released them on Carson Sink where they did famously.

"Some years later when Samuel Clemens (Mark Twain) returned to Virginia City after becoming world famous as a literary giant, his old boss, Sam Goodman, proprietor of the *Territorial Enterprise*, arranged a quail hunt for the former reporter.

"The sad fact was that Mark Twain was a punk shot and simply couldn't hit the quail.

"'Billy,' he declared, 'These little blue bats outa hell, or wherever they came from, are the fastest blankety-blank things on wings. Damn it, I missed again—there goes another.'

"At that very instant an old sage cock blustered off the ground and made a beeline for shelter following the little blue California quail. The big bird overtook the small comet and passed it easily before reaching the far bank of the Carson River.

"'Now there's just another case of betting on the wrong nag,' Mark drawled. 'A good, big horse can always beat a good little horse.'"

As we reached the higher altitudes, there was abundant evidence of Jack Frost's handiwork; lavish autumnal displays of crimson and gold. The air was pure and crisp and the morning updraft along the side of the mountains sent lacy banks and filaments of mist swirling through the canyons.

Now we were in the blue grouse country. The Judge headed toward a huckleberry patch as a likely cover for the birds. Spot must have sensed it too, because he strained at the leash and threw his head up with a clapping of flews while his tail cut the air. I knew what was in his mind, or in his nostrils, for I had seen the brainy fellow in action many times.

The Judge, tense as any fiddle string, cast Spot off. "Mac," I declared, "that little rascal's got birds in his nose."

Fast, and straight as a ruler, the pointer drew, head high in the air, as he caught scent from a distance. Once he hesitated and reared on his hind legs, the better to catch that evasive, fleeting odor. Then his rudder stiffened and like a flash he rushed forward another forty feet or so and froze. With a wave of his arm, the Judge shouted exultantly, "Dar he!" in southern black man accent. We moved in fast to cover the intervening distance to where the dog was standing like an alabaster statue among stunted huckleberry growth.

Not a doubt in my mind; I would have gambled my last shirt on the certainty that Spot had them. There was a catch in my breath, a bit of trembling around the knees as we hurried on and up for the rise. We shuffled to a station a trifle above the pointer, both of us ready for action.

Directly below us lay a steep canyon. It was almost certain that the grouse would bolt downward on a long flight to timber far below, perhaps travelling in a body. The Judge kicked at a wiry clump of huckleberry. That bush practically exploded with a thunderous bomb, and a mighty grouse broke cover and roared away. A hasty shot and a clean miss on the Judge's part. Then, after what seemed an interminable delay, a second sharp crack of nitro and the grand old blue mountaineer collapsed in mid-air while the Judge yelled triumphantly, "I got him!"

I fully expected that more grouse would attempt to get away in the confusion, but it wasn't until I had booted several likely looking clumps of cover that a feathered bomb tore loose and thundered away and downward on a tumultuous course. The shock of that bird getting up threw me off balance, but just in the nick of time, I recovered my footing,

94

lined up a good two feet under the sharply declining target, and at the crack of doom the big bird wilted.

Close by, a few yards behind us, Spot was locked up tight in another cataleptic trance. Out of the corner of my eye, I marked again for future reference the exact spot close by a clump of hardhack where my grouse had folded up. Then my eye was drawn back to the rigid pointer, and the Judge waved me on. "You take your shot," he said. I shook my head. "Go on," he demanded tersely.

"Stand by then," I said, setting myself for the flush. Coolly as possible, I set off the dynamite.

BOOM-M-M. This fellow did the unexpected thing. He twirled around our heads on a winding uphill course toward ridge timber. There was a lot of clucking as the frightened blue shifted gears and gained momentum. We got all tangled up in that skein of aerial maneuvers and it required a second broadside from us properly to grass the bird.

Spot staged the second act of this grouse drama on a beautiful alpine meadow hemmed in by stately spruces and firs. He nailed a covey at the edge of a tiny thicket of willow and sumac, close by the side of a small brook that meandered through the flat.

Mountain timothy, rose briers, and lush bunch grass afforded an abundance of ground cover, and small bars of sand and fine gravel provided dusting spots and grit which all grouse crave. The spot fairly shouted BIRDS.

Yonder stood a real bird dog on the point, adamantine and glistening among the briers. Finally, there was the concrete evidence when two lordly blue grouse folded up after the covey had taken wing; a single for each of us. We might readily have annexed a couple of scattered birds that we had marked down in ground cover a third of a mile distant, but we didn't follow them. Instead, we went after several blues which had taken to the big sticks close at hand. We didn't locate one of them in that mystic maze.

At length, from a vantage point on a high promontory along the far side of the mountain, we scanned another small world of blue grouse-hunting country. A great forest clothed the valley and the whole area was notched by countless small cross canyons extending into the far distant backbone of the mighty mountain range. Multiply what the eyes saw in this single barony of the dusky grouse family—yes, multiply it by the thousands, and you may gain a faint conception of the limitless wilderness empire to which the birds stand heir.

"Come, let's move on," urged my restless, tireless friend. "We can work out this timbered canyon practically down to the car. At this time of the year, the blues take to the big sticks after they feed. In fact many never leave the woods at all and feed mainly on buds and needles the year round.

"I've got up as many as fifty grouse on this one course, but you never can tell because grouse seem to be subject to cyclic periods of abundance and scarcity. Anyway, I'll parallel the upper fringe of the timber, and you keep abreast of me a hundred yards or so farther down. The birds that I put up are certain to dive downhill. There's little chance for dog work here."

Not very long after came the muffled roar of whirring wings, and a blue thunderbolt whirled past me on an angle. Too late! I merely clipped a handful of lacy needles from the intervening branch of a fir tree—the blue sailed onward and downward with the speed of a rocket. Twice more I missed other big grouse as they roared past me from above. It was difficult shooting and unless you watched your step carefully you would not allow for the vitally needed leads to make perfect contact with these dashing comets.

"Hell's bells," I said to myself, "these shots should be easy! There's plenty more open space around these birds than in ruffed grouse shooting in the brushy eastern covers." But I forgot that in ruffed grouse shooting a majority of the targets are rising birds, or practically on a level, and the average shooting distance is shorter than on these duskies. While it may be open to dispute, the fan-tails are not moving at any tremendous speed. Don't underestimate the rapid flight of the big blue grouse, when it is headed on a downhill course. It is true that blue grouse do less dodging than ruffed grouse, because of the generally wider spacing of forest aisles.

A studious friend and a careful observer has told me that with full steam ahead the big grouse can top seventy-five miles an hour downgrade. That's about one-half the speed credited to our fastest hawks when they step on the gas for a drop.

At the fourth try, and after I had passed up several grouse, I nailed a big fellow plumb in the middle and he landed in a salal patch with a thump—so dead that the customary dying flutter was omitted. He was a beautiful bird, fully four pounds in weight and as solid as any ring-necked rooster I ever killed. I spent a minute or more admiring that magnificent blue grouse and said in my pride, "Come on you blues! I've got your number!"

I had heard a shot or two from above, and wondered how the Judge was making out. Suddenly, I heard a roar of wings above and set myself for a shot, but the noise ended in a flutter, and not far away I caught a faint glimpse of a grouse as it landed high up in a hemlock—most likely an old timer who knew plenty of tricks.

These "hooters" are mighty hard to spot once they hide on the leafy end of a bough or flatten out on a limb close to the bole far up on some forest mammoth. They are thoroughly at home in such a lofty rigging, and far more cunning than the ruffed grouse hiding in similar environment. Again and again, as you comb the big timber, blues will flush out ahead beyond range, or they will hide so craftily on their lookout station that you pass them by without catching sight of them.

Mark a sticky bird down in some tall conifer, look for the bird carefully, and unless your eye lands plumb on him and he intuitively knows you actually see him, he'll hug tight as a leech to his hideout. Should a blue grouse in one of these trees dive down from his lofty perch, often as not he'll cleverly whirl around behind the trunk in his getaway. but that extra strategy isn't necessary. The mere act of dropping like a plummet and shuttling out behind intervening limbs is generally sufficient to take the big fellows to safety.

Shooting dusky grouse in the big timber country, if you can hit one out of four or five birds you are doing very well, and if you can smack down one out of every three you are really a crack grouse hunter.

There was a blue grouse somewhere in that hemlock. I knew it positively, but for the life of me I couldn't spot it. I spent several minutes on the job and heard the Judge calling a bit impatiently to determine my whereabouts; so I passed up that crafty bird and hotfooted it to a position in line with my friend. Not long after, I was successful in putting out one young blue, which obviously did not know its ropes. It plunged down from a high tree only to level off under the lowest limb of a big fir. The shot that it offered was soft—proverbial duck soup— and I socked it accordingly. Also, some time before we reached the end of the journey, I routed another grouse from tall rigging, but it spoiled the day for me, for the outcome was two clean misses.

In this one trip, I have given you some idea of typical hunting conditions on blue grouse to be found in grouse country. It is evident that these birds are being reduced in number and something should be done to conserve them. They formerly were very numerous from Alaska down to almost the California line. They still inhabit this country in goodly numbers, but nothing like the plentitude of other days. At the present writing, I'd say that British Columbia is the greatest stronghold of the dusky grouse.

Blue grouse were formerly plentiful in three counties of Oregon— Douglas, Josephine and Perry—where they were met up with in coveys and colonies in the mountain meadows and on the "marshes" or "ponds" which were open shots in the forests where grasses and wild fruits and berries were plentiful. In such terrain, the grouse were apt to scatter at the first alarm and then it was just a case of getting up singles as you threshed out the cover much in the same manner as you would hunt sharp-tails and prairie chickens.

In the Willamette Valley, it was quite common during the early days to find blue grouse in the stubble, in the mountain ash thickets and along the valley water courses, as well as in the deep woods. Their range extended also along both the coast range spurs and the higher Cascades.

Sierra members of the dusky grouse family differ but slightly from the other. Like all of his relations, the Sierra grouse inhabits the forest almost exclusively in the late fall and winter and is a tremendous feeder on buds at such times. In the high mountain country, the Sierra grouse provided splendid sport, because they would lie well to the dog.

And now I return to my original proposition, that the best hunter of the dusky grouse is the chap who knows the habits of the bird, is acquainted with the feeding ground, and has almost an extra-sense to locate either coveys or singles without wasting too much time. The blue grouse is tremendously partial to all kinds of berries and fruits, and the sportsman should not overlook that essential. The huckleberry is a favorite. Then come the elderberries, salal berries, blackberries, and snowberries.

All of the dusky grouse are extremely fond of the wild crab-apple or the thorn-apple. In the grouse country of New England, New York State, Pennsylvania and as far south as Virginia, the ruffed grouse also dotes on these tiny apples. And exactly like the ruffed grouse in the way it goes hell-bent toward certain cultivated crops, the blue grouse cannot resist a patch of buckwheat. It has many of the characteristics of the sharp-tail, invading the stubble fields to feed upon waste grain.

At certain times of the year grouse pine for animal life and will feed upon all sorts of insects, including grasshoppers. It is late in the season when the dusky grouse move away from the more open and marginal lands and take up their residences in the adjacent woods and along the courses of streams. It is at this time that they begin to feed on buds and other browse. When the tough winter comes and all other sources of food supply are cut off, grouse can thrive upon a purely vegetable diet made up of ninety per cent buds and needles.

Essentially, all the members of this group prefer the high country to the lower ranges. Up to the present time, this has been the salvation of the big grouse.

My study and familiarity with the blue grouse and others of the group have combined to show me that even in the logged-off parts of the West this fine fellow can hold his own and actually stage a comeback if he is not molested too much. Cutting away big timber always gives a break to wild life. It provides open patches where a new growth of berries and other food plants can thrive and where excellent cover is supplied.

In many parts of the United States, and particularly in Maine, New York, and Pennsylvania, where the second growth timber has grown to great height, state forestry departments are now opening up the timber to provide bird life and animal life with these favored areas.

The dusky grouse is a grand bird; one which the United States and Canada should conserve and foster in the interests of a classical upland sport with gun and dog. There is a wonderful charm connected with a day spent in pursuit of the big fellows among the forest and alpine highlands. The hunting is fine also in the midlands and you can find enjoyment in the lowlands.

If your ears are attuned to the strumming of wild life harps in the Druidical mystery of the forest, and you listen to the weird notes of the blue grouse, you will be thrilled by nature's strange melody.

To some, these ventriloquial sounds are uncanny and spooky when heard among the dim forest aisles in the land of giant trees, but to those who understand nature and appreciate the things that nature holds, the bird voices only speak in friendly and cheery accents—the mysterious language of our greatest woodland grouse.

Ptarmigan
by Bob Brister

Colorado has a huntable population of the small white-tailed ptarmigan. But Alaska is really the only state with first rate hunting for these grouse of the snow. Of the three species—rock, willow, and white-tailed—the willow is generally ruled most sporting. In fact, not many upland hunters realize just how good the willow ptarmigan can be before a gun.

The heavily loaded single-engine plane banked precariously close to the icy side of Peulik Mountain, and Ray Loesche dipped a wing at some scattered patches of white at timberline. He buzzed one of the white patches, and the whole side of the mountain seemed to take wing as big white birds fanned out and sailed down the slope like king-sized quail.

"They're in rough country this time of year, and you'll have to do some climbing," guide Hap Mathis shouted. He was crammed in behind me in the little plane intended for two, and with three big men, packboards, guns, and shotgun shells, I wondered if we'd make the climb out of that canyon and over the ridge.

But Loesche was once a glider pilot and is now considered to be one of the finest bush pilots in Alaska. At the last moment, with the mountain looming before us, he pulled up over the ridge and sideslipped back down the mountainside to regain flying speed.

Suddenly we were heading straight for a short, smooth cinderbed gouged out many years before during the volcanic eruption of Mount Peulik. Loesche pulled back the throttle, the oversized, low-inflation tires bumped ground, and we rolled and skidded to within 10 feet of the side of the mountain. At the last instant, he braked one wheel and the plane skidded to a stop.

"Short airport," Loesche grinned, possibly noting my blanched coloring. "With you guys out I can take off okay. Just be sure you take all your gear with you. Every pound of weight counts."

Hap rummaged around for his packboard, and I stumbled out into the snow with two cameras, a shotgun, shells, and a mountain climber's pack full of food and film.

It was a magnificent view. Far below, Loesche's base cabin on Ugashik Lake was a tiny dark dot in the willow brush. We were very nearly in the middle of the Alaskan Peninsula, some eighty miles south of the little fishing village of King Salmon and not far from the famous Valley of 10,000 Smokes in Katmai National Monument Park.

My friend Kenneth Campbell and I had planned our Alaskan trip for bear, caribou, and moose. But I'd been just as interested in checking out the stories I'd heard guide Ray Loesche tell about the fabulous ptarmigan shooting of the high slopes.

By flying Hap and me up to the timberline after birds, Loesche was free to take Campbell out for caribou, and we could have the whole day to hunt the ridges and work our way back down to camp. It was a straight-line distance of not more than ten miles, but closer to twenty figuring the ups and downs of climbing in and out of steep ravines every few yards.

101

As soon as we started walking, ptarmigan began taking off wild all over the side of the mountain. We'd spot a white patch of birds around the ridge of some brushy draw, but before we could get within 100 yards, they'd take off cackling derisively like big white chickens.

"They're strange birds," Hap panted as we climbed out of a draw. "They're grouse, you know. I guess you could say they're the far north equivalent of the ruffed grouse when they act wild, and more like fool hens when they think they're hidden. They're just now getting their white winter camouflage and I guess they don't have much confidence in it yet. They change from the brown color of a ruffed grouse to snow white. Right now you'll find some of them just about half and half."

I asked him about stories I'd heard of ptarmigan being so dumb you could kill them with rocks.

He grinned. "I've seen willow ptarmigan act dumb in a blizzard or when they think they're safe in heavy brush. But most of the time you'll earn every one you put down with a long-shootin' shotgun. Most of those stories you hear are about another species, the rock ptarmigan."

We sat down on a rock to rest for a minute and admire the magnificent Alaskan wilderness view. Within a few feet of where we sat wild cranberries, blueberries, and moss berries were growing.

"That's why the ptarmigan are all up here now," Hap explained. "Plenty of food. But that isn't doing us any good."

Suddenly there was a roar of wings from up the mountain and the air was full of ptarmigan sailing downhill straight for us. We sat still and they passed just out of range, made a sudden curving sailing descent, and dropped into the thick brush of the ravine below us.

A big bald eagle had cut one ptarmigan out of the flock and was right on its tail as the frantic bird twisted and dodged down the canyon. The eagle was fast, but not fast enough; the ptarmigan caught an updraft of wind and sailed off unhurt. The eagle came over us, wheeling and looking.

"Thanks," Hap waved up at the eagle. "Now you've set us up for a real ptarmigan hunt."

With that eagle around, he said, the birds would stick tight in the brush. All we had to do was walk in on them.

That proved a little more difficult than it looked. The sides of the brushy draws were almost straight up and down and distances were deceiving. The birds that had looked almost in our laps were two ravines away.

Hap insisted we work around and above them. "You can get a whole lot closer to 'em from above than you can from below," he said.

So we puffed and climbed and just as we topped out of the ravine there was a thunder of wings and a huge covey we hadn't seen exploded from the brush around us. It happened so fast I just stood there with the gun on my shoulder and a camera in my hand and didn't use either one.

"You can't stare 'em down," Hap said. "Let me carry that camera and you get ready. There'll be a few sleepers around here that didn't leave with that bunch."

We'd taken about five steps when a single burst out of the alders and swung downhill. I swung the barrel ahead of him, saw a shower of white feathers explode in the air, and the big bird went end over end down the mountain leaving a miniature snow flurry every time he hit the ground.

Then I saw it stand up, look around, and start running.

"What does it take to kill these things?" I asked. "I know I centered one."

"That you did," Hap said. "But these aren't Texas blue quail up here. That old cock ptarmigan has enough feathers on him to take temperatures down to 60 below zero. Those little 7½ shot you brought aren't big enough to penetrate unless you're right on top of 'em."

I thought about the advice I'd had from reading some ptarmigan hunting stories that recommended No. 7½ or 8 shot for a bird the size of a teal and seemingly with twice as many feathers. High velocity 6 shot would have been better than the field loads I'd lugged all the way from Houston.

After chasing that first cripple for half an hour down the mountain, I finally pinned him down in a little creek at the bottom of the ravine, and when I picked him up he was every bit as heavy as a ruffed grouse. The feathered legs didn't really look like bird legs at all, however. Even the pads of the feet were protected by tiny hairlike feathers so thick they more resembled the fur of a snowshoe rabbit's foot.

Hap whistled at me and pointed up the ridge. A big covey was running around in the open with the cocky, upright stance of quail. I climbed the ridge, circled to get above them, then lined up several alder bushes between the birds and my line of approach. Taking it slowly and quietly, I got within 10 yards of the alders when a big cock bird jumped, cackling out a warning, and the slope exploded white bodies with a deafening roar.

I pulled out in front of two birds flying side by side and saw them both tumble with the shot. A white cluster of wings were bunched together and I led the covey and shot. Two more dropped, and the third shot nailed a straightaway single.

"Now that was right pretty," Hap yelled, mocking my Texas accent.

"But was it luck or skill?"

Half an hour later we didn't think it was such great shooting at all. Of those five birds downed, three were up and running. After a lung-testing chase, I had to shoot one on the ground because it could run up the mountainside faster than I could. Hap helped me chase down another one and we were converging on the third when a dark streak whistled in over our heads and hit the crippled ptarmigan in a flurry of white feathers. The eagle had been watching, and must have realized the cripple couldn't fly.

Since we had to work down the mountain to get back to camp before dark, we had to leave the big flock. But we quickly began jumping other bunches on the way down.

Often there would be no warning. We'd start down into a brushy ravine and it would explode birds, sometimes a hundred at a time. I learned to pass up the long shots and concentrate on head-shooting the closer ones. That way they stayed down.

Once three birds jumped almost out from under our feet. I wanted to make the triple and rushed the first shot. The bird faltered, but I knew I'd hit him too far back. The other two curved enough for me to get shot into their heads and went down solidly.

When I walked down to that first bird, feathers were still floating down out of the air, and I couldn't believe it when another one cackled and took off right where the dead bird was supposed to be. I nailed him solidly because he was close and an easy straightaway, but then couldn't find the first one.

Hap was up on the ridge laughing. "You got your money's worth out of that one," he called. "Got two different rises out of him."

By the time we got halfway down the mountain, Hap was starting to complain about the weight of the birds, so we stopped and cleaned them. His packboard, with only sixteen of my twenty-bird limit, was starting to feel like lead.

Alaska has three species of ptarmigan—willow, rock, and white-tailed. But all that we saw were willows—the largest and most common variety.

Despite their abundance in many areas, getting a limit isn't usually easy. The day before I hunted, Loesche and Campbell had landed in the middle of an open country concentration which Loesche estimated at 500. Yet they'd been able to get within shotgun range of only two.

Our good fortune was the result of an eagle on the prowl, and later in the afternoon a gusty, howling wind which put the birds into the heavy alder brush where they would stick tight, thinking they were hidden. Often they were hidden. I blundered into several coveys that flushed fast downhill, and learned a downwind ptarmigan can be a most deceptive target—requiring a lot of lead. They make full use of the wind, much like chukar partridge. A short, fast burst of power was followed by a swift, sailing glide with plenty of sharp turns down the ridges.

When we finally made it to the beach of Lake Ugashik, I had nineteen ptarmigan and one shell left.

"Danged shame you couldn't have gotten to write in your story that you got a limit of these things the first time out," Hap said, puffing his pipe, "Would'a had it too, if that danged eagle hadn't stolen one."

About that time a shadow passed over and the eagle, or maybe its mate, swooped low over the brush and came back for another close pass.

It was getting late, but I was sure that eagle had spotted another bunch of ptarmigan, and we walked a quarter mile out of the way to see.

We were almost to the brush when ptarmigan took off in all directions, and a single came hurtling past us, wings set and sailing straight into the Alaskan sunset. At the shot it dropped—leaving a puff of feathers floating in the air.

"Now if that ain't the end of a perfect day," Hap said softly.

Chickens of the Prairie
by Ray P. Holland

Lesser prairie chickens and sharp-tailed grouse are the plains grouse of the West. The only place with a huntable population of the lesser prairie chicken is a three county region in southeastern New Mexico. The sharptail is best hunted in Montana. Both species are treasures. They are both critically dependent on vast, remote native habitat. Where civilization touches, these two grouse fade away quickly.

What is a prairie chicken? The answer to that question may be in the plural, as the term "prairie chicken" is applied to different species of grouse that live on the open prairies. Old-time gunners will insist that the only true prairie chicken is the pinnated grouse, or squaretail, but throughout the range of the sharp-tailed grouse this grand bird is universally known as "chicken."

Some years ago I was the guest of a rancher in Idaho.

"If you want to shoot some chickens," he told me, "go right out back of the barn. There's usually a flock or two feeding in the edge of the alfalfa. Take Shep; he'll put 'em out for you."

The land in back of the barn was watered, and even though it was late in the fall the alfalfa was lush and green. Around this field, Shep and I went. As a bird dog he wasn't much of a success, but he seemed to know what a gun was, for he kept running ahead a way and then running back and looking at me and the gun as though it gave him a great deal of pleasure. We jumped a couple of long-legged jack-rabbits that left the hayfield and bounced away through the sage-brush which grew at the edge of the great coulee bordering the far side of the field.

This wasn't my idea of how to hunt prairie chickens, but any kind of hunting beats no hunting at all; so I kept on around the edge of the alfalfa. Just as I had given up trying to get Shep to stir himself he began to bounce around and bark, jumping ahead as though he expected a rabbit to break out of the cover. It was not a rabbit, but several over-sized birds that finally clattered to the air. Two more got up before I could reload, and still another was nosed out by Shep after I had picked up a pair which I had killed.

These sage grouse were "chickens" to my rancher friend, and he knew a good deal about them. When I returned to the ranch house, he took the birds and cleaned them immediately, telling me that, if all of the entrails and the crop are removed, the meat of our largest grouse is as sweet as any game. These birds were certainly good eating, and my friend contended that even the old cocks were palatable if, when killed, the breast meat was immediately cut away and all the rest of the bird discarded.

The birds are so large and have such a time to get going that the sport they offer is about on a par with shooting toy balloons. When they are in sparse cover they will, of course, not let the gun approach as close to them as when in alfalfa. Usually they will flush at forty or fifty yards, and this fact alone is the only feature that would make their shooting sporty to me.

These sage hens look as large as turkeys when you see a flock of them walking across open ground. In fact, the cocks will weight eight pounds or more. Formerly these birds could be found in good numbers throughout the West wherever sage grew. Today there is but a remnant of the breed left. They were not shot out or trapped, although, of course, the gun played its part as the country was settled. There was, however, not enough enthusiasm for sage-hen shooting to make it a main factor in the disappearance of these birds.

Many claim that sheep are responsible. Where flocks of sheep pass over an area no ground-nesting bird could possibly incubate her eggs and rear her young. It is contended that when cattle ran the range the sage hen prospered, but that when sheep took over the birds quickly disappeared. Only in a few favored spots are sage grouse on the legal game lists today.

At one time the open lands of this country were covered with grouse. The heath hen, almost an exact counterpart of the pinnated grouse of the West, was so numerous that it interfered seriously with crops throughout the East. It was a common practice for farm labor to include in their contracts that they were not to be fed heath hen oftener than once each week. Today the heath hen is extinct. It passed out after many years of totally closed gunning seasons. Refuges were established in Massachusetts which contained what was thought to be a large enough number of birds to re-establish the species, but the pendulum had swung too far.

Pinnated grouse were just as numerous throughout the prairie states. Audubon tells of them and how easy they were to shoot and trap. The annals of the Middle West tell of the slaughter of these birds by the market gunners. Game laws with their seasons and limits were unknown. August 15 was the opening day of the first chicken law I remember, and at that time many of the birds were still "squealers." From a sporting angle, the only thing that could be said in favor of this early season was that it provided an opportunity for the grandest dog work imaginable. No bird will lie tighter than a young chicken that has been scared.

Prairie-chicken shooting today and yesterday are two very different sports. In the horse-and-buggy days two gunners would leave the railroad town with a team and wagon loaded with ice, camp-cook outfit and dogs. For many years the legal season opened on August 15. The weather was too hot in the middle of the day for both men and dogs, but in the early morning and evening the sport was perfect.

The usual thing was to hunt out away from town on the first day, camp on the prairie that night and hunt back the next day. In this way, birds could be iced and shipped back east while still fresh. Because of the high midday heat the chickens would have spoiled if an attempt had been made to stay out a third day.

108

A pair of dogs would be put down, and as your team walked or jogged along they would cover the prairie land or wheat stubble, as the case might be. There were no fences, and when a dog stopped, the driver simply turned his team over behind the dogs and the gunners climbed down and went into action. These young squaretails would stick so tight that on several occasions I have parted the heavy slough grass and caught birds that refused to fly. Birds were so plentiful that it was hard to imagine they would ever become scarce in the short-grass country of western Kansas.

Yet before the automobile had supplanted the old horse-drawn hunting wagon, we went north into Nebraska, looking for new pastures with more birds. Here we first saw a mingling of sharptails with the pinnated grouse, or square-tailed chicken. Occasionally we would kill one of the white-breasted birds in Kansas; in the sand-hill country of Nebraska, however, we found them not only mixed with the square-tails, but occasionally located flocks of them.

Today there are still prairie chickens in many of the states where their numbers once made them a pest; but in spite of man's best efforts, this grand game bird will probably follow his slightly smaller brother, the heath hen, to the shelves of our best natural history museums. The pinnated grouse seemed to increase and thrive with the breaking of the prairies and the planting of small grains, but as civilization settled down in earnest these birds were unable to adjust themselves to man and his ways.

For example, I first noticed a scarcity of chickens in western Kansas shortly after the introduction of alfalfa into that country. Old Bill Clellan, foreman of the big Baker Ranch, laid the blame squarely at the door of the new hay crop.

"This alfalfa," he said, "is just exactly the kind of cover that a chicken likes to nest in. They come for miles around to build their nests in an alfalfa field; and then cutting time comes just before their eggs are ready to hatch, and every nest is broken up. Some of them try it a second time, but the hay grows so fast that we will be cutting it again before they can lay their eggs and bring off a brood."

Today much of the old chicken country is overrun with that hardy foreigner, the ringneck—a bird that can prosper in most states where chickens were native. Many believe that, because of the pheasant's ability to cope with man under the most unfavorable conditions, he has been instrumental in pushing out the chickens.

Today there are many sections of Canada where the square-tail is still prospering and the sharptail seems to exist happily without signs of depletion. In fact, in recent years I have seen sharptails in greater numbers than I ever saw either chicken in the days when I was a boy in the West. Scientists claim their numbers are more or less controlled by nature, regardless of man. Possibly they are at the peak of the cycle at present and next year they will not be so numerous.

Both sharptail and squaretail migrate to a limited degree. Years ago, in the fall we always saw flocks of squaretails moving down and across the Missouri River, flying through a section where no chickens were to be found during the summer months. This same partial migration exists in Canada today, and now, as then, furnishes a very sporty type of chicken shooting, if you can locate the flyway.

The squaretails would also band up in the fall of the year, forming flocks of a hundred or more birds. At such time a man or a dog could never approach them. When they moved, they would go a mile or more, and hunting them was a waste of time—unless you knew how. A man on a good horse could drive these birds to cover by keeping everlastingly after them. Once they were tired out and sought safety by crouching in the grass, it was all over. A good dog could go to bird after bird, and a good shot could grass as many as he wanted.

Both sharptails and squaretails fly to feed each night and morning. Sometimes they will stay throughout the day in the fields where they are feeding. Usually, however, they will return to a place of their choice where they can dust and loaf during the middle of the day. There is no better way to locate birds in a strange country than to watch for these flights in the early morning and in the evening.

As a rule, the pinnated grouse will go out on unbroken prairie to loaf, whereas the sharptail will head for a thicket of scrub prairie brush. Either may choose to spend the day in a field of high weeds where land, once cultivated, has been allowed to lie idle. During the mornings and evenings, when the birds are in the stubble, a good bird dog will still give you the kind of shooting that will thrill any red-blooded sportsman. From the time the birds leave the grain fields in the morning until they return to feed in the late afternoon, a pointing dog can do little but wear himself out.

Both species are primarily birds of the open, but conditions have made them change their habits. There are places, both in the United States and in Canada, where squaretails can be found living in the woods. To a greater extent the sharptail also goes to timber. I have found them living in second-growth and budding just like a ruffed grouse. When either bird has become a woods dweller, you will find that hitting him is not the simple problem it is when he rises against an open sky out on the prairie.

Through the wheat lands of Canada, around old buffalo wallows, and wherever the ground is too wet to plow, you will find patches of willow and popple called "bluffs," or "clumps." The modern method of hunting the sharptail in the middle of the day is to drive from clump to clump and hope to find the birds at home. If you can locate a section of virgin prairie which is filled with clumps, you are pretty sure to find birds, especially if the day is warm. Here, in strictly sharptail country, you may also pick up a squaretail or two.

The usual method is to stop the car when within long shotgun range of the cover. A hunter drops out from either side and starts for the clump. One man goes down each side. Sometimes sharptails can be seen running around in the brush, and they will start getting up, often before you are in range. Always remember one thing—the chances are ten to one that they didn't all fly. Usually one or two birds, and sometimes three, will sit tight and let the other birds go on to wherever they are going. It is always a good plan, after you have walked around a clump, to let a good bird dog look it over—that is, if the cover is at all thick. Many times he will find birds that you have passed right by. When the weather starts to get cold, you will frequently see sharptails perched high on a straw stack. Sure, you can get up to within shooting distance sometimes—but if you have anything else to do, you had better go do it. The only way I know to get such birds is to have at least three hunters and a car driver in the party. Then, as the car circles the stack, the hunters drop off on all sides and lie flat in the stubble. With his men planted, the driver can then approach the stack from the unguarded side and someone may get a shot.

Sometimes a sharptail will perch on a telephone pole along the road in the early morning. Strangely enough, he will let you drive right up in range under such conditions. He may look you over in a disinterested way as you approach with gun ready. You may even have to shout and throw a clod at him before he will fly.

Here is a suggestion. When you see a nice fat chicken sitting on a telephone pole, be a gentleman and let your companion do the shooting. Tell him you insist that he kill this bird. Then you get out of the car and go along just for the walk. Have your gun ready. The shot at the top of the pole is a tough one, but I am not planning that you should wipe your friend's eye. Let him kill his bird or shoot both barrels at it and miss. Your job is to kill the bird or two that are probably sitting tight in the grass near the pole. They aren't always there, but it is a good gamble that, when your friend's bird flies and the gun pops, another bird will flush.

This, of course, will also build up your prestige as a good shot, for your friend will probably miss his bird that launches into full flight from

111

the top of the pole, and if you are any good at all you should bag your bird coming out of the grass at your feet. The reason the pole shot is a hard one is because it is unusual and the gun must be held low to connect. In flushing from the pole, the bird will usually drop a little. It may slant straight down to near-by cover; but even if it goes away on a level with the top of the pole, the gunner on the ground must shoot considerably below the flying bird in order to intercept its flight.

Both chickens fly with an alternate flapping and sailing; both come out of cover with a roaring flush, not so disturbing as the flush of their cousin, the ruffed grouse, but more so than the clattering rise of a pheasant. Neither is a difficult mark, yet both will occasionally be missed by the best shots. Both roll in flight, the sharptail more, I believe, than the squaretail. It is very easy to miss a rolling bird if he starts to roll away just as you pull the trigger.

Then, again, there is that old friend of all game birds, the wind. When the wind is blowing, and it generally is on the prairies, a sharptail boiling out of a clump and heading down-wind will call for some gun-swinging. With the late open season, all the birds are full-grown and full-feathered—able to put on plenty of speed. Their rise cannot be compared with that of the Hungarian partridge or the quail, or, for that matter, with the ruffed grouse; but when once under way, they have plenty of speed.

Gunners are likely to form opinions on the speed of birds that are not based on anything more substantial than guesswork. There is no possible way to clock a rising bird and tell how long it takes him to fly the first fifty feet because we can't do more than guess at that fifty feet. I have felt at times that the ruffed grouse was the fastest flushing bird on the game lists; and then, when my nerves were cold, I have occasionally flushed one out in the open away from cover and promptly changed my views. One afternoon in Saskatchewan I flushed a ruffed grouse from the stubble, a good hundred yards from cover. Apparently he wasn't a bit faster than the squaretails we were shooting.

By the same token, take a try at either one of these prairie grouse where he has taken up temporary quarters in timber. You will find that he can, without too much effort, dodge and twist and make you miss him. And just as soon as you miss a bird or two you will begin to give him credit for extra speed.

A friend of mine who has always belittled the sharptail as a game bird, claiming that shooting them was akin to shooting feather pillows, got mixed up with a flock of sharptails living in fairly large second-growth. For the next two weeks he tried to argue me into admitting that they must be different species of grouse.

112

When I am shooting chickens, I like to use my favorite shot—7½ chilled. It does the work for me perfectly, although some will argue for 6's. I do like a little more powder behind those shot than you get in the regular trap load. The 3-dram load is all right for the first barrel, but if it is necessary to reach out I like to have 3¼ drams pushing the shot. Imagination? Probably! But, nevertheless, that is what I like, and no man can shoot good unless he humors his whims on such important subjects as shot and powder. You are licked before you start if you haven't full confidence in your ammunition.

Have that first barrel bored improved cylinder, and even then you will have to wait on some of those big grouse to keep from cutting them all to pieces. After they are out a way, especially on that second barrel, you can use all the shot you can put in them, for no one likes to see a hit bird fly away. Have that second barrel as tight as it can be bored.

Many epicures claim the sharptail chicken is the finest food of all feathered game. Broiled over hardwood coals, they will tell you, it is food for the gods. Possibly this is sacrilege, but I would rather get my eating-chicken from some farmer's barnyard.

And yet I remember camping along the Solomon River, out in Kansas, when I was a boy. Jess Stewart broiled chicken breasts for supper, and he broiled them over hardwood coals. That night Gene Howe and I slept under the wagon, and before it was good and light Jess broiled more chicken breasts for breakfast. Were those chickens good to eat? The best food I ever ate!

Through the years, that has survived as my high spot in gastronomical pleasures. Maybe I was hungry. Maybe circumstances added to the charm. There was a moon that night, and we could hear the winnowing of wings as ducks flew along the river. Jess Stewart had a good cowboy singing voice, and after we had gone to bed he sat by the camp-fire and sang about Dolly Gray and going away. But we can't count those birds anyway, for they were squaretails, and not the famous sharptails that the gourmets rave about.

Shadows on the Prairie

by Charles F. Waterman

Unfortunately our largest grouse is now in trouble over much of its former range. Once very common, many populations are gone or nearly so. Only Montana and Wyoming still harbor populations that can be deemed huntable. It is to be hoped that they remain on the game list in the years to come.

The largest grouse—the sage hen—must have sage, and sage depends upon the price of wheat, the need for coal and the living space that man demands.

Before the buffalo and the cattle grubbed down the tides of grass, the sage existed mainly on only the higher ground. But the shrub spread its range where the grass gave way and some of the grass eaters changed their life styles. The pronghorn was one. But the sage hen seems always to have favored the sage brush.

Because of its sameness the sage seems endless, and where it still stands man has left little mark. The double trails of rattling pickup trucks are not much different from those of creaking wagons with grunting oxen and the landscape of brush and towering sky seems even more lonely when it is broken by the tiny cipher of a monument. "Sheepherders' monuments," we say, although any lonely man on any timeless mission could have built one—a little tower of stones that was likely to be the most permanent mark he would leave upon the world— to last longer and to be seen more often than his gravestone, if he was to have one.

I think of sage hens and "monuments" together as I think of sage hens and prairie-dog towns, distant antelope and drifting coyotes, turning golden eagles and the sandhill cranes going south. And although it can be that way, I find it hard to remember sage hens flailing at sage and rabbit brush at my feet in a touch-and-go duel with gravity—the procedure that causes better gunners to say this is no game bird.

I think of sage hens as moving shadows a quarter mile ahead on stony ground that has kept the sage thin. I know they are watching me and probably will not wait, and I can remember them flying higher and higher to set their wings briefly and choose a course, whereupon I always say exactly the same things.

"They're leaving the country."

And there is the little bunch at great height, flying against a chilling backdrop of snow-promising sky and over a white spine of the Rockies toward some winter range I do not know.

When the history books first spoke of the "prairie chicken" they undoubtedly meant sage hens part of the time, but after Lewis and Clark met the grizzled, hump-backed bear they were not likely to go deeply into the taxonomy of plains bird-life. And the mountain men and then the settlers who came afterward saw the plains' birds as essential though sometimes infrequent meals. Some were simply larger than others.

Then there were graceful rifles that came from Pennsylvania by way

115

of Kentucky, and there were a few sleek fowling pieces; but it is likely that more of the sage grouse fell to nondescript guns remade from muskets of the Revolution, and few birds were shot in flight. When man is a stranger, sage hens are fools.

Only a few years ago the sage hens became so scarce that it seemed hunting them was gone forever; but then they came back to open seasons over much of the West. The farthest north I have killed a sage hen was in southern Alberta.

The danger now is the immense articulated diesel tractor that can rip up sage-covered land the pioneer's sod plow could not turn. That will depend upon how beef and wheat profits compare and how the cattleman judges the use of chemicals for pastureland. Sage grouse are primarily leaf eaters, although their rather flimsy gizzards may contain some grain. Although they may search for green shoots in stubble fields and love alfalfa, the sage is never far away.

Few know sage grouse except from the pictures taken or painted during the grouse's big scene in early spring as the snows are going and the cocks gather at their strutting grounds in displays only the wild turkey can rival, but only because he is larger. Indian costumes for ceremonial dances were made more in imitation of the sage grouse than of the eagle. Except for the mating ritual the bird merges with the sage and excites no magazine covers.

Crawling sweatily through a dry wash toward a herd of antelope I had stalked for almost two hours, I saw my first sage grouse, apparently either a seven-pound quail or the product of a rebelling nervous system. I was crawling on a plane with jackrabbit droppings and an occasional dried bone of indeterminate origin, and he seemed to tower above me as he stood with upstretched neck. When I described him as a seven-pound quail an editor deleted it with no stated reason. I submit the comparison again as a sort of test.

Like gunners who assign a certain speed to each game bird and do not concede he can go faster or slower, casual observers of sage grouse make factual pronouncements that startle more careful students.

A sage hen will sometimes stand and watch a hunter's approach with no effort at concealment, leading to the instant conclusion that he can neither hide nor run, but he does both very well.

Bobwhite quail that move 200 yards under the frustrated supervision of pointers are called "running birds." A bunch of sage grouse will go just faster than a man's walk for two miles—and when a hunter or his dog finally gets too close it may be that only one or two birds go up, the rest having disappeared in cover somewhere along the route. But you may hunt sage hens for years without such an exhibition.

There are times when birds of the year will make a foolish attempt at concealment in close-cropped grass several feet from the sage, but the adults hide well when they try, and a hunter sometimes brushes a five-pound bird with his foot before it batters its way into the air, a disconcerting experience that sometimes results in ridiculous shooting displays. Remember that in early season there may be alert rattlesnakes in sage grouse range.

The giants are the cocks, perhaps even seven pounds, while the hens are more likely to weigh a little more than two. When they walk, the cocks have a tendency to waddle; the hens walk evenly, their feet apparently put down with deliberate caution. But in the air the hens execute a violent twist at intervals as if one wing might have failed momentarily—and when it occurs as a shot is missed the gunner is likely to feel he has a hard cripple. This twist-in-flight appears not only in escape. I have watched it in birds flying so high that I might not have identified them otherwise.

To most gunners the sage grouse is an incidental bird to be pursued only the first day or two of the season, and the methods used are hardly aesthetic. A row of shooters in skirmish order will kill sage grouse, especially early in the fall, and the score is aided if they have a flushing dog or two. Birds of the spring hatch make mistakes in the direction of flight they choose.

Where early-season birds are fairly plentiful and the sage spotty, binoculars work for hunters who simply park a truck and scan surrounding hills. If the birds move about, they can be seen, slow-moving dark spots against sun-cooked grass; but if they are resting, a long inspection reveals nothing but possibly a drifting coyote or antelope or a searching hawk.

There are formulae, however, for resting sage grouse. In typical sage habitat they are most likely to be in the draws—where the sage is heaviest and not far from water; and if the water's edge is muddy, their big tracks are a sure thing in an uncertain business. Then, of course, there are the droppings to look for, subjects of endless argument, for no one knows just how long sage-hen droppings will survive the seasons. A year? Two?

The shredding grey ones, widely scattered, mean simply that a sage hen (possibly long dead) has walked that way. If there is some green and black in the droppings, they are fairly recent. If they are clustered in piles, the birds have rested there, each leaving his own collection. And "caccal droppings," black liquid that hardens in temporary blots on the ground, mean fairly recent bird presence.

Last fall we went to new sage country and we were late. The first shooters had driven the Bureau of Land Management roads in eastern Montana, and here and there the sun glanced off empty shotgun shells in or near the trail. Several times we found scattered feathers where someone had dressed his kill. It was warm and dry despite our lateness, and more than a mile away a film of dust rose over someone's cattle herd being relocated for the late fall. Dust swirled inside our truck, too. But dry weather can be a help, for although it may be that sage hens can live on dew, they will try to stay near water.

We came to a classic spot, a valley with heavier sage along the nearly dry creek, bare shoulders on some of the slopes and little grooves with thicker sage and rabbit brush near the ridge crests. On the ground was scattered winterfat, the earth-hugging little plant sage grouse are supposed to favor when the northers drive buckshot snow across the flats. There were no really high hills, just several knobs with their miniature walls of rimrock, and some irregular white dots near the horizon instantly translated into a band of antelope who had watched us since we first entered the basin. And to make us feel at home, there was a solitary herder's monument, like an overweight fencepost on top of the highest hill.

I put down the dog, an orange and white Brittany with more steam than judgment, and I watched him tear up along the nearly dry creek. An orange and white dog is discord in purple sage, an interloper where canines should be grey and ghostly.

I found fresh sign within a hundred yards and watched my emissary hopefully as he left the bottom and swept the slopes, one slithering stop and stylish point crumbling to embarrassment as a lazy jackrabbit loafed off ahead of him, loping sidewise. On some days the dog might have chased with urgent yips, but this time he pretended not to notice.

The basin bent to the right and the dog came back to heavier brush near the bottom and was out of sight. Then part way up the slope he reappeared to point so far ahead of me that I despaired of getting there in time. Fidgety dogs do not display their staunchest qualities when large birds stroll about them like field-trial judges assessing form.

Several birds went up in a scatter—bulky forms skimming the sage at first and then towering slightly to spread out and soar over the hilltop. The dog, evidently feeling his primary mission had been accomplished and that it was now time for a bit of relaxation, then methodically put up a dozen more, one at a time, while I screamed helplessly.

But by then I was within a hundred yards of him and he eyed me with some apprehension, loped off to one side and pointed rigidly. When I was still 20 yards behind him a sage hen went up ten yards ahead of him and I killed that bird. Then the same thing happened again, after which came a humiliating miss with both barrels.

We turned back toward the truck, for some of the birds had gone that way, and I cut across a hill to shorten the trip and, as usual, was amazed to see that the truck was only a blue speck. Until then my legs had not seemed tired. Now I was thirsty and even contemplated the grimy canteen I had brought for the dog.

Back at the truck the panting Brittany circled a little and pointed scarcely 50 yards behind it. Then we were really in sage grouse and they went up all around me, all seeming to eye me as they chose escape routes. I killed the third and final bird of my limit and wondered how so many had moved into the area. I investigated the sign and recalled the direction my dog had gone when he first struck the ground. He had simply missed them, and a dozen limits of sage grouse had been there all the time while I had tramped miles of sage.

There are, of course, perfect places for sage grouse that never seem to hold them, and other areas that seem no different from a hundred surrounding square miles but that have had sage grouse for the 20 years I have hunted them. There is one such place, a little island of sage brush half a mile distant from thousands of acres of solid growth. The little island of brush sits in grassland, and there a little bunch of sage hens has been for 20 years, possibly a hundred years for all I know. Perhaps some of them were part of the winter meat for the homesteader whose cabin slowly crumbles in dry wind beneath the ridge a mile away.

It is the fall and winter concentrations that most confuse sage-hen hunters, and an area that has been hard hunted with scanty result at the season's beginning may suddenly be alive with birds at some later date. It happened to me in good antelope country when I came back to a sage-grouse hunting spot as the pronghorn season opened. There was spitting snow where the sun had broiled me and a pair of huffing dogs a month before. And there were several hundred acres of sage grouse, seemingly spaced for the hunter's convenience and going up with predictable regularity. I assume they had moved in for the winter but the location of such a rendezvous is not always the same.

And such a concentration is not necessarily hunter's heaven. Last year, confidently hunting country where I had killed early-season grouse without much difficulty, I found the area seemed suddenly deserted. There was probably six square miles of it with all the sage-hen necessities, including two herder's monuments and the remains of a weathered homestead.

We had hunted all day without sight of a sage grouse and the ones we finally saw went up wild. Wild for the dog who could not hold them and very wild for us, the flushing birds gathering others as they went until there were a hundred against the evening sky and they became specks and disappeared with no sign of alighting. And this time there were no sleepers, no sluggards to wait us out and croak up under our guns. All of them were together and all of them had gone.

When roosting, sage grouse tend to stay fairly close together, but the average flock put up in daytime will be spread out, perhaps over 50 acres or more and scattered so thinly that I cannot say how they get together again. The "sleeper" is the bird most frequently bagged and he is nearly always there if the flock is big. Perhaps he may move hardly at all in the 12 hours after the main flock leaves, and many times I have returned after a long hunt to try once more where I had previously given up, and found one or two birds still there. Of course, occasionally they have returned after flushing earlier in the day, this being a rendezvous point.

But it is his home that lures me after the sage grouse—a country scorned by sightseers and called simply "empty" by passersby with their eyes on distant peaks or singing forests of pine.

There was the trip with Charles Eustace in eastern Montana. A game biologist, his job was to catalog the sage-grouse population, and he took us hunting; but he mentioned a spot where he wanted to eat lunch and was almost insistent although it seemed to be out of our way. He was a new acquaintance and I humored his whim.

It was a rather steep grade that the old Blazer clawed at briefly and then we were at the base of a butte, a flat-topped promontory thrust up at the edge of an immense sage flat that seemed to extend forever through thickening haze toward North Dakota. Around the stony base were Indian designs, many of them the reproductions of animal tracks, and there was the childish hacking of a few modern vandals.

Then we climbed to the top, a winding way of only a few yards and of no great difficulty although there were no steps.

And on the top, carefully designed to cover attack from any direction, were rifle pits—appearing haphazard at first, but laid out with geometric precision so that no attacker could approach the natural fortress unseen.

"No, I don't think Indians ever dug rifle pits in this country," Eustace said.

So who, I wanted to know, gouged out the deadly little trenches? It had been long, hard work. I waited for the answer. Ranchers fighting cattle thieves? Cavalry standing off Indians? Outlaws making a last stand against an awaited posse? Range war?

"I don't know who dug them and I can't seem to find out," Eustace said.

And I don't really want to know who did it. I have seen documented and landmarked battlefields.

Eustace looked off toward the Dakotas and endless sage. "Certainly is good sage-hen country," he observed.

Very Easy Birds to Miss

by Ted Trueblood

Idaho's Ted Trueblood is best remembered as a fly fisherman. But he was also a bird hunter of almost nonpareil stature. He hunted most of them, and wrote of them. While reading this, one can quickly draw an image of the lanky westerner reaching down to take a valley quail from his pointer's mouth. Trueblood was truly one of the best, and with the valley quail found one of the best.

I was in trouble. Willard Cravens and I were hunting California valley quail and I couldn't hit them. This was nothing new really. The valley quail is a very easy bird to miss, but today I was setting a record.

We were in quail heaven. A meandering creek wandered for a mile down through a shoestring ranch. On both sides were narrow fields of corn, hay, and small grain. Along their outer borders were irrigation canals that carried water to the crops, and beyond the canals lay endless miles of sagebrush and greasewood. Each canal was rimmed by a strip of splendid cover. Wild roses, sumac, sweet clover, weeds, and willows, some of them in groves 30 feet tall, grew along the creek. With water, perfect cover, and abundant food, the quail had everything they wanted, and they had wandered in and out of the surrounding desert until the place was crawling with them. But an abundance of game wasn't helping me. My trouble started when, on the first scattered covey, I put up seven singles in a row without getting one shot. Two or three birds flew toward some nearby cattle; others buzzed behind the tall brush so fast I couldn't get on them.

This no doubt made me overanxious. I got to straining, and every old shotgunner knows you never put meat on the table when you try too hard. Finally—but only because there were hundreds of birds and I had enough ammunition to start a war—I managed to bag the ten quail the law permitted. Willard was through long before I finished the shameful exhibition. He walked along and watched me miss, but was kind enough not to offer either sympathy or advice.

The proper thing to do after such an experience is to forget it—and the sooner the better. I can't seem to do that, however. I keep trying to figure out why. By the time Willard and I went back to quail heaven, three days later, I had come to the conclusion that my eyes were to blame. After all, they're certainly not what they once were, and in dim light valley quail *are* hard to see. They're small and fast and they blend into the usual background like sugar into oatmeal. I decided to wear my Kalichrome shooting glasses, which increase contrast and would, I hoped, enable me to pick up the flying quail more quickly. I'd previously found them a real help in seeing big game under poor lighting conditions, but somehow had never tried them bird hunting.

We left the car about 4 o'clock. By 6 I was explaining to Willard just what my trouble had been for all these recent years. I had killed ten quail in eleven shots and a lot of them were in heavy cover. That's about as good as I ever hope to do. The glasses were the answer!

It's too bad life is never so simple. The next three or four times out

123

I shot my usual average. Then I had another bad day. The glasses had nothing to do with it. In the long run I shot just the same with them as without them. The trouble lay in me—or maybe in the valley quail. As I've already said once and may say again, they're very easy birds to miss.

I think the valley quail is the trickiest and fastest upland bird in America. A shade smaller than a bobwhite—about 6 ounces—a valley quail is flying full bore by the time it's 2 feet off the ground. And it may never get any higher! In sparse cover a favorite stunt of the quail is to flip over or around a bush and buzz away behind it. You shoot the tops out of a lot of bushes when you're hunting them.

In the fall of 1958, the upland birds in the desert areas near my home were incredibly abundant. We had a lot of rain during April and May in 1957 and the cheat grass grew knee high; 1958 was also an excellent year for spring moisture. With two good nesting seasons in a row, the recently introduced chukar hit their first peak. So did valley quail, which were also exotic to this area. The native mountain quail population exploded too. I made up my mind to hunt every day of the open season if I had to borrow money to do it, and I almost succeeded—on both counts!

I soon discovered that shooting chukar, mountain quail, or even Huns, which had been introduced many years before and were also abundant now, was no training for hitting valley quail. We'd get into a covey of them after doing fairly well on the other birds, and I'd invariably find myself shooting yards behind on every crossing shot. And where the little speedballs had halfway decent cover so they could flip around or buzz over waist-high brush, I had to step up my shooting tempo about 50 percent before I began to connect.

Incidentally, we killed a lot of birds that fall, but we might as well have killed a lot more. The last day of the season on Chukar mountain, we shot our limits and saw hundreds of chukar and quail. Next season, we couldn't find one bird there!

Along with the rodents—jackrabbit, cottontail, and mice—which also built up to a tremendous peak in 1958, the chukar, quail, and Huns experienced an almost complete die-off during the winter of 1958-59. This, coupled with a dry spring, made the 1959 season the poorest I can remember.

Valley quail are hardy and adaptable. If water is available in a creek, spring, or stock tank, they thrive in desert surroundings so harsh and barren you wonder how they find enough to eat—much less raise their broods and elude their enemies. Yet they also thrive on irrigated farmlands where food and cover are a hundred times more plentiful than on the desert.

In the rural neighborhood where I grew up, we once had good hunting for bobwhites. Clean farming, which started during World War II and has grown steadily worse, was too much for Bob. As the weedy fence rows and brushy corners disappeared, he went with them. There are few coveys left. But about ten years ago valley quail from a stocking 30 miles away drifted into the area, and the quail shooting now is as good as it ever was.

There are—or were—two subspecies native to California and southern Oregon. One inhabited the lush coastal country from San Francisco north to Grants Pass. The other was resident in the more arid interior valleys and foothills, but trapping and transplanting have extended the range of both so greatly that they are now thoroughly mixed.

Most hunters prefer a light, fast gun for valley quail. The boring should be open—improved cylinder and modified in a double, either of these two chokes in a pump or automatic. The only thing gained by shooting high-brass ammunition is recoil; with a bird the size of a baseball, pattern is what counts. I use No. 7½ shot, partly because my gun patterns them better than 8's and also because we often find chukar in the same area.

When you're looking for a place to hunt, remember that you'll seldom find valley quail more than a quarter mile from water until the fall rains come and turn every cow track into a drinking fountain. Unlike bobwhite, they don't roost on the ground. A few high bushes, shrubs, or trees near water fulfill two of their requirements. The others are food and sufficient cover to protect them from their enemies.

The young eat insects, then shift to weed seeds, green plants, waste grain, and berries. Newly sprouted grass is an important food after the autumn rains. It is at this season, with food and water everywhere, that coveys wander across country to restock depleted covers. Once fall moisture brings up the new grass, you may find quail anywhere.

One day several years ago, we saw a big covey—probably a hundred birds—as we were following a pair of wheel tracks across a greasewood flat. There was no grass at all and the brush was scattered. Ninety-five percent of the ground was bare. By the time we stopped the car, got out, and loaded our guns, the quail were a block away, flowing over the flinty soil like an army of blue-gray bugs. We followed with the dog at heel.

Alternately running and walking, my companion and I chased the quail across the flat, over a rise, and down into a swale on the other side.

Here the cover was better. There was some big sagebrush along the bottom and a few weeds. By the time we reached it, the covey was disappearing over the next rise 200 yards ahead, but we paused to let the dog hunt out the bottom.

When a covey of quail is running, a few stragglers usually drop out in any cover where they have a chance to hide. This was the case here. We collected six, but by the time we reached the top of the next hill, where we had last seen the remainder of the covey, they were long gone.

I have friends who don't like valley quail because they run. I don't share this feeling. If I were a quail and had nothing whatever in which to hide, I'd run like hell. The difference between valley quail and pheasant is that pheasant habitually run away and flush out of range, even in good cover. The little blue birds with the forward-tipping plume stick as tight as bobwhites where they have a chance.

One day last fall while Willard and I were hunting the quail heaven mentioned previously, he hit a bird that scaled down into a 50-foot-square patch, of thick, tangled alkali weeds beside the creek. Knowing it might be hard to find, we put both dogs in. A minute later, his Brittany pointed. "Queenie's got it!" he exclaimed, then added, "Dead bird. Fetch."

But Queenie didn't budge and when Willard waded in, a perfectly healthy quail flew out. I shot it.

To make a long story short, we eventually tramped around in the weeds encouraging the dogs until one of them found Willard's dead quail. But before that, they pointed five others, all birds from a covey we had flushed 100 yards up the creek a few minutes earlier. These quail, the very same birds that run like antelope in the desert, had stuck like leeches in good cover.

The best hunting strategy depends on the type and extent of cover and the time of day, but as with most other upland game, it usually pays to follow the edges. Valley quail leave their roost quite early to feed. Where food is abundant they never get very far from the tight brush that provides safety from their enemies, but where the pickings are slim they may have to wander a long way before they can fill up.

By noon they're usually back in thick escape cover where they loaf in the shade during the hot part of the day. They feed again in late afternoon, working toward their roosting trees or brush just before dark. All movements normally are on foot.

You can generally get within range of a covey in decent cover, and about half the time it will scatter enough on the flush to provide good singles shooting over a pointing dog. Where the ground is bare, coveys always run and it would take an Olympic track star to push them into flight. A dog can do it, however, and for my money the best valley quail dog is one that sets them if they'll set and makes them fly if they won't.

But any dog is better than none, especially after the shooting. Dead birds are hard to find, and cripples in thick brush are all but impossible for a man to catch. In fact, I think it's little short of sinful to hunt this splendid bird without a dog of some kind.

If you have to knock down fifteen to bag ten, you're wasting one day's limit for each two days' hunting. Any game deserves a better break than that!

Concerning a Certain Blue Bird

by Capt. Edward C. Crossman

For many years almost all articles on valley quail contained some type of comparison of this species to bobwhites. Crossman's 1925 article follows these lines. He was also an early champion of small gauge guns, his favorite being the 20.

This," said the pointer, sitting down on his tail and fixing his master with baleful glare, "is one hell of a bird. I dunno who told you it came under the head of game. The chief difference between it and a jack rabbit is that you have some show to run down the rabbit, while this thing finally starts in to fly just as you are going to grab it. If you want to play the coursing game instead of bird hunting, why don't you buy a greyhound?

"The dambushes have an inch of dust on 'em; the plants are covered with thorns; it is hotter than the hinges of Hades, and the last water I saw was when you took a swig out of your canteen and forgot to slip me any. If you want to hunt any more of these so-called quail, you go and do it alone."

So saying, the pointer turned his indignant tail and made for the automobile a mile away. If you never heard a pointer talk this way, or any way, then it is merely because you never owned one.

Now there is some justification for the attitude of this Eastern-bred pointer dog. Our blue-plumed deceiver doesn't operate along bob-white lines, nor does he inhabit bob-white country. The dog finds this out more promptly than you do because you are not running through brush about as high as your head, and getting your paws full of cactus thorns and your sensitive nose full of dust and your soul full of bitterness when you come to a beautiful point—and the pointee blithely continues to scratch gravel on his merry way. Likewise you do not, in your leisurely sauntering, get up a temperature like a flivver topping a grade, and you do not seek hither and yon for the spring or the brook at which the pointer slakes his thirst in the bob-white ground—and never find one.

But you have never heard a California-trained bird dog talk about Eastern bob-white shooting, or the long-time hunter of the California blue quail comment on the measly little bunches of a dozen or so birds, hidden out in the briers and refusing stubbornly to move without the aid of the dog to show you precisely where they are. The trouble is not with the bird or the country; it is merely that the denizen of either does not "sabe the burro" concerning the other.

Probably the greatest game bird haunts in North America were the brushy flats and the washes of southern California prior to the '80s. Never had there been a hard winter to decimate the flocks; feed was plenty; the semi-desert bird knew where to find water in the driest season; the most active of the few bird killers could not take appreciable toll from the flocks. They were remarkably prolific, often nesting twice in one season; and in spite of their numbers and their freedom from danger, never did come under the fool-hen classification. The plumed darling that decided to quit running and look you over, and on closer inspection didn't fancy you, would fly just as fast and as hard as the most shot-over bird of the present day.

With the breeding season pretty well over, say about September, Bill Jones and his frau and the little Jones children would meet up with Sam Smith and his flock of misbehaved kids, so characteristic of other people's families. Presently the Jones and Smith families would foregather with the Browns, and then this covey would move up and mix with another; and presently there would be a band of anywhere from 100 to 1,000 birds. In the good old days the number was more often the thousand or several thousand than the hundred.

Then when the festive hunter, plodding along through the brush and without any more dog than a high church wedding, because he didn't need a dog, fell over one of these bands, the brush broke into thunder and the sky immediately ahead of him was blotted out with the great cloud of hurtling slaty-blue birds. That was not the end of the tale, outside of much and joyous shooting. Not at all, the difference being one which has caused much language on the part of the inexperienced or Eastern variety of shooter. Because if the hopeful and astonished huntsman continued to plod along to where he saw most of the blue cloud alight, his course would take him through the most quailless country he ever saw outside of 42nd and Broadway.

Paradoxical as it may seem, the first flight of a great band of quail serves merely to stretch their legs. They strike the ground running, and they continue this reprehensible method of progress until the danger seems to have been left behind.

Then they raise their little voices in song, chanting in their sweet throaty tones something like "Co-co a-a-ah ca," which, like every other bird note translated by printed letters, means nothing unless you have heard it. Every hunter of the plumed blue bird has his own version of the quail note, and not infrequently some discouraged tramper of the dry brush says that quail note is "You d-a-am fool," which is not unlike it in syllables, but requires a late afternoon and bagless frame of mind to hear plainly.

Presently the band is again foregathered and is sitting cozily in the shade, if it is after ten o'clock, the birds so situated scratching in the dust like hens. Earlier in the morning or later in the afternoon they are engaged in the endless task of putting away, where they will do the most good, several hundred seeds flavored with suitable bugs.

Now the before mentioned huntsman, if a wise and California-bred huntsman, is not alone; likewise is he not plodding guilelessly in the wake of the retreating band and never catching up. The secret of successful hunting of the California quail is first finding the covey, and then breaking it up and making the birds lie, which is done by such hurried measures as wild yells, firing all available guns into the mass when it erupts, and then by immediate dash at top speed into the middle of the band where it alighted.

When the little blue brother has the same amount of scare thrown into his system as pervades the colored person who sees something white moving in the burying ground, then, but not until then, do his legs give way under him, and he takes to the nearest cover. This is probably the roots of a gray bush, situated about six feet to your rear and four feet to your left.

When the arrangement is as I have stated, then the quail decides that it is time to go away from that place. The combination has sprained many a good man's back and fractured many good resolutions as to swearing out loud. Sometimes the patience of the bird gives out a little sooner, and he erupts, with totally unexpected and frightened twitter and a horrifying roar, from the bush into which you're preparing to plant your front foot.

I have hunted over dogs, and enjoy watching a dog work. I am not sure that I don't prefer the dog method. But the pointing of the dog gives the snap away; you know that when you unfasten the lid of the box, the jack contained therein is going to spring up with the horrifying squeak so terrifying to the small boy.

If you want real thrills—unexpected, hair-raising thrills that rock you backward on your astonished heels and move your hat straight upward—then hunt our quail without a dog.

The first job is the hard one—scaring the birds and making them lie. It is much harder than making the hunter lie, as you have probably noticed. Shots, yells and the approach of several hunters from different directions usually terrify the birds and freeze them to the scanty cover of the low bushes in the open flats. I am talking now of ideal quail country.

Sometimes, in these days, the cover consists of rocks larger than a piano and brush eight feet high, in which event you had best decide that you haven't lost any of those birds and come on away before St. Peter starts putting more rubber stamp cross marks in the account opposite your name.

Four hunters are more efficient than one, both because, opened out in skirmish order, they cover more ground in the preliminary covey hunt and because they can dash at the flushed covey from various sides and make the poor quail think there are at least forty men out there. I say that four hunters are better than one, but should add the proviso that all of the four be cool and trustworthy parties who will not forthwith plaster you in the subsequent proceedings with a load of 7½ chilled.

I have known of a great many such cases, one particular chap, a friend, getting not only one barrel, but two, at the range of about sixty yards. The boys took him down and washed him up, and picked out some of the shot; then they returned to camp and told his innocent wife that he had fallen through a barbed-wire fence, to explain his somewhat mussed-up appearance. I don't know what the good lady thought a barbed-wire fence looked like; but if any fence put as many beauty spots on a fellow as those two loads of 7½ shot, it must have had more barbs than a porcupine.

Once the birds of a broken-up band decide to lie, they lie with a consistency that would make Ananias resemble George Washington. You can cross and crisscross the low brush wherein they sought cover and only those birds that you fairly kick out will flush.

There appear to be two or three standard incentives for a lying California quail to burst into flight. One of them is to kick the bush in which he is hiding; another is to walk past it a few feet; a third is to stop, which seems to make all the birds round you nervous because they cannot locate your position; and the fourth is to get nicely astride of a large bush or a rock so that you are in the worst possible position to shoot. The standard procedure in this last instance is for the bird to fly straight down hill, if there is a hill. After you fire both barrels over the top of his back, then two more flush from a patch of utterly bare and vacant ground in front of you, and sail leisurely away, the only time when they do fly in a leisurely manner.

I have often taken a limit of twenty-five (old days) from a single broken-up covey on a brushy flat, and seen two or three other fellows do likewise. In fact, I am not sure that those low-lives didn't get more than the limit. I am the fellow writing this story.

In the old days the ideal bird shooting was out in the flats in low brush, hardly more than knee deep. Water was invariably within a mile or so, because quail and water are not too far separated during our open season.

132

Not one time in a hundred flushes did the hunter ever see the bird before the soul-stirring roar announced the going away of the quail from that spot. The only time he saw the birds was in the preliminary flushing of the entire band, and possibly in the occasional open patches the glimpse of a running bird, passing with ease such slow-moving animals as the jack-rabbits, cottontails and other such little talented denizens of the brush.

Our quail runs just as enthusiastically as he stays put when finally scared out of a season's growth, all of which is so demoralizing to an Eastern-trained bird dog.

Not one man out of five, in the old more or less pre-automobile days, bothered with a dog. In the first place, the dog was of little aid in finding the band which you had to break up, because when either of you got close to such a band you had no doubt about its being there. He aided little in the breaking up and scaring of the birds, and when they were so broken up, all you had to do was to keep walking around about three or four acres to get your limit—or shoot yourself clear out of shells, if that's the sort of a shot you were.

The chief value of the dog then, as now, was to aid in finding the shot birds, because the California quail not killed outright, or with his landing gear mostly shot away, regards being shot as merely an incentive to speed in running. And shot practically dead, the last fierce struggles of life passing out of that beautiful and virile little body would nearly always take the bird into the roots of a bush if one were available.

The slaty-blue color of the bird's back blends in wonderfully with the prevailing color of the cover in which you find him. A deplorable number of birds are lost by the most skilled hunter merely because of the bird's running habits and his protective coloration, or at least his accidental blending with the shade of the brush, have it as you choose.

Regardless of the temptation, oblivious to the deliberate insult of another bird flushing and knocking off his hat with the wind of its eruption, the old-timer goes straight to the spot where his bird fell and he finds and picks up that bird before any further business is attended to. It may take him two or three minutes to find his bird, or as much to come to the hateful conclusion that it was merely wounded and got away; but he attends to that job first.

If conditions are right, a double, one to each barrel, is permissible, particularly if the first bird is in plain sight or the ground is very open.

Herein does the tenderfoot mark himself apart from the old California quail shooter. The novice or the hog proceeds to shoot just as long as anything is getting up as he proceeds in the direction of the first bird downed. He may get down five birds before he finds the first one—if he ever does find it—but he will rarely find more than three out of the five, and often not that many.

In this sort of work the dog is valuable. Opposed to it, however, is the objection some men have to the inevitable currying of the poor dog's paws for cactus spines, the constant need of the dog for water, and the advisability in some localities of washing out the dog's dust-filled nose.

With the covey worked out—which more often means that the outlying birds have finally plucked up courage to sneak off through the brush—the hunter has his option of seeing another band, which may be miles away, or sitting down and eating lunch and cocking up a weather ear for little voices. Sooner or later a bird lifts up his voice and wants to know if anybody has seen those dod-gasted hunters the last hour or so, and where is everybody, anyhow?

And to this another bird a half mile away replies with more uncomplimentary remarks about the hunters, and says that he's right over this way; let's get together down at the bunch of mesquite. So pretty soon is another covey ready for the hunter, except that, being made up of veterans, it is quite likely to keep a weather eye out and to flush wild, which adds to the difficulty of getting it broken up again.

The story of our quail is pitiful. Talking to the old boys who shot our quail thirty and forty and fifty years ago, both amateurs and market hunters, one is inspired to repeat the famous remark of Carlyle, with some modifications—that the United States of those days consisted of about 60,000,000 people, mostly damned fools. That any set of legislators would permit the slaughter that went on in this country from the Civil War to the Spanish War passes understanding, and our quail situation is merely one more instance.

One market hunter, a fine old chap whose love for the gun is such that he now shoots clay birds for his recreation, told me of killing 2,200 dozen quail for the market within a few months. He said that he and his partner shot 1,500 dozen from one enormous band in one single location, without apparently lessening the number of the birds. If you will put this on your slide-rule, you'll note that 2,200 dozen means 26,400 quail, and that 1,500 dozen means 18,000.

The market hunter is not at fault; you and I might easily have been market hunters had our love for the gun been what it is, and the birds available, and the supply apparently inexhaustible. They had no such "back-sight" to guide them as we now have; they loved to shoot, and that was a legitimate way of making a living into the bargain. No foresight could have shown that the quail or other game would disappear seemingly over night.

Our amateurs went out and staged quail-killing races in the '80s and '90s, within sixty miles of Los Angeles. Individual bags of four and five hundred birds in a day were not uncommon in such races. It is not meet to pan the market hunter, when our best amateurs were giving an imitation of a game hog that would make said hog take to the woods in disgust.

With any protection at all in those days, a bag limit of, say, 100 or some such neat figure, and a closed season of nine months, California would have magnificent shooting today, and fifty years from today, because our quail cover and quail feed and breeding grounds will always be with us. We still have many quail but, like the coyote, the birds have changed their habits in self-defense. They stick close to rocky hills and high brushy cover, and pile into it at the first gun-fire. Paved roads and a million automobiles in the one state have run the birds ragged, what are left of them.

In the old days, the brushy flats, with springs or some stream trickling down a draw, were the quail haunts. In the early part of the season they are still found on the lower shoulders of the brushy, rocky hills, roosting in the high bushes out of reach of vermin, departing for feed and water with the first glimpse of the sun, then hunting shade for the hot part of the day. Old vineyards used to be great quail haunts.

The skilled quail hunter, preferably with his dog, still gets good quail shooting in the state, but he knows where to go and how to hunt. He does not start up over seven miles of rocky, brushy hills as devoid of water as the middle of the Mojave Desert, because he knows that quail like food and water just as does a human being, and won't be found more than a mile or so from such supplies. Likewise does he refrain from getting into high brush, because he can neither see the birds if they flush nor can he make them do other than run in most cases.

For fifteen years of annual quail hunting, outside of four wasted years in the army—so far as hunting was concerned—I have carried nothing bigger than a 20-bore, and for ten years have shot a little 20-bore single trigger, of 6 lbs. with 30-inch barrels, both full choke, and with 2¾-inch chambers. It is plenty of gun and plenty of load in it.

The *sine qua non* of successful retrieving of your birds, lacking the dog, is to kill them just as near to you as you can, not to mention the fact that they are then easily hit before they have time to start curving off hither and yon. Much of the work is in the hills; always the weather is hot, and your shells heavy, and your boots full of feet.

135

All of which prescribes the light, small bore gun; not necessarily small bore, I admit, but at least light. One of the most successful quail hunters I know shoots a 30-inch 28-bore, but his gun weighs as much as a full-grown 20-gauge.

The canny quail man sallies forth with light boots, twelve-inch top or higher, or puttees, a skeleton coat without sleeves, a small light canteen with water in it, and two boxes of shells, 20-gauge shells if he is wise in his gun selection. If he's going to get quail, he has got to drill; and when he drills very far under the California fall or winter sun in the quail country, he will understand why the Latin word for baggage, or supplies, is impedimenta—"that which checks the foot"—likewise which produces copious perspiration and a large pain at your lack of judgment in the things to carry.

The Valley Quail of California

by T. S. Van Dyke

This 1892 article by Van Dyke was among one of the first "how to" articles published on valley quail hunting. It is interesting to note that he speaks of habitat decline even at that time.

B efore the great "boom" turned into vineyards and orchards so many of the best game preserves of Southern California, and opened with railroads so many of its remote corners, valley quail abounded in incredible numbers, especially in the county of San Diego. The bevies of this quail run together in the fall, forming flocks of many hundreds, and even thousands. But in its movements and habits it is so different from the well-known "Bob White" that the most experienced shot from the East may be bitterly disappointed at first if left to his own experience in shooting them.

To elude pursuit "Bob White" depends first upon hiding, whereas this quail depends first upon its legs, next upon its wings, and hides only when thoroughly scared and scattered. After being overtaken and flushed a few times, especially if fired at, it concludes that legs and wings are a failure, and then resorts to hiding, when it will often lie well to a dog.

But by the time the birds are worried into this frame of mind, the dog, unless kept behind or tied up, is liable to be demoralized with the rapid running of the birds or spent with heat or thirst in the dry air; so that when the birds are in condition to enable you to use him to advantage he may be quite worthless. And if so steady and well broken that he cannot be demoralized by the swift running of the numerous birds he may be too slow upon all, except those that lie the most closely. The proportion of these to the whole number is so small that you cannot well confine your shooting to them while for the others you must move too rapidly to keep your dog in good order.

Fortunately a dog is not generally necessary (unless birds are very scarce) either to find a flock in the first place or to find most of the birds when scared enough to make them hide. The flocks are generally so large and so noisy and keep so much on open ground that one can either see or hear them farther than a dog would be apt to catch their scent.

The best way to seek them is on horseback or in a wagon, riding until a flock is found, and then tying up the horse and going after them on foot. If the ground is good it is often best to charge upon the flock upon horseback, firing over them as they rise, following them up on a gallop and firing over them before they find their feet. As their flight is short this is generally an easy matter. After two or three charges the flock breaks, bewildered, into hundreds of slate-blue lines, darting, wheeling, chirping and buzzing in all directions for a moment or two. Then suddenly all is still, and hundreds of birds are scattered over ten or fifteen acres of thin brush about waist high. This scattering of the birds may also be done by a single person on foot. But he must move rapidly and will be much aided by a companion going ahead of the flock and firing into it in front when it rises.

If you have scattered a large flock on ground not too rough and where the brush is not too high, you will now have some two hours of shooting on one of the most gamy and saucy of American birds, and if you can keep cool and shoot half straight you will have all the birds you can carry.

At your first advance into the place where the quail last settled in confusion, a dozen or more rise in front of you and as many more on each side, and from five to fifty yards away. They burst from the brush with rapid flight and whizzing wing, most of them with a sharp, clear "chirp, chirp, chirp," in the tone of which there is more of defiance than of alarm. Some dart straight away in a dark-blue line, making none too plain a mark against the dull background of brush, and vanishing in handsome style, unless you are very quick with the gun. Others wheel off on either side, their mottled breasts shining in the sun as they turn, and making a beautiful mark as they mount above the sky line. Some wheel and pass almost over your head, so that you can plainly see the black and white around their heads and throats and the cinnamon shading of their underwear.

At the report of the gun rise ten, twenty, perhaps fifty more all around you at from five to one hundred yards and even more; sometimes all at once, sometimes in groups of three or four or a dozen, one group following the other. And the report of your second barrel arouses perhaps half as many more from apparently the same bushes from which the others rose. You may be an old and skillful shot and fancy that you are extremely cool, but now you must be careful or your California companion, who is perhaps an inferior shot on most other game, will leave you far behind on the score. Many a man who has stood with unruffled calmness on a "duck pass" in the Western States when during the "evening flight" the air trembled beneath the beat of wings, or on a "deer drive" has heard the music of the hounds rolling toward him in a tumultuous *crescendo*, yet felt not a shiver gambol up his spine, has lost his head completely on his first introduction to a large flock of these quail.

Supposing that you are cool and make a handsome double shot right and left at the very first rise of the birds and send two of them whirling down out of a cloud of fine feathers; when you go to pick up the first one you may find only an exasperating sameness about all the bushes, with perhaps a few feathers on the tops of some of them. Meanwhile a fresh bird breaks with a squeal from a bush at your feet, scuds a few yards along the ground with wondrous speed of foot before rising, and at the sound of its wings buzz, whizz, whir! chirp, chirp, chirp! go half a dozen more from the ground all around you. The temptation to shoot is irresistible and down goes another bird. And perhaps two fall with another shot, of which you feel very proud. But if so you may be worse off than if you had shot only one. For now you are quite sure to forget where the first two fell, and still more apt to lose sight of the spot where the last two fell, and your confusion is increased by the whizzing and darting and chirping of more birds all around you.

Nor would you be much aided by a retriever, unless a very good one and one used to these quail; for he easily becomes so worthless that you cannot scatter birds all around the points of the compass and depend on his finding them without any aid from you. The art of killing these quails so quickly that they do not flutter several yards away from where they fall, of landing them where they are easily marked and found, of remembering where they fall and going directly to the spot and picking them up at once without any loss of time or distraction of the attention by the rising of fresh birds, is fully equal to the art of hitting them in the first place. The extent to which this skill is cultivated by some of the best quail shots is quite marvelous, while many never become skillful in that way, but always lose a large proportion of the game actually killed.

Meanwhile away go the birds, here, there and everywhere, some whipping out of the brush after you have passed them, some rising on the sides, and more rising ahead far out of reach of any gun. Up hill, down hill, across, in front, straight away and curling around behind they go, buzzing and chirping as if they would never stop. So numerous are they that you can select your shots, if sufficiently cool, and take only long, crossing shots which call for the greatest amount of skill and calculation. Up the slopes and on the other sides of the gullies you can see them in the open places, scudding along on foot, some going nearly as fast as if on the wing, others trotting slowly along, stopping occasionally to look at you, some single, others in lines of half a dozen or more, trailing along one behind the other. And nearly all are traveling up hill. Many of these are birds that rose but a moment ago and flew but a short distance before alighting. The flock is such a large one that they are all around you. Perhaps fifty or sixty bevies have run together to form it, and though you may take home a hundred out of it to-day, yet to-morrow you might start it again without noticing any difference in its size.

The rapid rising of the birds lasts from fifteen minutes to half an hour, according to the size of the flock, the nature of the ground and your management of the scattered ones. Suddenly the shooting tapers off, and one might think that the game had all run away. Many birds have indeed run away, but many still remain, well scared and closely hidden. Now, if you had a good dog, fresh and cool instead of excited, heated and thirsty, he would point plenty of quail on the very ground you have just been over. Yet fair shooting may still be had without any dog, and you may take your time at it. Backward and forward for a dozen times you may now traverse the same ground, getting a shot every three or four minutes, instead of every few seconds, as before. The birds rise nearer than before, many almost at your feet, and nearly all of them singly, the interval between the shots growing longer until it reaches a point where it is better to find another flock if you want more birds. But one large flock will generally give all the shooting a reasonable man should want.

Before you have spent many minutes among these quail you find you have to deal with one of the toughest birds of its size on earth. Here one rolls whirling down out of a cloud of feathers, yet when you go for it it is not where it fell perhaps, but twenty yards down the hillside, fluttering, bouncing and gyrating. As you stoop to pick it up it flutters away again, and even after you think it is dead it spins around in your pocket. Another sheds a handful of feathers at the report of the gun, yet instead of falling or even wavering in its flight it seems to fly all the better for its loss. Vainly you watch it, expecting to see it fall. It buzzes swiftly away, sweeps majestically up the next slope, sets its wings and sails over the ridge out of sight. Another twists and wabbles with a broken back as the gun rings along the hills, then settles a little, then rises again, and swinging up and down finally alights some two hundred yards away. Go there and perhaps it will rise wild and actually escape you again.

A fourth suddenly changes its course as the shot sings across its path, mounts rapidly upward forty, fifty, perhaps a hundred yards, winding up in a spiral line; then poises for a moment with fluttering wings and bill pointed skyward; then suddenly closes its wings and descends with a thump to earth. Unless you have an unusually good dog, a wing-tipped bird is generally as safe as a well one. All you see is perhaps a dark line vanishing in a twinkling in the brush, and generally you do not see that much, unless the bird falls very near you. The gun must be loaded heavily with powder and with the finest shot that the gun will shoot the most evenly and with the least scattering. Then there is no suffering except that of instant death.

Strangers are often troubled by the quail flying into cactus, and seem to think they must give them up at once. There is cactus enough here that would stop a rhinoceros, but there is also some that offers the very finest, easiest shooting in the land. Take, for instance, one of the hundreds of little valleys from forty to one hundred yards wide and

141

from ten to fifty feet deep, half filled with prickly pear and surrounded by low hills or table lands quite bare of cover. The prickly pear grows in clumps from five to fifteen feet or more across, and from three to six feet or more in height, its broad green lobes thickly set with spines like cambric needles. This fearful stuff the valley quail prefers to all other cover. The flocks roost in it, fly into it and out of it, and even run at full speed up the limbs without being hurt by it. Such ground was always certain to contain plenty of birds before so much of the country was cleared up, and where sufficiently open to allow ready walking between the clumps of the cactus it is the very best of all places to make the acquaintance of this lively little bird. On such ground it is quite easy to break and scatter the flock, and as the open part of the ground is generally quite bare you will have little trouble in finding birds that fall on it, but the great advantage is that if the tract covered with cactus is large enough, and the hills around are quite bare of cover, the quail will not leave it, but fly to and fro in it.

Often you will hear the sharp "whit, whit, whit" of alarm before you fairly enter such a place, and down the winding openings catch a glimpse of a dozen or more birds scudding darkling away in the forbidding array of thorny green. You quicken your pace and suddenly a quail rises with short and intermitting stroke of wing, mounting by successive strokes as if only climbing higher for a better inspection of you. At the report of your gun he sinks perhaps into a sheet of roaring blue that the sound has aroused from below. A snap shot from your second barrel into the thickest of the mass fills the air ahead with a cloud of white and blue feathers, and half a dozen birds are hung up on the lobes of cactus or are fluttering and spinning around among its roots. You see at once that such work will not do. You must so select your shots that the birds fall dead upon the open ground—another of the fine arts of shooting.

The flock scatters along the prickly pear some two hundred yards ahead, and in a moment all is still. And now as you move down the winding spaces amid this grim shrubbery, that stands so silent and savage around you, birds by the dozen come chirping and fluttering from out its shaggy arms. Some scramble rapidly to the highest point of the cactus before taking wing, while others come whizzing out under full headway. Some curl around over your head, others dart out on the opposite side, just rising into sight for a moment in a dark-blue curve, while others dart along the ground on foot to the next clump of cactus.

As before, there is no time lost in waiting for a shot. At every step ahead there is a whizz on one side, a buzz on the other and a "chirp, chirp, chirp" ahead of you, or even behind you, and the report of the gun

142

is followed by a dozen blue lines curving and twisting out of the same clumps of cactus from which but a minute before half a dozen perhaps rose. Your gun rattles as fast as you can load it, stricken birds bounce fluttering and spinning upon the open ground, others rise whizzing and chirping as you go for a dead one, still others burst from the cactus beside you as you stoop to pick it up.

But, as before, this intensity does not last long. In fifteen or twenty minutes the climax is reached and the roar and confusion are suddenly gone. But the shooting is by no means over. It has only settled down. For two or three hours yet you may traverse the open places of this strange covert, and from out the thickest and most threatening parts come bird after bird as you pass it again, again and again. Never shall you see the valley quail show to better advantage than when he bursts from the outer edge of this stuff and tries to go around you to enter it again. His rapid wings make a bluish haze, through which you see plainly his mottled breast, his little blue neck and black and white head outstretched to their utmost length, with the long dark plume bent backward by his speed. He looks too pretty to shoot as he cleaves the warm sunlight or, setting his little wings, glides like a falling arrow full into the thickest mass of the thorny cactus.

143

Quail? It's a Gambel

By William J. Schaldack

The spacious desert of Arizona still offers excellent quail hunting. The species is the Gambel's. It is a runner, hard on dogs and men. Things haven't changed much since Schaldach's 1941 article. When a covey of seventy-five plus quail come up it's memorable.

Nine days of steady driving had brought us to the Arizona desert, nearly three thousand miles from our Vermont home. We were entering the saguaro-cactus country, and on each side of the old Silverbell Road the weird giants reared in grotesque shapes and designs, sprawling their twisted arms in crazy contours. To our Eastern eyes it was pure fantasy.

Nearing one of the innumerable dips where the road passed through an arroyo, we spotted our first Gambel's quail. A procession of twenty or more birds raced across the road a hundred yards ahead of the car. Anxious for a closer view, I stepped on the gas, rolled down into a dip and struck inches of loose sand. The front wheels wedged, a shiver ran through the car, the motor coughed, died—and there we were!

It took some manipulating, but we finally crawled through the fifty yards of loose stuff by keeping the car in low. On the other side we met a cow hand, who seemed amused. I asked him if they had a road commissioner in Arizona and, if so, whether he knew about that sand trap back there. He just grinned and said: "Why, mister, that's a right good road. You just drove through the Santa Cruz River."

"The Santa Cruz River? I didn't see any water."

"Not now you didn't . But two days ago she was running a flood. Starts in Sonora, down in Mexico, and when it rains down there the water gets here fast. After the surface water runs off, the river keeps right on flowing. It's there just the same, but you can't see it. Follows an underground channel beneath the bed of the stream."

We thanked him and drove on, suspecting that we were being kidded. But we found out later that he had told the sober truth. A few minutes later we arrived at the home of our friends who had, two years before, left New England for good to settle on a unique and lovely desert spot, surrounded by giant cactus, paloverde and mesquite. Here we were to spend the winter.

Black clouds rolled up out of the west, casting weird shadows on the ridges and slopes of the Tucson Mountains. The wind shrieked a gale, and the air had a rawness that spelled storm. I said so, but was promptly squelched.

After all, we were just green Yankees, and what did we know about Southwest desert weather, anyhow? It was going to clear; anyone with a real weather-eye could see that. And darned if it didn't—in less than an hour!

Rivers that flow underground! When it looks blackest, cheer up, the sun is about to shine! Apparently we had a lot to learn. Take the matter of wildlife and its habitat. We all know that a ruffed grouse is pretty spry when it comes to dodging in and out of thorn-apple trees, catbriers and blackberry bushes. But these are smooth as satin in comparison with, for example, the cholla. Nature never developed a more vicious spiny device. The Mexicans say that a cholla will jump at you as you pass by. But road-runners, desert mocking birds and a dozen other species of winged creatures fly full tilt into the maze of needles, walk around on the branches and actually seem to enjoy it.

"Adapt yourself or die" is the watchword of the desert. Water-holes are infrequent, and any running stream west of the pecos cannot be depended upon to perform more than half the time. So the desert creatures, including Gambel's quail, live from month to month with practically no moisture other than what is obtained from the vegetation and insects on which they feed.

During much of the year temperatures range up to 110 degrees and stay there pretty constantly. There are wild thunderstorms in the summer, frost and ice in the winter. Add to this many natural enemies: prairie falcons, other hawks, owls, coyotes, skunks, rattlers and many species of non-venomous snakes.

The very nature of the terrain would be enough to discourage a foraging beast or bird unused to the country. The desert floor resembles nothing so much as a gravel pit, cut through irregularly with large and small washes and arroyos. There is no lack of vegetation, but it is not the lush and succulent growth of the East. Here a bob-white, transplanted from Carolina, would starve looking for an edible seed or insect with which it was familiar. But the little chestnut and blue waifs which are the Gambel's quail thrive and multiply.

During several winter months I had the rare opportunity of studying this little desert game bird at close range. Back of the cottage in which we lived there was a large windmill. When this overflowed, as it frequently did, the ground became saturated and made one of the few wet spots to be found anywhere around. Once or twice a day a pack of as many as two hundred quail would come trooping up out of the mesquite and paloverde to drink, dust themselves and have a siesta. Since they were protected in this territory, the birds were quite tame and would allow a fairly close approach.

But out on the open range, away from habitations, the story is quite different. Here you will find the Gambel's quail well able to fend for itself against its natural enemies, including man; those who have hunted these fast little fellows will say, "particularly man."

All that applies to the hunting of other species of blue quail—valley, scaled, Massena—fits the Gambel's bird. To be really successful the gunner should be an able sprinter and possess the lungs and heart of an athlete, the nerves of a tight-rope walker. Then, if he can combine with these virtues the agility of a tap dancer and the limberness of a contortionist, he is fairly well equipped.

To the uninitiated this may sound discouraging, but it is always well to present the darker side of the picture first. Any desert quail hunter will tell you that the bird's name might just as well be spelled "gamble." It is wholly unpredictable. You may roam the desert throughout an entire day without finding a covey; or, more frequently, finding the birds, you may fail to get a good break on shots and return empty-handed. But there are full days, too, when things break well and sunset finds you with your pockets bulging. Such days are in the majority.

In the section of Arizona with which I am familiar, dogs are seldom used, though a smart pointer would, I am sure, contribute vastly to a day's fun. Hunting alone is practically useless, discounting the rare lucky stroke of coming suddenly upon a pack of birds in a hidden wash. Field tactics call for the carefully planned cooperation of two or three gunners, just as coyotes hunt in pairs or trios.

Having located a covey—more properly a pack, as the birds often number from forty to a hundred—the strategy is to follow slowly, keeping in full view of the moving birds. When the quail stop feeding, it is time for the man following to stop too. The pack may break from nervousness. Meanwhile your partner, or partners, are executing a flank movement designed to cut off the birds and place themselves within reasonable range when the quail flush.

In sections where vegetation is thick—and this applies to much of the desert—these guerrilla tactics are quite successful. The gunner dodges from mesquite to greasewood, bends low behind a clump of prickly pear, takes advantage of any friendly wash. He keeps moving and hopes for the best. When a close approach has been made, it is time for action. A warning whistle from the scout informs the gunner driving the pack that the magical moment has arrived.

Brace yourselves, boys! Things are about to happen!

The driver takes a deep breath and runs; he runs as though the devil were after him, straight at the birds. If he is lucky, he may have a long shot or two at a detachment of birds which swing in his direction. But usually he must watch with what philosophical calm he can summon as his friends hurl charges of chilled 7½'s at the roaring, speeding mass of chestnut and smoky blue forms.

The Gambel's quail is as much a part of the earth as any of its four-footed neighbors. It loathes flying, and if left to its own devices would probably never take to the air. But once awing, it is a fast and efficient flyer, getting out of range as promptly and effectively as bobwhite. If, upon breaking up the pack, the gunners have succeeded in scattering the birds into several small groups, they may count themselves lucky— provided, of course, the positions of the birds have been fairly well marked.

No time must be lost, because there is nothing permanent in the life of a Gambel's. He is just as apt as not to remember that he hasn't seen his cousin in Rillito for some months, and now would be as good a time as any to make a social call. A quick sprint, on the part of the gunner, to within a hundred yards of a clump of chaparral suspected of holding quail and then a moderately fast walk will, at least half of the time, result in that delicious feeling of seeing two or more birds break into the air with the sweet innocence of bob-whites.

If the gun is held right—well out in front—and a double comes to earth, a feeling of peace descends upon the gunner. After all, the game is worth those twisted ankles, scraped shins and prickly-pear spines in the seat of the pants.

But the element of mystery envelops scattered birds, too. On many an occasion I have dashed hopefully up to a clump of cactus which I knew held a pair or more of quail, knew it because I had seen them plop in seconds before. I had started sprinting before they lit. The next nearest cover was fifty yards away. I had not seen them run to it; yet, upon arrival, panting and sweating, I failed to find a single trace of a bird.

The Mexicans and Indians speak knowingly of kindly spirits that protect the creatures of the desert. Perhaps it is as good an explanation as any.

Having failed to locate scattered birds, the sensible thing to do is sit down quietly and enjoy the desert sunshine, meanwhile keeping the ears attentive for the musical, inquiring note of the scatter call. For the desert quail have a scatter call as distinctive as that of bob-white, though it is quite different. To me it sounds like "quir-r-t? quir-r-r-rt?" though I am not at all accurate about those things and an ornithologist would probably disagree. It is often possible to follow a pack again, after it has reassembled. But the chances are that the birds will be wild, having been shot into.

Most gunners prefer to go on tramping and locate a fresh bunch of birds. The experienced desert man will know what type of cover is most apt to hold birds at a given time of day. But an even surer method is to listen for the voice of the pack. Gambel's quail are extremely talkative, chattering steadily as they move along and feed. In the evening they are usually to be found near thick cover—clumps of mesquite, paloverde, ironwood and greasewood—in which they roost at night.

The dogless gunner has his work cut out for him in any kind of country. Unless he becomes expert at marking down birds out of the tail of his eye, he is bound to lose much game—even birds killed outright. In the case of cripples, his problem becomes magnified many times. This is particularly true in the desert, where the plumage of the Gambel's blends surprisingly with its surroundings. One simply must learn the trick of marking hit birds, approximately at least, while in the act of swinging at another angle on a second bird.

Having one or more birds down, the thing to do is to get over there at once and start looking. To take the eye off a particular rock or clump of cactus is fatal, because everything looks alike.

In the case of cripples, the wisest procedure is another shot. You are no match for a running Gambel's, particularly on stony and thorny ground. One fellow out there has the right idea. He takes a springer along with him. The dog is taught to follow at heel until sent on to retrieve. That gunner and his friends seldom lose a bird. But during much of the season the heat is too great, and a dog can only be hunted for a few hours during the day. Water for the dog should always be carried, since it is an arid country.

The Eastern grouse and woodcock hunter, accustomed to snappy fall days in the field, will find the desert quite a different matter. He must dress for heat, which means light clothing—a skeleton shooting coat and, above all, stout footgear.

Footgear is by all odds the most important consideration. Tramping mile after mile, part of the time running at top speed, over the rough and stony desert floor calls for boots made of stout stuff. On the other hand, weight is a positive encumbrance. A third factor enters into the consideration of proper underpinning—the chance that you might plunk down full tilt on to a coiled rattler. In fairness it should be said that this is a rare possibility. Nevertheless it does exist. And if you feel the way I do about venomous snakes, you wouldn't be any too happy with much less than stove pipe on your shanks.

In the desert region extending from Phoenix to the Mexican border rattlers are supposed to go into hibernation from late October to mid-November, not emerging again until the following April. Inquiry seemed to prove that this is almost invariably true; yet I met several persons who stated that they had found buzz-tails at large while quail hunting in early December. It is better to play safe, and certainly far easier on the mind. Since most of the desert rattlesnakes are of the smaller species—sidewinder, or horned rattler, and green rattler (the big diamondback is seldom seen)—stout leather shoes with leather puttees are favored by most hunters.

The last consideration of equipment, and probably the most important, is one about which the discreet man will keep his mouth shut. It concerns the gun. And the very mention of guns among shooters anywhere is apt to stir up a hornet's nest of argument, unless the speaker be extremely tactful. On the desert, as in the quail country of the deep South, or the forested grouse lands of the North, men shoot every make and bore of scatter-gun. Each declares his choice to be the best. And for him it probably is.

It all boils down, I think, to what a man is capable of handling proficiently and confidently. Desert quail do not often offer close, easy shots. The rule is usually a 30-yard flush, with birds being taken at forty, forty-five and fifty. Some men will do wonders, and do them consistently with a 20-bore. Personally, I want heavier artillery.

One point upon which everyone agrees is that open chokes are out. Nothing wider than modified for the right barrel, and a good full choke for the left. And there is probably a definite advantage in shooting nothing but a full choke, as near birds can always be allowed to get off into safe range for a close gun. Once in flight, the Gambel's quail takes a bee-line; he knows nothing about the twisting and dodging tactics of the snipe and the woodcock.

The little blue and chestnut fellow can take a lot of shot and carry it a long way, too. So shells must have plenty of wallop. The most popular shot size seems to be 7½, though some gunners prefer 8.

The slanting rays of the desert sun bathe the rugged slopes of the Santa Catalina Mountains. Brilliant orange and vermilion at the top of Mt. Lemmon, 9,000 feet in the air; scarlet and maroon along the belt of canyon oaks and pines half-way down; purple, cobalt blue and pale green at the base, where the rocky giants rest on the desert. Color such as Easterners never see.

We drop down from the low plateau on which we have hunted to the sandy, cactus-covered bottomlands of the strange stream that flows underground. A roadside sign tells us where we are. It reads: CAMINO DE MAÑANA. Since tomorrow never comes, what better invitation could one have? There will always be this rocky, half-forgotten little desert road, and for those who know, and care, a band of brave, saucy Gambel's quail at the end of it.

Mountain Quail
by H. L. Betten

The mountain quail is our largest quail. Many people rate it as the most striking. Still others speak of this species as the most difficult of any North American upland bird to bag. Betten's book chapter from the 1930s suggested that this species would remain for future grandchildren. Happily it has.

Higigh up in the Sierras of the Pacific Coastal Range there is a bird—largest of the American quail and little known outside of the mountains that slope toward the western coast. It is the mountain quail, cousin to the valley quail and the Gambel's quail.

Although there have been efforts to popularize the mountain quail east of the Coastal Range they have been uniformly unsuccessful, and it is probable that very few hunters even as far west as the Rocky Mountains have had any experience on this bird. In fact, many sportsmen even in California think that the mountain quail is a poor excuse for a game bird, but my own experience has been something different. This bird really deserves to be better known than it is, and I am going to devote a few words to the busy little fellow.

Get this. The mountain quail does not inhabit the highlands exclusively, but it is most often found higher than two thousand feet. And it can enjoy itself and increase in numbers up to an altitude of twelve thousand feet. I do not know of any quail in this country that can endure such altitudes. Mountain quail are of a migratory nature, leaving high altitudes when snow flies to descend to elevations which—in a severe winter—may be as low as twenty-five hundred feet.

If the bobwhite quail of the East and the South could handle itself one-tenth so well as the mountain quail, there would not be the terrific losses that we find following a series of deep snows.

Some years ago, it was permissible in the Coastal states to shoot mountain quail as early as October when they afforded the acme of sport along the alpine range in the Sierras. Perhaps this was opening the season too early, and now we must be content with shooting in late November and December. Fine though it is at times, the sport hardly measures up to the thrills which we formerly had during the Indian summer on the highlands.

The shooting season of today is apt to find us facing winter storms coming up very suddenly and developing a decided element of danger. One-way mountain roads hang precariously over deep gorges and canyons—the trails become slippery—there is always the possibility of being stalled by a landslide or a breakdown. This is a brief picture of what the mountain quail hunter meets.

Not many seasons ago I went through one of these sullen, difficult wintry adventures, and I look back upon it with a vivid recollection. December storms had swept the mountains for weeks. Finally there was a lull of several days followed by a spell of delightful weather. However, the open season was slipping rapidly away, and I wanted at least one try at those romantic highland quail before it was too late.

There are some winter trips that no sportsman wants to try alone.

Perhaps it is an elk hunt; maybe it is a trip after deer; perchance it is a drive through the rains and the sleet and the mist to some favorite spot where there is duck shooting.

When you meet up with such a situation, you usually discover that it is difficult to interest others in a prospective outdoor trip. Comes fine weather and you have fair weather friends. Comes the gloom and dashing rains and the cold winds and you walk or drive or hunt alone.

In the end, it was Doc Crane who had the fortitude and the courage and the will. Doc is a dentist, and you know how dentists are. There was a great deal of mercurial Irish blood in him and no end of recklessness and daring. I doubt if Doc Crane was afraid of anything or anybody or gave a second thought to dangers he might face. As for narrow escapes of the past, he just laughed at them.

We started for the mountains at midnight in Doc's car after I had made sure that we had two sets of chains, a stout rope, a shovel, and other equipment aboard. Doc was doing the driving.

"How's the windshield wiper, Doc?" I inquired, because there came to my mind a rather bitter experience of other days when a windshield wiper had failed to function.

"Okay," answered my friend blithely.

"How do you know? Have you tried it? Let's see if it works."

"Aw forget it," Doc exploded impatiently. "I know it's okay, and besides we won't use it anyway."

But I insisted, and a try-out showed that he was wrong. So we stopped at an all-night garage and had the gadget fixed; a mighty lucky thing for us.

We passed through the famed mining town of Angel's in the mother lode country. As we rolled between the houses the good burghers were still sleeping in peace. Then we slid along the mountain road to Ebbet Pass. It was a clear night, with the stars shining brilliantly and indications pointing to a beautiful, calm day. As we began to climb the mountain side the grades became steeper and steeper and the highway grew narrower and more rocky and bumpy.

I wonder how many of you chaps who've travelled through the hills by night on a hunting expedition have ever missed the fork in the road? Gloom and the fog and the uncertainty of distance combine to confuse you. Well, we missed the road and had to double back and we wasted considerable time searching for the trail that we wanted. When we did locate a spur road, we could not be certain it was the right one; but that didn't bother Doc. Morning was just breaking.

"Why worry?" he asked. "What difference does it make if it's the wrong road or the right road? It's getting us somewhere, isn't it?"

There was really no answer to the Doc's philosophical question but I did plenty of speculating and considerable worrying while my companion went on his reckless way without a care in the world. We were high up in the mountains with ghosts of forty-niners all around us. We passed a mine dump; you can see thousands of them in the Sierras; every hill and canyon is pock marked with these reminders of the glories of the gold rush of ancient days; they are strewn along every road; they are historic.

"There she is. Right where I expected to find her," said Doc. "The directions say, 'Turn left into a cross road, see mine dump left side, about two and a half miles, continue four and a half miles to end of road, see tumble-down cabin.' Well, there may be room for doubt but there's the mine dump to start with."

I watched the speedometer anxiously as we slipped down the narrow snaky road in the early morning; four miles and at last we came upon a deserted shack. The trail had ended; Doc had hit it right.

And now, here we were high in the Sierras of an early winter morning—in the mountain quail country. It appealed to me. There was a deeply notched canyon which widened out in the form of a terminal basin of a hundred acres or more, while its steep, sharp-spined ridge on the far side gradually leveled off and flattened into a kind of mesa, studded with patches of chaparral, sagebrush, and outcroppings of rocks, together with many great round boulders. An occasional stunted piñon pine stuck up to add variety to the landscape. Here and there along the length of this table land were barrancos or dry washes which extended down to the basin, brushy cover along their beds and the banks to afford a safe hiding place for birds. This is the ideal set-up for mountain quail.

Not long after our arrival I gave the word to Clementine, excellent daughter of that famous old pointer Plain Sam, and I waved her away on a long cast across the bottom. I did this to take off the wire edge before she tackled the serious business of the day.

The exercise did her plenty of good and she settled down nicely as Doc and I worked up on the mesa and took a fairly level course just under the crest so as to command the upper end of each dry branch. Clementine combed the country above us. In the East and among the Appalachian ranges you could say that Doc and I were working the first "bench" below the top of the ridge.

Right at this point I know there will be plenty of readers who will understand our strategy. They know just as I knew that day that the mountain quail is a fiend for running uphill when disturbed. Nearly all varieties of grouse will fly uphill when flushed on a mountainside. If you can head off the mountain quail you have them puzzled; they'll scurry this way and that way in an effort to reach the crest. Once they realize that they have been balked, they become bewildered. Here is where the well-trained, wise, and capable dog comes in. If he is a master in the art of roading and circling coveys he will head them in. If he is not, and if they break through your interference, then you are on the losing end of an uphill marathon. Up and up they'll go, and they'll keep on going, and where they'll stop nobody knows.

This may, and I believe it does, clear up the reason why so many good sportsmen curse the mountain quail and refuse to have anything to do with him.

All went well with us that morning. Clem had done her part well. She nailed coveys and she stood scattered birds. Doc and I puffed feathers with considerable regularity and our hunting-coat pockets began to bulge. The air was cool and bracing, our enthusiasm was rampant, and we moseyed along through the high Sierras without thought or care for the future. After a little while we rested briefly on the crown of a hog-back; a world of fine looking quail country confronted us on both sides, miles upon miles of real shooting terrain.

Now, while we sat there at peace with the whole world, a faint haze crossed the sun. It grew thicker. Then, suddenly, the air became chilly. You have premonitions before tough weather breaks, and I turned to Doc and said, "You know, I think we've gone far enough. Let's work back to the car covering some of this likely looking high country on the way."

"Oh, thunder with that," Doc swung back at me. "We're up here now. We had a lot of trouble getting here, so while we're here let's cash in. However, if you want to, you can head back. I'll sample that side hill yonder and catch up with you probably before you reach the car."

He had hardly finished speaking when there came a spit of snow; it was followed by a deepening of the shadows among the hills and to any one familiar with the growth and development of a storm in the western ranges it spelled trouble. I started to back track and within a few moments the snow was on in earnest. It didn't occur to me then that Doc, bull-headed and arbitrary, might continue on his way regardless; I fully expected him to be on my heels. After a spell I stopped and waited. Fifteen minutes passed, but there was no Doc. Now the landmarks were being blotted out. That's the moment among the mountains when even the experienced traveler begins to feel uneasy.

There came to me with a start the recollection of what a friend of mine had once told me concerning Doc. "That little so-and-so has absolutely no sense of direction. Every time he goes deer hunting with us, he gets lost, and one of us has had to track him down. Honest, I've never seen a dumber cluck in the hills in all my life!"

Just the thought of this sent a chill down my spine and I trembled to think what Doc's fate would be if I didn't catch up with him pronto—and him with the keys to the car in his pocket too. I knew darned well that there would be no vestige of his tracks back where we had parted, but I hurried to the spot anyway, intending to fire some guiding shots to bring him in. Then it occurred to me that if I could make my old dog Clem understand what was uppermost in my mind she would pick up Doc's trail, snow or no snow, and lead me back to that perhaps hopelessly lost sheep.

I didn't have a thing of Doc's that might give Clem a whiff of scent, but I did manage to uncover a half-smoked cigarette he had tossed away and I held it to her nose. "Clem," I whispered, "go find Doc! Go find Doc!" The old girl searched my eyes with her earnest amber lamps and whined in a high-pitched tone which was her way of answering when you talked to her. Then I waved her off in the general direction my compadre had taken. She trotted away and I felt that she understood.

Although the scent was partly smothered by the snow, Clem trotted unerringly to where Doc's tracks were faintly discernible. These led straight away for a while, but eventually I sensed that in following them I was swinging in a circle. I fired two shots in quick succession and shouted, but there was no answer. Less than ten minutes later Clem dashed off at an abrupt angle and her excited barking and whining led me to a badly befuddled Doc. He stopped short, looking at me foolishly and finally came to his senses. No leech ever clung closer than he did as we back tracked to the car.

I doubt if my hunting companion on that trip after mountain quail could have found his way back, and it is a question whether I could have located the car through that smother of snow without the guidance of Clem.

Right here, I want to say that a seasoned dog as well as a horse possesses an inherent homing faculty that no human being ever can hope to attain. It was with tremendous relief that I saw the deserted cabin loom before us, and even then it was not until I peered through a frosted window of Doc's sedan and saw my coat lying on the back seat that I really felt we had arrived.

Why am I dwelling upon our difficult experience of that day? Oh, just to show you that hunting mountain quail isn't all peaches and cream. We had reached our destination; we had enjoyed a real hunt; we had taken our share of birds, and we were still facing dangers, inconvenience and troubles. The return trip was to be just as tough and perhaps a little worse than the journey up to the table-lands.

In his usual harum-scarum manner, Doc had driven in without resort to chains, even though parts of the road were very slippery. Now with a deep snow facing him, he realized that he must use them to get out. We laid them out on the ground and attempted to start the motor. More trouble. A low, practically dead, motor quit cold on the job. Fortunately, there was a crank in the car and we took turns swinging on the gadget until we were blue in the face, but all we could raise was a weak cough or two from the engine. This was a mess. The prospect of hiking a good thirty-five miles to the nearest mountain settlement wasn't inspiring—not even comforting.

Maybe you have forgotten, although I hope you haven't, but it is possible to put life in a frigid motor by the heating process. I am passing this tip along to you. We found a battered water bucket in the shack and after plugging up several holes, we heated water to the boiling point on a rusty old stove. Two doses of hot water into the radiator with endless rocking and continuous cranking and then, glory be, the mummified motor turned over. It sputtered. It stuttered, and then it went into a roar that took a great load off our minds.

To this day the return trip over the Sierras and the grinding up and down terrific grades remains a dreadful nightmare to me. We never could have accomplished it without the chains and several times we barely made slippery grades and navigated sharp turns in low gear. Often we came within scant inches of slipping off the road into deep caverns. But after what seemed an age, we came to the secondary highway and for the first time in many hours Doc burst into song. So great was the relief that at one spot when a covey of mountain quail scurried across the road and sprinted for cover on a big mountain meadow, we halted the car on an incline, got out and took after them. Clem nailed them in a clump of willows beside a piney creek and gave me an unforgettable picture as she stood like a statue with the snow sifting gently down in great flakes. Ten feet away from her the covey had bunched and the birds loomed black against a snowy background, the long plumes on their heads waving slowly while from their throats came the sound of a low musical "quoink, quoink."

When Doc and I circled the covey to put the birds in the air, they changed to the warning sound "whit, whit, hit, hut, hut!" Then they roared aloft. We fired. Out there on the snow field one dark form was inert while another quail beat its wings into the blanket of snow. Clem retrieved beautifully and with obvious pride handed each of us a stately quail.

To hunt such a bird, under conditions and amid surroundings that

157

only can be found in the Cascades and Sierras of the Pacific is to open a new chapter in the volume of outdoor life.

In a general way, the range of the mountain quail extends from Vancouver Island on the north to the southern extremity of Lower California in Mexico. It is to be found also on the mainland of Mexico down through Sonora. The birds have their habitat in the highlands of the Sierra Madres, the Sierra Nevada, the Coast Range and the Siskiyou Mountains in California together with numerous spurs in western Nevada. Also the Cascades in the Coast Range of Oregon and southern and southwestern Washington.

You will find the mountain quail in the highlands of Santa Barbara County, as well as in the other mountainous counties of San Luis Obispo, Monterey, Santa Cruz, Santa Clara, Sonoma, Memdocino, Lake, Colusa, Glenn, Humboldt, Del Norte, and Siskiyou. Some of us have run across the birds on the higher ridges on the west side of the San Joaquin Valley from Kern County to Mount Diablo. Some years since, I met them on Black Mountain and the high ridges of Tomales Bay in Marin County.

The range in Oregon embraces every bit of the coast country together with the Willamette Valley and the Cascades from the California line to the Columbia River.

It is difficult to believe, but mountain quail once were trapped by the thousands among the foothills in Oregon and were sold alive in Portland markets at two dollars and twenty-five cents to three dollars and twenty-five cents a dozen. Today, of course, they cannot be bought or sold in the open market, and even as prized possessions of earnest hunters, they are becoming scarce.

In former days, there were spots where mountain quail were extremely plentiful. It is difficult to explain why, but I have a hunch that the most reasonable explanation is introductions from exotic birds. In other words, in some way specimens were placed or found their way to new territory and there spread rapidly.

Any sportsman knows that if you will place a new type of animal or bird life in a favorable terrain there will be an abnormal increase in population and that this will continue for a number of years until nature strikes a balance. In the United States, we have had an illustration in the spread of the English sparrow and still later the extension of the starling. This latter bird, which now is to be found today beyond the Mississippi River and from Canada to the Gulf of Mexico, started from less than ten birds released a half a century ago on the outskirts of Brooklyn, New York. This also may explain why the Chinese or English pheasant has spread so rapidly in the United States.

I want to tell you a little story to illustrate my point.

I had heard that Whidby Island in the Puget Sound literally swarmed with bobwhite quail together with an even greater concentration on San Juan Island. This latter, beautiful gem of the San Juan archipelago in the Strait of San Juan de Fuca, became the talk of many sportsmen. Naturally, I arranged an expedition.

Together with several crates of gun dogs, I embarked at Seattle early one fine autumnal morning to visit this sporting Utopia.

On arriving at Friday Harbor, I quickly learned that the reports had not been exaggerated one bit, but I learned another thing—that these birds were not bobwhites but were mountain quail. Where they came from originally, nobody seemed to know, but that there had been an exceptional increase in number was generally admitted.

I had with me several seasoned hunting dogs. They were familiar with every wile of the cagey grouse, the deceptive prairie chicken, and the clever ring-necked pheasant. They were setters particularly adapted to the fine science of stopping running birds by the circling or heading off system, a method which anchors game tightly.

Compared with those other cunning, tricky birds, the mountain quail in the Pacific Northwest is comparatively easy to handle. The main difficulty is to find the birds. The members of a covey feed in the open only a short distance from convenient dense thicket. In this respect they somewhat resemble the large native quail of Maryland and Virginia.

My veteran dogs solved the problem of handling the birds by skirting the very edge of the woods and coming to a point with a suddenness which fairly mesmerized the mountain quail.

My approach upset them still more, for when they flushed they seemed to lack the unity of purpose and action which marks the flight of a covey of bobwhites. You remember that the little bobwhite moves and acts in unison with his companions and when a bunch get off the ground they all head in approximately the same direction and at about the same speed.

Your mountain quail are itinerants; in their bewildered haste it is a case of every bird for itself and the devil take the hindmost. When they flush they fan out in all directions, which is a very confusing thing to the shooter who meets up with them for the first time. The bobwhite knows exactly where he intends to stop and you will find almost the entire covey will alight within a very small space. Mountain quail will drop off at any place that the spirit moves him and then may do a bit of running before he settles down.

In the damp, humid atmosphere of the Pacific Northwest, this will

159

be toward patches of ferns, salal, rose brier, second growth slashings, among low rocks and even the branches of pines and other conifers.

The great trick in handling mountain quail is to head them off from the thick timber; once in the dense stuff, your chances of finding the bird are tremendously reduced.

The mountain quail has absolutely no similarity in appearance with the bobwhite. Its slate color is more associated with the valley quail. However, it is larger than either bird and is strong of wing. Its head carries a really attractive and graceful plume which is observable even when the mountain quail is standing stock still. In mountain country it affords an often difficult mark because of curving flight, or an abrupt uphill or downhill course, and the treacherous footing. The average hunter will do better on bobwhite.

As a lad, Uncle Billy Dormer crossed the plains from Wisconsin walking almost the whole distance to California by the side of an ox team drawing a covered wagon. His parents had settled in Sierra County among the high ridges where mountain quail and grouse were both plentiful. When he grew to be a man, Uncle Billy left the hill country, but there was a magnet that drew him back in his later years— the memory of the days when as a youngster his dearest friends were the mountain quail and Sierra grouse.

So it was that Uncle Billy and I used to team up to test our hands and eyes on the highland game, or to cast flies for rainbow trout. There is a wealth of hospitality in that section of the country that has been carried down from the days of the pioneers. Uncle Billy knew everybody living in the section and had a scale by which he addressed his friends ranging from "Lord Henry" down to plain "Hank."

He got this "Lord Henry" business from a local character. A highbred Englishman, a member of the British aristocracy, had drifted into Billy's home town of Downieville during its palmy mining days. He arrived with a substantial poke, or stake, and he had the quaint idea of investing the money in what he called "a mining plantation." While there, the town character became strongly attached to him and acted as his retainer or squire. He followed the Britisher every place he went and was most deferential and attentive, always addressing him as "Your Lordship," or "My Lord Henry."

This kept up until the Englishman, after stirring encounters with ferocious tigers in gambling joints and thrilling adventures with bartenders, threw away all his money and was strapped down to his last farthing—or it might have been a tuppence. Finally, when he was completely broke and without even credit, his once faithful retainer deserted him and bade him farewell with the brusque remark, "Well, so long, Hank, you old lunkhead. See you later."

My old pioneer friend had associated with every type of individual in that section of the country and knew every variety of wild life like a book. Many a time as the early rays of the sun were glistening on the castellated peaks above timber line, Uncle Billy and I, after taking on a cargo of breakfast, would call our dogs and start on our way to the hills for a hunt on mountain quail. Knowing the habits of the birds, we always steered, of course, for some extensive bowl or basin, or what the boys in Colorado refer to as a park. Our favorite location was the area which narrowed down in canyon formation and dropped off to join the main gorge of the Yuba miles below. A depression hemmed in by hills clad with conifers.

From past experience we knew that this selected area constituted a migratory path for a considerable army of mountain quail; birds that moved from the alpine peak to the lower levels and then back again to the heights. Here too, mountain quail could find an abundance of the very special kind of food they crave—mountain rye and timothy, wild oats, clover, sage, and the delicious wintergreen berries, huckleberries, blueberries, and wax berries. There was a particular kind of lichen, *Selaginella*, a plant related to the horse-tails, growing in the recesses of the rock. It had the appearance of a moss and the mountain quail doted on it. All wild life, and particularly bird life, will thrive where there is plenty of food, and the capable hunter studies the food supply first of all when he goes on a hunt.

Up in the high ranges, it is not every spot that will provide sustenance for birds or animals, and often the search for mountain quail leads the outdoor man into dangerous situations.

Billy and I knew and understood the country and had no trouble either in getting around or in finding coveys. Like the clan chieftain of old, Billy could stand on a knoll and declaim, "My name is Magreagor! I stand on my native heath—" We would follow a well-marked trail with our two setters ranging ahead, and as they combed out the country with liberal sweeps we kept our eyes peeled for signs of birds.

That rugged old white setter out yonder was the son of an early National Champion, a grandson of both Count Noble and Antonio; full brother to Pin Money and a grand dog in his own right. He was a slow developer, that fellow. It took three years to bring him to the height of his career, but the blood of champions, plus individual ability counted in the end.

There was another big going setter, a son of his field mate, The Old Man, and the apple of Billy's eye. "I never owned, I never saw, I never judged, a better long-haired hunting dog in my life," he used to say.

"His name was Rock and he was as steady as any boulder resting on these mountains."

Rock cast over a distant spur while his sire tended to his own knitting. The Old Man expertly cut across a series of dry branches along the ridge then suddenly swung at a sharp angle and drew rapidly fifty yards or so uphill, flashing to a stand in plain view.

"Hi, Bill!" I shouted. "The Old Man nailed 'em!" Before I could arrive on the scene, the old dog broke his point and made a quick circuitous dash uphill to head off the birds, then swung down upon them. He froze again, but once more the birds began to sprint, this time moving out to the side. Another dash was made around and in front of the running covey by the clever setter. This time he locked them up proper. There he held them, his head swinging a trifle as he showed the white of an eye and seemed to say, "Those twerps thought they could pull a fast one on me! Well, here they are, now you boys sock them!"

Billy came up and we moved in on the covey huddled in close formation, hypnotized by the dogs. We walked almost into the midst of those birds before they exploded and buzzed off in all directions, each quail taking its own sweet course.

Two of them wilted and dropped in a halo of cut feathers, while another slanted down and hit the ground at an angle. Our shots brought the other dog in on a double quick. Forty or fifty yards below, he crossed the track of the sprinting cripple and quickly caught up with him and brought him into camp.

He carried that mountain quail so gently that when he placed it in Billy's hand not a feather had been displaced.

It was fast hunting, with plenty of returns. A few seconds later, both dogs had driven into points on widely separated singles. No sooner had we accounted for them than The Old Man made a bee line for another bird and after trailing it fifteen or twenty feet locked it up until Billy drew in.

That day we hunted in leisurely fashion, doing important business with four or five different coveys. All in all it was a fine, profitable day.

Some scientists hold to the view that the Lower California subspecies of the mountain quail is in a distinctive class, but outside of the fact that it is to be found on higher ranges than the usual mountain quail it differs but little from the birds of the Sierras.

I don't think that the mountain quail will disappear. Wise laws are protecting it; it is to be found mainly in hard and difficult hunting country; it is able to take care of itself against deep snows, heavy rains, and even severe droughts. It is a prolific bird, the females laying from eight to eighteen eggs, and it has a strong tendency to remain in family groups very much like the bobwhite quail. It has endured through the ages and may continue to provide rare sport for our children and our grandchildren into the dim and distant future. Who knows?

Jumping Jacksnipe

by Frank Dufresne

The few hunters who go afield especially for snipe do so knowing that they will encounter a superlative gamebird—both before the gun, and on the table. Dufresne's 1955 article is an interesting one because it was published after the re-opening of a long closed season on the species (1941-1953). He noted that most hunters had forgotten the snipe. This is still much the case. And for those of us who are keen to hunt the bird, this situation is excellent.

Every time Deskin or I popped off with our small-bores, the duck hunters in their blinds along the bay shore stood up and stared our way. You could see they were puzzled. They'd swivel all around, scanning the storm clouds. Then, seeing nothing, they'd settle back out of sight again. They must have thought we had rocks in our heads.

That's where they figured wrong, because we were ankle-deep in prime bog shooting. For Deskin Reid, especially, it was just about perfect. He'd been waiting twelve years for a day like this, he said. It was like good old times—birds all over the soggy flats; scary little fizz-crackers flashing away in crazy, zigzag spurts like no other feathered game in all the world.

As we sloshed across the marsh we kept punching holes in the gusty mist with charges of No. 9 shot. Deskin's black Labrador female, Smokey, sprayed right and left through the puddles to fetch, and the duck hunters in their blinds kept standing up to see what all the noise was about.

We ran out of targets when we reached the sand dunes, beyond which lay the open Pacific. But we heard other gunners at work. Above the dull roar of the foaming surf came the steady *whoom! whoom!* of exploding magnum shells, where green-slickered waterfowlers humped behind curling breakers in a reception line for incoming Alaska geese. The sea winds brought fragments of their cries to us across the rustling sandhills. Between honker arrivals we heard the grating croak of black scoters and the thin, nasal whistle of sprigs riding the high air turbulence down from the arctic icefields. Now and then a susie mallard in the murk would let go with lusty squawks.

And there was still another wild call, a strangely exciting, nostalgic sound that few of the younger hunters had ever learned to identify. It was a rasping *scaip! scaip!* as hard to locate as a jet plane because the smallish, needle-nosed bird that uttered the cry was far ahead of its own call. Like a detached arrowhead, wings half closed, it came zooming down through the ocean storm clouds to its first landfall in hundreds of miles.

As a small boy just busting into his teens—that would be about the turn of the century— Deskin had trudged these Western tideflats with his father. Now the drumming of Pacific October gales across the dunes was bringing back memories long buried. Jacksnipe! His first gun! The twain were as one, because his father had taught him how to sight, swing and squeeze trigger on these double-jointed dodgers. And when the lesson was learned, young Deskin discovered that few other birds would ever offer a greater challenge to his skill; that no man could ever ask for finer wing-shooting.

But beyond that there had been the thrill and the mystery of the snipe itself. No stodgy homesteader was the long-billed jack, no hedgehopper settler in the field corner, but a global cloud-roamer whisking from arctic tundras to Southern swamps with the calendar. The whole hemisphere was its home. The steppes of Siberia and the rice paddies of China had felt the probe of its hinged beak. Fowlers of Europe had long paid it homage as royal game.

The new crop of hunters, however, hadn't learned about snipe, said Deskin. How many of them could distinguish the jack from sandpeeps, yellowlegs, plovers or godwits? How many young gunners realized that today, for the first time in a dozen years, it was once again open season on the matchless little Wilson's snipe?

A wave of the oldtimer's arm embraced a hundred hunters along the beach waiting for geese; as many more squatting in duck blinds; not a single walker on the marshes. Deskin had his answer.

It was much the same way all across the land the fall before last when the U. S. Fish and Wildlife Service opened a 15-day shooting season on jacksnipe with a bag limit of 8. The bans had been on a long time—ever since the Gulf Coast deep freeze of 1941. The bitter zero weather that wiped out tens of thousands of woodcock in Louisiana, Mississippi and Alabama also did it for Wilson's snipe, which have similar feeding habits. While the woodcock favors cut-off forest lands, and the snipe likes open places, both need soft, moist earth in which to probe with long bills for worms. They had found ideal wintering grounds until 1941 in these three Southern States. Then they died like frozen flies. When the news came, a lot of sportsmen crossed shorebird shooting off their lists for a long time. Some even said the two longbills might never again be offered to gunners.

Both woodcock and Wilson's snipe normally lay clutches of four eggs; so recovery potential should have been about the same. But it didn't work out that way. The woodcock came back much faster because, Federal biologists will tell you, second-growth forest succession was extremely favorable in the Great Lakes-to-New Brunswick regions, where most of the timber-doodles nest. Food and cover conditions were just about right. Two or three years was all the woodcock needed to climb back on the sportsman's roster.

But the jacksnipe ran into fresh obstacles. Even now, fourteen years after the big freeze, they're not back to oldtime numbers. That's only half the story. They never will be, and this time you can't blame the hunters. Something a lot deadlier than occasional charges of fine shot has hit the snipe where it hurts worst. Somebody has swiped their marshes. Somebody has drained their bogs to grow spuds and spinach. Somebody has built airports armored with acres of concrete, or factories, apartment houses and filling stations on the wet spots where jack once spaded for angleworms. So now only reduced numbers of snipe can drill for a living. The flyway scientists have a phrase for it. They say the jacksnipe has tapered off to a new, lower level of population. When they opened the season, it was a tipoff that the ceiling may have been reached.

Up north there's no trouble. In their spread across the continent from Greenland to Alaska—close to 4,000 miles—the jacksnipe find plenty of ideal summer nesting sites. The bind comes when the birds start bog-hopping southward in an ever-narrowing funnel that finally pinches almost to a tip near the mouth of the Mississippi. Too many of their old picnic places have been nailed shut by man. That's why there had been no increase for four years, and that's why the Fish and Wildlife Service decided to let hunters gather in the annual surplus going to waste each winter for lack of board and room.

But what the Government snipe scouts didn't know about was the strange disappearance of snipe *hunters*. When the season opened in 1953, after the twelve years of protection in the United States, you could find jacksnipe if you knew how to look for them. But you couldn't find hunters.

Why? Well, it's just that an army of new shooters has taken to the field. Talk with these young gunners, and you find that almost none of them know the flight-mark differences between a jacksnipe and the still-protected shore birds, such as dowitchers, plovers and curlews. Nor do the new hunters care much—not enough to take a chance on being nabbed by a game warden for peppering the wrong bird. To them, all shore birds, except the distinctive buff-colored woodcock found in grouse cover, were taboo. That's the way it had been ever since they shouldered their first scatterguns. Picking one species of marsh bird—the least conspicuous of the lot—and suddenly tagging it fair game didn't make much sense to the younger hunters. Deskin knew why: "My dad taught me snipe shooting. But when my own son was ready, it had been outlawed."

So, while most of the new license holders couldn't tell a jacksnipe from a fillyloo bird, the few men you met splashing the snipe marshes— the fellows with gray hair, or perhaps no hair at all—knew exactly what they were doing and what they were looking for. It was a bird slightly smaller than a quail, brownish-colored, with stripes like blades of dead grass down its back. It was a bird of amazing protective feather pattern, a bird that squatted unseen until you were almost upon it. You rarely saw it until it darted away across the bog, uttering its scratchy *scaip! scaip!* It corkscrewed insanely, as if it couldn't make up its mind whether to go east, west or straight up, and it was the sportiest shooting a man could hope to find. You'd hit one dead center. The next one you'd miss from here to third base.

For the oldtimers of the West, like Deskin, who knew their snipe from away back when, it was a fine season. It was still better in the Eastern States, where hefty migrations poured down from the Maritime Provinces of Canada. There was a good supply of jumping jacks along the Mississippi, and heavy concentrations once more along Mobile Bay, where the dead bodies had piled up during the deep freeze of 1941. Even in the mountain regions, where you found low spots you were almost sure to find snipe borings during fall migrations. The birds soon cleaned up the small pockets—here this morning, gone by afternoon. With so many of their old marshes blotted off the map by bulldozers, the snipe were working every wet spot they could see from the sky.

As the Pacific flight whirled down from Alaska that October the jacksnipe started spiraling from the storm clouds behind the first sand dunes of the Washington coastline. "We've caught 'em just right," said Deskin as he cocked an ear to their scraping calls overhead and now and then caught glimpses of brown streaks whipping through the overcast. "Next week they'll be scattered all over the cow pastures from here to the Rockies. But today they're here, and we have 'em all to ourselves."

A lone jack overhead went *"scaip! scaip!"* and came swooshing downward at dizzy speed. Deskin threw his gun to shoulder, then started swinging the muzzle downward in a wild attempt to sight ahead of the brown streak. Just as the snipe shot out of sight against the marsh he touched off a barrel.

"Good try," I said.

"Better than that." Deskin waved to his Labrador. "Fetch, Smokey!"

The black female charged across the bog into a tangle of cattails, snuffed noisily for a couple of minutes and came back, head high in the air, with a winged jack.

It was a time for bragging, but all Deskin said was, "One of my dad's favorite shots. You got to shoot about twenty feet under."

Another jacksnipe squirted out of the dead grass and started zigzagging away in crazy dipsydoos. Deskin's 20 double leveled quickly and hesitated while the bird straightened its flight. Then the open barrel spoke sharply. A few feathers drifted free. The snipe turned end over end and skidded across a puddle.

"No use to shoot while they're twisting, not unless you're a lot faster on the trigger than I am," offered Deskin. "Best wait for them to

168

straighten. You don't have to hurry. They'll still be in range."

Smokey retrieved on command, then started hunting in a short half circle ahead of us. It was the black Labrador's first experience on jacksnipe, but already she had worked the project out.

"Some of the old snipe hunters liked their setters and springers," said Deskin, "but give me a dog like Smokey." At the mention of her name the black female wagged her heavy tail and came back to thrust a wet nose against her master's hand. "They can have all their fancy breeds," said Deskin. "Give me a Lab like Smokey."

Three more snipe, all on my side, whistled up and I made my only double of the day. Deskin waited until I had shot my wad, then picked off the third jacksnipe forty yards out with his choke barrel. It was a clean kill. Smokey, watching it plummet into the bog, fetched it to her boss while I did my own retrieving.

The midday lull had hit waterfowlers along the beach and bay shore. Most of them walked to their parked cars for sandwiches and vacuum bottles of coffee, but a trio of young fellows came out to intercept us on the flats. They flushed several birds. One came our way like a leaf in a gale, and Deskin grassed it neatly. We emptied our game pockets and counted up the score; I found I had three to go, Deskin one. The duck shooters moved in to peer over our shoulders.

"Those little dickeybirds?" One of the young hunters picked up the first snipe he had ever seen at close view. "Is this what the shooting was all about?"

Deskin swung around to face the youth, tolerance in his level gaze. "Ever try it?" he asked. All three heads shook, and that's when Deskin remarked dryly, "Well, I've shot plenty of ducks." The boys seemed to get the point.

While we were poking the snipe back in our game pockets we heard the rasping *scaip! scaip!* of another loose flight arrowing down from the dark wind clouds to a green-rimmed pothole behind the dunes. The black Labrador, intently watching the spot, felt Deskin's hand on her shoulder. "Come on, Smokey," said the oldtime snipe hunter, "let's go get the rest of that limit."

With the Canvasbacks of San Pablo

by J. P. Cuenin

Almost all canvasback hunting is immediately associated with the eastern seaboard—Chesapeake Bay in particular. There are valid reasons for this: there were once a lot of canvasbacks wintering in that region. They were prized for the bag, and a lot of hunters sought them. And almost all outdoor writing for a roughly 75 year period was done on and about the eastern side of the Mississippi. What is not fully appreciated today is the fact of just how good canvasback hunting was on the Pacific Coast. This 1915 article is an insight.

When the duck season closed (January 15, 1914), Buster and I began figuring on the shooting for the fall of 1914. Now some folks would think that rather early to begin, and to us it would have been if it had concerned some such common thing as business, but when the subject was the wary duck bird we had something demanding much thought and preparation. And without the pleasant dreams of the coming season and the pleasure of getting ready, how would it be possible to live through the nine months of closed season?

There was a duck-boat to build, more decoys to make, and others to be repainted with "can" colors.

The boat was the subject of many talks between Buster and me. You see, we wanted a low boat in which we could hide well in the tule grass; it must be reasonably dry on the choppy waters of San Pablo Bay; the stern should be decked, and broad enough to hold about forty decoys, and, above all else, the boat must be so shaped that it could be easily pushed over the mud flats. To get these qualities into a fourteen-foot boat required the use of many sheets of paper in the making of plans, and after the model was finally decided upon and I had built the boat, I was not disappointed in the result. And you duck-hunters who simply order a boat lose a great deal of pleasure by not building your own, or at least having your ideas built into the one you buy.

When the boat was finished, I went to work on the decoys, of which we had about three dozen—mallard, sprig, and bluebill. As we were to hunt canvasbacks principally, we wanted most of our decoys to resemble that bird, so I cut off the long, pointed tails of some of the sprig, and painted them, as well as the mallards, with the black, white, and brick red of the canvasback, using a very dull, chalky paint.

Next I made eight large decoys, great big fellows, at least three inches longer and about two inches wider than the factory-made article; and if I could carry them on the little boat I would have about forty such, for I believe that a flock of large decoys will give one many more shots than one would get over the same number of the undersized decoys sold by some dealers of sporting goods.

We rented a small ark at Black Point, shipped our outfit, and then sat back to await the arrival from the north of Mr. and Mrs. Canvasback and their relatives.

Although we didn't expect much shooting, we were out on opening day (October 15th) and were lucky enough to get three widgeon and four ruddy ducks. Two weeks later we decided to try 'em again. Of course, we knew that it was too early to expect the northern ducks, but the season was open, and an open season is to us like money, in that it

171

is no good to us unless we use it. And then there was a chance of getting a shot or two at local birds, mallard, sprig, and teal, that were using the baited ponds.

We failed to get any of the home-raised ducks, but we did get a shot at one bunch of "cans," killing three of the fine, big birds as they streaked it over the decoys; and, what was of more importance, we saw a number of large flocks of "cans," come in over the mountains, which meant that the flight was commencing, and all that was needed to bring them south in great numbers was a cold snap or storm in the north.

Back in the city again, we watched the daily Government weather reports with great interest, reading of unsettled weather along the Gulf coast; another time, there was a Northeaster in the making, off the New England States; and then one day it was reported that there had been a general falling in temperature over the Northwest. That was the kind of a notice we had been looking for.

We waited impatiently while three days passed, allowing that time for the birds to reach here, and then boarded the 4:45 P. M. boat which carried us across San Francisco Bay to Sausalito. On the way over, we saw high in the sky two big flocks of southbound geese. Those geese made us feel pretty good, for were they not proof that we had figured correctly on the cold wave up north sending the ducks down to us? But it didn't require much to make us feel good that day, for it would be impossible to feel otherwise, with the prospect of the next day with the "cans."

Arrived at Sausalito, we boarded our train, and sat down to enjoy the twenty-two-mile run to Black Point. We have been over that section of road a number of times, yet it never grows tiresome as do some suburban trips. Perhaps to the poor souls who do not hunt it is a weary journey if they make it often, but hunters must always find it interesting.

From the car window one can at all times see a bit of either San Francisco, San Pablo, or Richardson's Bays, on which bodies of water a duck-hunter is sure to see flocks of coots and bluebills; and then there are strips of marsh where a hunter (I say "hunter" because other folks wouldn't notice such things) may see a few sprig, teal, or mallards jump as the train rushes past. And there are spots on the sides of old Mount Tamalpais and its foothills where quail can be found; and just beyond San Rafael (only seventeen miles from San Francisco) there can be seen a rugged piece of mountain where deer are killed every year. Yes, I can truthfully say that we always enjoy that trip.

At 6:20 P. M. the train rolled into Black Point, and ten minutes later we were aboard our ark, which was anchored in Petaluma Creek.

172

With the fire going nicely, and Buster preparing supper (not dinner), I began getting ready for the work of the morrow. I say getting ready for the work, but "work" is not the word. What is a four- or five-mile row to a fellow who is expecting to see canvasbacks, see them with their wings set and comin' in with a rush! The only ones who might find it to be work are the market-hunters, and they felt differently about it when they shot only for pleasure.

Well, as I said before, I began getting ready. I took old "Duck Soup" out of his case, and after oiling his vitals, put him in the gun rack. Then "Susan Jane," Buster's light 12-gauge, was treated with an oil rub, and placed next to her "side kicker." The shell-case was pulled out from under the bunk, and into its four tin-lined compartments was dumped some feed for "Susan Jane" and "Duck Soup." "Susan" is a light eater, and her favorite meal is 24 grains of powder and 1 ounce of No. 6 chilled. She kicks mighty hard if more is given her. Old "Duck Soup" is not so dainty, and 28 grains with 1⅛ ounces of chilled o's fills the bill for him.

Stepping out on deck, I pulled the boat alongside, and after adjusting the decoy rack, began loading the decoys.

As I worked, there came sneaking out to me through the open door the sound of sizzling from the fry-pan, and a coaxing odor that kept whispering in my ear of good things to eat. I couldn't quite make out just what was being cooked, and my mind went a-wandering. While standing there, idly holding a decoy and dreaming of what I wanted to eat, Buster sang out: "Supper's ready. If you're hungry come a-runnin'."

I didn't wait to set down the decoy, didn't even wait to drop it, but just came away and left it there in the air. Some time after I was seated at the table I believe, though, of course, I'm not positive, I heard the decoy fall on deck. At any rate, I did hear a loud bump about that time.

And the meal! Veal cutlets, breaded and fried in butter, with a tomato sauce that had in it some fried onions and green peppers; and then there were baked sweet potatoes—not ordinary baked sweets, but slices baked with a big lump of butter on 'em. And then there was—but this is supposed to be about ducks, and not a page from a cookbook.

At four o'clock next morning the sweet-toned alarm-clock (sweet-toned at the shooting shack, but a howling monster when calling me to work in the city) chirped its little piece, and we crawled out immediately.

My first move was to get on deck and have a look at the weather signs. Over head and to the north it was clear, but turning to the south I was pleased to see that the stars had about them a hazy appearance,

173

which might mean a southwester later in the day. Hoping my guess as to the wind was a good one, I went in and started the fire, and then Buster went out to pass judgment on the weather.

Her idea was the same as mine (no, that HER is not a misprint, for Buster is my un-silent partner until death or Reno judge steps in), except that she predicted a southeaster; "because," she explained, "the sky looks exactly like it did the morning we had such good bluebill shooting at Mount Eden, last season."

"Well," I thought, "let it be southeast or southwest—it wouldn't matter much as long as we have enough of it, but wind we must have."

Breakfast eaten, the guns, shells, an' sech in the boat, we got under way, and out in the open we felt a faint touch of wind that came from the south.

A twenty-minute row down the south shore of the creek, past many shacks and arks, whose lighted windows showed that others had intentions on the "cans," brought us round the last high, wooded point and out on San Pablo Bay. From this point on, we started many flocks of ducks, and though it was still very dark we could often tell just what kind had jumped. The little ruddy ducks would allow us to get within a few yards, and then, with much splattering, off they would go. The coots, in getting under way, would splash along about like a ruddy, but louder, of course, and with quite a wing whistle. Then a bunch of "cans" would leave the water with a great roar, but less splatter than either the coot or ruddy; and the sprigs, with one splash and no splattering, would be up and away.

In the darkness we couldn't see any of the ducks, but, judging from the sounds they made in getting out of our way, most of them were "cans," and that was as we hoped it would be.

As the eastern sky began to show signs of the coming day, we arrived at the point from which we were going to shoot, and, pulling close to the tule grass, I stood up to select a tall, thick patch of tules that would make good cover.

I began setting the decoys, dropping the first one well up wind, and then working down, scattering the others so that the main part of the flock would be up wind, and with the farthest decoy not over thirty-five yards from us when we were in our hide.

While this setting-out process was going on, we could hear ducks passing overhead and see others against the brightening eastern sky, and when the last wooden deceiver was in the water, I pushed the boat into the tules and dug out my watch to figure how many minutes we would have to wait before the sun would rise and give us permission to shoot.

Out on the bay, about a quarter of a mile from shore, there were great rafts of ducks, thousands of them, with here and there a few small bunches flying. To watch so many ducks was a great sight, one that we shall never forget, but with such numbers of them on the open water to attract any that were flying, we stood a small chance of getting good shooting. Those big flocks would have to be driven farther away, I thought, and while making up my mind to run out and chase them, the sun popped up from behind Mount Diablo, and it was time to be prepared for visitors.

"Susan" and "Duck Soup" were brought out from under the deck, fed, and laid across the gunwales within easy reach. Then began a period of "watchful waiting."

Overhead, but too high to kill, sprig were passing every few minutes on their way from the fresh-water ponds to the middle of the bay, where they would remain until sundown should make it safe for them to return to the ponds. Occasionally a small bunch, lower than the others, would whiz by, but when low enough they were always too far up, or too far down the shore.

Keeping well down, we were squinting through the tules to catch some of the low-flying sprig, when a loud splash behind brought us round with a jerk, and, just outside the decoys, with necks stretched to what seemed a foot in height, sat four drake "cans."

Whispering to Buster to take one on the right, we "riz" above the grass, and up jumped the ducks. "Duck Soup" spoke, and one "can" dropped, then, with the slide handle working like the piston of a mile-a-minute engine, the old pump made a speech, but the ducks went on their way.

I turned to Buster, and was surprised to see the expression on her face and her lips moving. Now I don't believe she was swearing, but, though I heard no sound such as I should make under the same conditions, I think her expression was evidence that her mind was running in that channel.

"I had the safe on," exploded Buster, "and I almost broke the trigger trying to make 'Susan' say something."

After reloading, we shoved out to pick up the dead bird, and, as it always happens, just as the boat was clear of the tules, a flock with set wings and heading straight for the decoys, saw us and turned off.

Back in the hide again, we made resolutions to do better with the next shot, and I began excusing myself for hitting only once when I had fired four shots. I was positive that my holding had been correct, and all that kind of stuff, and was telling Buster so, when—swish! Right smack over our heads went a pair of sprig, and they were not over ten feet high. Of course, I grabbed my gun and stood up to shoot, but that pair of birds were well over a hundred yards off by the time I was ready.

"Well," I growled, as I sat down, "we aren't doing much with these duck birds, but you watch the next one that tries to knock off my hat."

"If the safe hadn't been on," alibied Buster, "I am sure I would have had that 'can'."

A half hour passed without excitement, during which time I noticed Buster look at and try the safe slide on her gun no less than ten times, and I was holding the pump at ready, waiting to smash the first duck that showed up.

Glancing down the bay, I saw a dozen or so, coming, and it looked like a sure chance for a shot, but the big raft of birds on the bay drew them away from us. The same thing happened four times in the next half hour, and we were peeved about it. To sit there and look at such vast numbers of ducks as they loafed on the water was very nice indeed, but we were there to get a little shooting, and intended getting it; and, besides, there were shooters at other points along the shore who might enjoy seeing thousands of ducks resting on the bay, so I rowed out and told the big flock to move along. I don't suppose the shooters down on Long Point, near where the flock alighted, appreciated my thoughtfulness, but then some folks are hard to please, anyway.

We didn't have long to wait for a shot after getting into the tules again, and this time it was eight "cans." We saw them when they appeared as mere specks away out over the bay, and for some time could not tell whether they were coming or going, but coming they were, and fast, too. When about two hundred yards out and a little down wind, they saw the decoys, and, wheeling sharply, came in on set wings.

We were ready this time, and rose when the birds were about twenty yards away. We each killed with the first shot and missed with the second. My third shot stopped another, and then the flock was too far out for sure kills, though I might have knocked one down if I had tried, but a crippled "can" is hard to get, and I have given up trying to stop them beyond forty-five yards.

Our next visitor was a mudhen, who dropped in among the decoys and then had an exciting time keeping clear of the bobbing wooden blocks. Judging from his actions this mudhen must have had rough treatment at the hands (or rather, bills) of canvasbacks, for the little fellow would keep well away from the large decoys, but did not seem to mind swimming close to the female bluebill variety. When the mudhen swam close to shore, I waited until he appeared through an opening in the tules, and then took his picture, which sent him splattering off down the bay.

While I was reversing the plate-holder, Buster glanced back over the marsh, and saw a pair of mallards circling above a small, shallow, salt-water pond. For five minutes they flew about that pond, first high and then low, and at last decided to alight, and were just about to drop into the water when a shot fired some distance off sent them up into the air again. Now they were coming our way, and we crouched low, hoping to escape the sharp eyes of these wary birds.

Slowly they came on, with every action showing that they intended alighting at the first favorable spot. At sight of our decoys the slow wing-motion stopped, and in a graceful downward curve the beautiful birds came within range—not of the gun, but the camera.

The click of the shutter startled them and they flew off up-shore, but not with the climbing flight of frightened mallards. The pair went on for perhaps a quarter of a mile, when the female turned and began working back. I didn't suppose it possible that she would come near enough again, but still, I thought, neither bird seemed to act as though they had seen us. Hastily changing plate-holders, I was ready for another picture just as this obliging "hen" mallard, with wings straight down under her body, sailed by and dropped into the water a few yards up-wind.

Thinking Mrs. Mallard might again pose for her picture, I quietly reversed the plate-holder and motioned to Buster to keep still, which she failed to do, but for a good reason. I was watching intently the movements of the duck on the water, while Buster, it seemed to me, was doing an unnecessary amount of squirming in her end of the boat. Sitting with my back toward her and eyes glued on the duck, I reached my hand out behind and held it in a position which indicated silence, but instead of keeping quiet, Buster slapped my hand and exclaimed, "The drake mallard is coming!"

Of course all that happened in a few seconds, and Buster's warning, though it jumped the female, gave me a good picture of her mate as he began to climb into the sky.

"Well," laughed Buster, as the shutter clicked and we had the picture, "that was the most accommodating pair of ducks I ever saw."

"And now," I exclaimed, "I'll get a canvas-back picture that we can dream over all during the closed season, one that will show the birds coming in, with some of 'em splashing in the water, and others of the flock with their big gray-black feet hanging down!"

The getting of that "can" picture wasn't as easy as I thought it would be. You see, I was figuring on the nice way those mallards posed for us, and, knowing how much wilder they are than "cans," I naturally had the idea that my luck was running good.

With camera and guns within easy reach, and the warm sunshine upon us, we sat in the boat waiting for THAT picture. The wind had shifted a little and was now blowing on shore and against the ebbing tide. This combination of wind and tide quickly kicked up a choppy sea, and the birds commenced moving nicely. One flock of about fifteen passed down-wind and near enough to kill, but, thinking they would turn to the decoys and give us a chance for a picture, we allowed them to go, which they continued to do until out of sight.

The next bunch of "cans" also came down-wind, going like feathered eight-inch shells. Seeing that they would pass too far out for the camera, but near enough for "Susan" and "Duck Soup," I gave the word and we popped up above the grass and let 'em have it, I pointing about six feet ahead of the leader. Nothing happened at the crack of my gun, so I swung quickly to a lead of something like ten feet, and pressed the trigger. Down came that bird, and so did the next one I pulled on.

Buster fired twice, but didn't connect, and explained the miss by saying that the flock were too far for her light loads, which showed that she knew the correct excuse to use.

Now a gray sort of haze was being pushed over the bay by the wind, and I feared it would settle any chance for pictures, but decided to try a few plates at a trifle longer exposure. While releasing the tension on the shutter, Buster called attention to four "cans" coming up-wind. Judging from the way they were turning in close to shore and then out again, and flying very slowly, I figured that these birds would come in nicely for a picture, so made ready with the camera and "shot" as one of the four stuck out its feet preparing to alight.

Then came five, and this little flock brought out in me the desire to kill. I enjoy taking duck pictures and get much pleasure out of those that are fairly good—a pleasure that lasts long after that which I would derive from killing—but, for some reason or other, I haven't arrived at the stage where I can lay aside the gun.

When this bunch of five "cans" came into view, I fully intended using only the camera, but when they were just outside the decoys, I jumped up, took the picture, set down the camera, and then grabbed the gun and killed one bird. It was foolish to take a picture when the birds were so far out and still coming, but I couldn't resist using the gun.

Believing the light too weak for the short exposure necessary to "stop" a duck in the air with a camera, I placed the instrument in its water-tight box and settled down to shooting.

The next chance we had was at a pair of "cans" that came along hunting for company, which they thought they had found upon sighting our decoys. This pair came in without a sign of suspicion, and I told Buster to try for a double.

"Wait until they lower their feet," I whispered, "and with your first barrel take the farthest one."

She centered that bird and crumpled it nicely, and then made a pretty shot on the second as it turned.

"Good shooting!" I yelled, when the last bird struck the water, and then, shaking Buster's hand, I added, "I'll make a shooter of you if you follow my teaching."

"Oh, you will," she replied in a very superior tone of voice, "and how many birds have you killed to-day, and how many misses did you score?"

"Huh? How many did I kill? Well, let's see. I have six dead, and five misses."

"And I," put in Buster, "stopped three, and missed an equal number." "Now," she continued with a laugh, "where did you get the idea that you could teach me any more about shooting?"

"You win," I answered, "and I'll be good, but I'm glad you don't shoot a pump gun."

"Why?" asked Buster.

"Well," I said, "some day you might slam three shots into a flock, accidentally kill three birds, and then, I suppose, you wouldn't speak to a common shooter like me."

About three hundred yards out we could see many flocks skimming over the waves and heading into the wind on their way toward Gallinas, where they would find quiet water in the lee of a high range of hills. Those birds were too low to see our decoys, so to attract their attention I threw a dead bird into the air. Some flocks didn't seem to notice, and others would rise fifteen or twenty feet from the water and then drop back without a break in flight.

Then I tried a new stunt. With two dead birds close at hand, I waited for a flock and flung a bird as high as I could without showing myself above the tules. The flock rose, and then I threw the second dead bird so it would fall among the decoys. The bunch of "cans" broke, some wheeling toward us, and the others going on, but in an instant the whole flock of about forty were coming in as fast as their wings would bring them.

Seeing that they were going to alight, we allowed the first few to do so, and then opened up on the others, I getting two with three shots as the confused flock scattered, and then I went after those that had alighted, taking two as they hurried after the others. Buster knocked down one with her second barrel, admitting that the big flock rattled her at first.

We now had fourteen of the big ducks, and decided to have one more try at calling 'em with dead birds. They didn't come like the first lot, but after a half dozen attempts, a pair fell for it and came in. I killed my bird, which was on the left, waited an instant for Buster to shoot, then killed the other. I knew she had her gun to shoulder, and wondered why she didn't shoot; then it struck me. A few days before Buster had been reading an article on quail shooting, and ran across the expression "wiped his eye." I recalled explaining what it meant, and now Buster had held on that bird, hoping, no doubt, that I would miss.

We agreed that sixteen big canvas-backs were enough for one day's shooting, and picked up the decoys and rowed back to the ark, where we enjoyed a good lunch, prepared things for our next trip, and then walked to the station to catch "the 4:20," which would drop us in the city at 6 P. M.

The rocking of the train, combined with the long day on the water, soon had Buster nodding, and as she drifted off into the duck-hunter's dreamland, I heard her murmur, "I made a double!"

180

Lucky Limit
by Frank Dufresne

Frank Dufresne spent most of his adult life in Alaska. He wrote
extensively of the far north. This 1953 gripper was one of his best.

G ive me a squally day on a marsh. At dusk I'll come slopping out of the muck oozing good-will to all. Ducks or no ducks, I'm relaxed and satisfied. I've had a grand-stand seat at my choice of the great outdoor shows. If I haven't fired a shot, there is still the lingering excitement, the scalp-tingling memory of wild wings stitching their mysterious patterns across the overcast.

I like to shoot, sure. I'll burn my share of gunpowder. I'll brag when I smack a high-flier dead-center. Nobody will top my alibis at the misses. But I'll not make a maximum bag limit my yardstick for measuring fun in a duck blind. There'll be no straining to rack up the biggest score allowed by law. Like a lot of other waterfowlers, I'll rate a full bag limit second to the stirring sight of waterfowl racing in the skies.

And yet I remember a certain howling November day in Portage Bay when it became a matter of life and death to shoot a limit of ducks and geese. It was a lucky break for me, too, that the ducks were mallards instead of teal. The white-cheeked geese that came along in late afternoon filled a desperate need.

I was hitchhiking a 100-mile boat ride along the steamer lane from Petersburg to Juneau on an Alaska Game Commission vessel when a prowling sou'easter came charging out of the Stikine back channel, twisting its tail and looking for trouble. Churning the sea into white fury, the storm snarled down upon us, laid brutal hands on the 40-foot patrol vessel and started bouncing it around like a cocktail shaker. Skipper Severin was a hardy Norwegian, but he knew when to run away. His narrowed blue eyes scanned the purple-black clouds rolling ominously toward us, and he swung the *Grizzly Bear* hard aport to head for the nearest shelter.

For an hour we staggered through the tide-rips, one rail and then another scooping green water while crockery crashed in the galley. Through the foaming bore that guards the entrance to Portage Bay the vessel plunged like a spurred bronco, then raced along on spume-topped swells until the water became too shallow for further retreat. Skipper Severin slacked off on his controls, turned into the wind and signaled for the deck-hand to drop the hook. He straightened his cramped fingers from the spoked wheel and helped himself to a wad of snoose.

"Aye turn no more vheels today," he declared, glaring around the pilot-house as though expecting an argument. Then he added, "Now is gude time for everybody sleeping."

With this I could not agree. Not on the last afternoon of the waterfowl season, when the ill wind that always blows somebody a little good had laid the *Grizzly Bear* alongside one of southeastern Alaska's fine duck marshes. There was not another boat in the bay. I would have it all alone, because neither Skipper Severin nor any of the three crewmen appreciated the sweet joy of standing in cold sea water facing a whistling deluge of icy rain, the perfect combination for duck shooting. But they were glad to put me ashore in a speed boat, and they told me they'd eat all the ducks I could shoot. When Severin set me on the beach with a promise to pick me up at dark, he reminded, "Gat the limit." I'm glad he said that.

It was a mile walk across the bared mud at low tide and around to a small river delta partially sheltered by a spruce-timbered point. As I neared the mouth of this salmon spawning stream williwaws ripped patches of kelp and widgeon-grass free and sent them bowling like tumbleweeds across the open flats. Ducks jumped, squawking, into the gale and went whizzing downwind. Here in the eddying gusts and down-blasts was a feeding area crawling with waterfowl. Mallards, baldpates, pintails, shovelers and green-winged teal dabbled in the puddles. Goldeneyes, bluebills, scoters, butterballs and mergansers dived for feed in the salt-water channels. They spattered aloft, filling the blustery air with the swish of their wings.

Between the forked mouth of the river where the current ran no more than ankle deep at ebb tide I saw a ready-made, natural blind floated into perfect position by a previous high water. It was a grotesque cedar snag offering both windbreak and hiding place. I hadn't been there a minute when a greenhead came pedaling past, folded when it ran into a charge of chilled 6's and fell close enough for me to make a vest-pocket catch. I held the glossy drake by its orange feet and shook it hard. Nothing snapped out of the open bill except some seeds and green shoots. Satisfied that it had not been gorging on salmon eggs—a nasty mallard habit in late season that imparts a horrifying flavor to the flesh—I decided to try for a full bag of these handsome big drakes.

It was almost like shooting fish in a well, Given enough shells, a man could have raked down a hundred ducks on that zesty afternoon. The cedar snag seemed to have a sign on it for waterfowl only: "Portage Bay Duck Inn. Dinner now being served." It stood in the exact center of the local flyway. For every greenhead I missed, two more crossed over the snag within easy gunshot. Once they had landed, the birds didn't want to fly against the buffeting wet gales any more. They waddled around on the muck flats while more ducks bucked in to join the party, and I snapped the rain out of my eyes and swung a bead on the fat drakes.

The shooting disturbed a gaggle of geese up the river valley. After each volley from the 20-gauge autoloader I'd hear their honking complaints. Finally they lifted up for a look, then went circling around the valley against the green wall of timber, talking strategy. Next, the entire flock, two hundred strong, swung into line and headed straight for the cedar snag, touching off chords like a spread of low notes on an organ. They spotted me, though not soon enough. The lead gander had already collapsed before the white-cheeked birds flared. A tail-ender joined the downed leader, and then the thrash of wings died away in swirling mist. While I was gathering the brace an umbrella of milling duck wings formed overhead, out of which a wing-tipped mallard came spinning down to join others on the duck strap.

The tally after this exciting action stood at seven ducks and two geese. I had three more mallards and another pair of honkers coming to fill the bag limit of that year. The tide had turned and was foaming in across the mud-flats, hurried by the wind. By the time I got back to the stump with my downed birds salt water was lapping against my rubber boots. A scattering of mallards pumped past, spaced just right for a triple on drakes. I retrieved two dead birds and chased down a flapping cripple to complete the legal limit on ducks. The water had risen knee-high around the snag, a warning to which I should have paid prompt attention.

But with the incoming tide waterfowl came tumbling in from all points of the compass. A couple of hours of daylight still remained. I decided to let the tide reach its flood stage and start ebbing away before trudging the mud-flats to the meeting place with Skipper Severin. After all, this was the last day of the open season. It would be a long time before I would see the likes of this afternoon again. Also, I still had two more geese to go before reaching the four-bird limit. Two of these honkers I hoped to meet again when Severin's Norway-born wife served them old-country-style, browned, tender and swimming in hot spiced pickle sauce.

Absence of exploding shells must have convinced the geese that an armistice was at hand, because what appeared like the same flock I had thinned earlier in the day now came battling the wet storm back to the river valley. Flying low to avoid the full force of the blow, the heavy birds labored over the cedar snag scarcely fifteen feet up. It was no trick at all to pull down a double.

As I waded out to gather in the plump pair I was surprised to find the water still rising, lacking only an inch or two from spilling over my boot tops. This meant, clearly enough, that out in the river channel that I would have to ford to reach the main shore the tide would be running no less than belt-high. I shinnied atop the cedar snag to wait until it started draining away again. It seemed that simple. I hadn't a thought

184

of danger as I crammed my pipe, blew smoke into the breeze and gave myself over to enjoyment of quacking, squawking, whistling waterfowl.

The first doubt came when a breaker smashed solidly against the snag and I felt it lurch against the bottom. Soon there was another bump, followed by an even heavier smash. The snag heeled over and rolled back again. Scrambling for holds on its slippery surface, I was jolted by the sudden suspicion of big trouble looming. Belatedly it became clear that the cedar snag, which had been deposited on the river delta in the first instance by an extremely high tide, was due to be skidded free by another—and today might be moving day.

Now I was quite sure the tide would not change in time to do me any good. This was in the full moon of November, when the maximum flood tides of the year fell due. There would be close to twenty-five feet of rising sea between minus low and peak high level. Worse yet, with a raging wind to heap it still higher there was now no question but that the cedar snag would be carried away. Then what?

I had three chances, none of them very encouraging. One was to try to stay with the floating duck blind; try to ride its wave-washed surface as it went drifting off into the salt current. What I didn't like about this plan was the certainty that tide and wind would sweep it out into mid-channel and in an opposite direction from the *Grizzly Bear*. What next, then?

Could I, by using the gun as a third leg, hold my footing as the tide rose and fell? It might take several hours. I doubted my ability to endure the test long enough to try the third choice. This was to leave the snag and attempt to swim across to the main shore, now about two hundred feet away and much too deep in spots for wading. I would need help. A drifting sawlog appeared to offer the necessary equipment. It came bobbing toward the blind as though by special delivery. If I could reach it and climb astraddle, it might get me over the river channel.

Shivering and anxious, I watched it draw closer. Then, while yet several feet beyond my grasp, the log started turning away in an eddy. Slowly it changed direction and moved away into the whitecaps. As it drifted away the cedar snag under me reared off the bottom again. Time was running out. It was zero hour for Operation Duck Feathers.

Hastily I pulled the ten mallards and four geese together and bound them around and around into a bushel-basket-sized mass with some cod line out of my hunting-jacket pocket. The water was waist-deep when I struggled free from my rubber boots, slicker and canvas jacket. Placing these items on the ball of feathers, I added the shotgun and started pushing the odd raft toward shore.

Soon the chilly sea rose to my armpits and I was forced to rest against the bale of waterfowl to keep balanced. Then the bottom sloped off abruptly. The river channel! Could I make the next forty feet? Would the trussed birds hold under my weight? There was no turning back now. All the answers were in front of me. My wool-socked feet kicked off the squishy bottom and I started flailing the briny flood with numbed hands.

As my chest fell across the bundled ducks they spread and settled almost to the water-line. My feet rose to splash sea behind. Waves broke against my face, strangling, frightening, and the chilling shock of icy water pouring down the front of my wool shirt was almost unbearable. When I could stand it no longer, when I could paddle no farther, I stood on end to tread water. That is when two wonderful things happened. The ball of ducks and geese lifted high on the surface. My feet touched bottom. I was across the river channel!

A few feet farther stretched the weed-lined shore of the bay. Wading clear with waterfowl, gear and gun sagging across my shoulders, I struggled into the heavy timber for protection against the stinging williwaws. Soaked though I was, this was no time to stop. A game trail punched by tracks of bears, wolves and deer led along the contour of the bay under a canopy of giant evergreens. Before heading along this path I stole a glance back toward the flooded river delta. The cedar snag was gone. It was far out in the open bay, twisting and dipping in clouds of spray.

It wasn't the first time in my Alaska experiences that I'd been thoroughly dunked, and I knew what to do about it. When I came to a dead tree that suited me, I flung off my heavy load and went to work. Where half-rotted roots branched away from the base there was a good-sized opening through which my exploring hand encountered an accumulation of pitchy splinters. Crushing a few handfuls just inside the entrance, I fumbled off the threaded top of a waterproof case and whipped an old-fashioned sulphur match into flame.

The oily chaff spluttered, smoked, fizzled and at last broke into a puny blaze. As it grew stronger most of the fire sucked back into the hollow tree and started licking on hanging splinters. It wasn't long before the standing shell of the dead giant was roaring warmly. In its red glow I stripped off my sopping clothes, wrung each garment and dried it reasonably well.

As daylight waned, the scudding clouds lowered and began spitting snow. The fire blew itself to king-size. From its open top, forty feet above the forest floor, the hollow trunk started erupting like a volcano.

Now and then, as the hot flames melted out new pitch pockets, dense black smoke rings belched forth to be whisked away in the snow-storm. Since there wasn't the slightest danger of the fire spreading in such a drenched woodland, I was enjoying the fireworks.

My clothing was getting drier by the minute when the sound of an outboard motor drew closer from out in the storm-lashed bay where the *Grizzly Bear* bucked at its anchor chain. The motor cut off in the gloom below me. I heard Skipper Severin's boots smashing through a wind-row of clam shells. He came up to the red-lighted perimeter of the flaming spruce skeleton, hefted the ducks and heaved them over his shoulder.

"You gat a limit, feels like," came his hearty shout over the wind as he swayed away toward the shore-line. "By golly, you vas lucky."

Lucky? Wait till he heard the rest of it!

Mira Monte Memories
by Lee Richardson

S.C.

Lee Richardson spent most of his life fishing and hunting along the Pacific Coast. He traveled in elite company and was a frequent guest at the best private duck clubs in the nation. In its day the Mira Monte Club was noted as about as good as there was in California.

From Roaring Twenties times until a bittersweet moment alone in a duck blind during a late December sunset in the early Sixties, I was privy to a waterfowler's Utopia in marshes of mid-California. Focal Point of my privileged experiences was confluence of Cordelia, Goodyear and Suisun Sloughs—historic havens for waterfowl and shorebirds, mostly unfit for agriculture due to tidal flushes and so preempted by waterfowlers.

The duck club buildup became possible after the Central Pacific, in 1869, provided first access, other than maritime, to the marsh's northern perimeter. As clubs sprouted, a "Duck-Hunters' Special" made flag stops at Teal, Sprig and Jacksnipe. Later an electric train, "Sacramento Northern," connected Berkeley with the state capitol, serving the marsh's south side with stops at places like Mallard and Honker.

On walls of Pacific Valley Club in Irrigation District 10 is a picture of California's first *organized* duck club, chartered in 1880 by ten San Francisco sportsmen and in continuous operation to this day, as far as I know. Originally part of the vast Chamberlin tract, it was called the Cordelia Shooting Club. Numerous clubs formed around it, best-known and certainly most lavish being the Mira Monte.

Until a clubhouse arose at the confluence, members' yachts served as living quarters. Mira Monte was built entirely of redwood, as were blinds and walkways that led to them.

Among early members was A. B. Spreckels, a name synonymous with sugar. His private railway car, an exhibit at San Francisco's Panama-Pacific Exposition, later was barged to the confluence, where its rose satin and velvet-upholstered lounge served guests until its demolition in 1943.

Mira Monte's 640 acres, shaped like a foot, were bounded on three sides by sloughs and, on the fourth or north side, by a dike separating it from the Tule Belle Club. The prestigious 1,400-acre Joice Island Club was east, across Suisun Slough. Members, who included Dean and Jack Witter, Al Swinerton, Frank Noyes, Bill Roth, Spencer Grant, Sr., occasionally dropped by.

South, across Goodyear Slough, was Bud Ehmann's Morrow Island Club, later acquired by Ward Dawson. The Henshaw's family club was on Cordelia Slough, by the railroad. As roads improved and vehicular access became common, Mira Monte and Joice Island Members and guests were met by their launches at Pierce Landing and conveyed onward.

In those early times, daily limits of 25 ducks and eight geese were readily obtainable by proficient gunners. Clubs' members didn't know it, but never again would they have it that good.

Accessibility and diminishing natural habitat increased competition, but the double-barreled and near mortal blast was economic collapse in the early Thirties, concurrently with the Canadian prairies drought where seventy percent of the continent's waterfowl were produced. Ducks Unlimited's well-conceived and executed programs ultimately stabilized waterfowl population, but discontinuance of live decoys and more especially, cessation of feeding, were to adversely effect the Suisun.

Final blow, as far as early-day Mira Monte members were concerned—nearby residents' opposition to the annual mosquito curse. With support from newcomers, an abatement ordinance was enacted, calling for drainage of all surface water during the mosquito breeding season.

For Mira Monte that was catastrophic, ending in eventual destruction of a fine native stand of threesquare bulrush, plus tule and sedge cover beloved of mallards, gadwall and teal. Unlike nearby Joice Island and the famed Folger circumstance for canvasbacks in another area, Mira Monte had no deep water ponds, and local mallard broods were obliged to swim across to neighbor's property as their water home vanished.

In 1940, with war imminent and with an aging membership unwilling or unable to cope, colorful Mira Monte was offered to the highest bidder—with few potential takers.

Enter now, Uncle Bill Cole. He had been shooting at Doc Ward's Van Sickle Island Club near Honker, but had long envisioned a club of his own. As a sales executive, he knew customer relations opportunities weren't limited to just a golf course. When his immediate superior, Preston Levis, agreed, he made a ridiculous offer on Mira Monte and, much to his surprise, it was accepted.

Mira Monte was a many-splendored place where gentlemen indulged the genial hour in a relaxed atmosphere of light-hearted banter that would be difficult to recapture today. Anyway, most of the original cast is gone. For sheer elegance of appointments, cuisine and service—even to an English gamekeeper—few duck clubs could match it.

The east wing, or clubroom, was furnished with deep leather chairs and couches, billiard-cloth-lined poker tables, bar, fireplace, gun racks and enormous wrought iron chandelier. Its sister wing housed the dining room, fireplace, kitchen, refrigerator, and keeper's quarters. Connecting wings was a hallway with individual bedrooms and Simmons mattresses, if you please. Rooms bore names like Spoonbill, Gadwall, Redhead, etc., to correspond with matching gun rack designations. Sanitary facilities were so elaborate and spacious as to prompt at least one guest to comment:

"What? No barber?"

In back were kennels to accommodate four Labradors and a pair of goldens, a pumphouse and a tower like that at Utah's Bear River Duck Club. Frequently, guests assembled there, glass in hand, to watch the evening flight as it funnelled into ponds, that raising their blood pressure decidedly.

A typical shooting day began at the usual outrageous hour, gamekeeper stomping down the hall, throwing doors open and turning on lights, predicting in sonorous tones that "... there will be smoke on that water today." Occasionally, one who came mostly for amenities (ducks be damn'd) and usually the last to bed, would object strenuously:

"I'm not mad at those ducks! Don't you so-and-so's *ever* shoot 'em in the afternoon?"

Uncle Bill's breakfasts were as talked about as his dinners. On the sideboard, beneath Tommy Brayshaw fish prints, were pitchers of freshly-squeezed orange juice and slices of most delicious and aromatic Crenshaw melon, accompanied by lime wedges.

Then came the gamekeeper, towel over arm in most approved maitre d' fashion, with the lightest, fluffiest hotcakes, maple syrup and tender sausage cakes especially fashioned by Robert's Market on California Street.

On the back porch, to take to the blinds, were water flasks, Washington Apples, flit-guns and duck straps, so all that was required of a hunter was a license, duck stamp, shotgun and ammunition. As the Jeeps pulled away, Uncle Bill admonished all hands to "... please be out of the trenches by noon. Let 'Buck know if you want a lift back and he will come for you."

Among Uncle Bill's friends, Jules Cuenin, who wrote the outdoor column, "Rod & Gun," for *The San Francisco Examiner,* in December, 1957, reported as follows:

"Last weekend I had a new experience duck hunting at Bill Cole's 'Mira Monte.' I have shot waterfowl on many areas in the state, but this was the first time I was ever given a retriever to take out . . . with me.

"Bill has a full kennel of Labradors and goldens for his own use as well as that of his guests. The dogs are all superbly trained and perform in a masterly style.

"When Bill asked . . . would I like to take a dog . . . , I hesitated, because I never like to hunt over the other fellow's dog, whose commands I might not know.

"'There are only two commands,' Bill assured me, 'the first is

"Fetch!" when you want him to go get the bird, and the other is "Charge!" when he delivers it.'

"Arrived at the blind, my dog, "Tar," a black lab, immediately took his place under the brush on the platform alongside me. The first duck I dropped fell out in the pond. Tar was alert but never made a move until I uttered the magic word, 'Fetch!,' when he was off like a shot, delivering the drake sprig to my hand in the most approved form. Then, without waiting for the command to charge, he immediately sat. Not once did he move as ducks flew over and I fired, only when I gave him the magic word, 'Fetch!'

"After he had retrieved my sixth bird and we started for the club-house, he immediately followed at heel. Tar performed for me just if I had trained him from puppy days, a novel experience."

A frequent guest was the old, retired Winchester man, Charles Knight, no mean shot in his own right. Charlie endeared himself to the management by arranging a "clergyman's discount" on shotgun shells and unintentionally contriving to lose more often than win at poker. He was at his best during the hour of small talk when, without much persuasion, he discoursed on an uncle who was said to have been with General Lee in the Civil War, as follows:

"Is Sergeant Knight here?" the distinguished warrior is alleged to have asked.

"Yes, Sir!" Sergeant Knight assured him.

"Very well, then, let the battle begin!"

Among Charlie's idiosyncrasies was one his host couldn't abide, his insisting he never shot a bird anywhere except ". . . in the haid." It got to be a joke.

"Nice string of ducks, Charlie," someone would venture, "all shot in the head, I presume?"

"Friend," was his certain answer, "you've never seen such a bloody-headed bunch of ducks."

Which would bring forth acid comments from Uncle Bill:

"Aw, the old wind-bag! Last year he gave me a brant, killed at Bolinas—'head shot,' naturally. I picked every damn feather off that brant, and the only shot mark was in the middle of the back. Didn't phase the old blowhard one bit. He explained the pellet entered one of the bird's nostrils, went down the neck, and out the back!"

Uncle Bill's greatest retriever, King, was a gift from his old friend and glass jar customer, Marcus Nalley, founder of the pickle empire in Tacoma, Washington. When asked the animal's bloodlines, "Uncle

Mark" wrote that all he knew was the mother was a Chesapeake, adding:

"His father must have been a traveling salesman who wasn't mokussed. Like some of your salesmen, he just kept on going."

Regardless, King was a birddog-in-a-million and, under Uncle Bill's strict indoctrination, became one of the all-time great retrievers. Because his master so seldom missed, King was trained to "break shot," which is to say, when the gun went, so did he, so in event of a cripple he had that much head start.

As powerful as he was brainy, King rarely lost a bird, no matter how far away it fell, just as long as he could see it. Countless tales were told of his remarkable feats and this one, especially, bears repeating.

Shooting at Mira Monte, in conformity with most clubs, normally was confined to Wednesday and Saturday mornings, with a few exceptions, especially near season's end. On one such occasion, Uncle Bill suggested to his friend, Carl Thompson, he take King out to blind No. One as it shouldn't bother the next day's shoot. Carl departed with retriever at heel but, in less than an hour, the dog came back—alone.

Later, when his guests returned, Uncle Bill asked why, and Carl countered by asking for an ounce-and-a-half of "Old Rarity" before he answered:

"You know my shooting, Bill, even when they're decoying well, I'm usually only good for one out of three. King got all wet for nothing when I missed the first shot. And it seemed to me I got a dirty look when he resumed his platform beside me.

"When I didn't touch a feather on a couple of hen sprig, King's nose went skyward and he sounded off a most doleful lament. The humiliation so unnerved me, damn'd if I didn't let the old bastard down again, missing a cock sprig, both barrels! King moaned, emptied his bladder on No. One and buggered off to the clubhouse. Pour me another shot!"

My personal diary of October 21, 1956, describes a duck hunter's sensations at a Mira Monte dawning, a time and place never to be forgotten:

"A sickle moon is mirrored in the pond where coots fret and skitter away as the gunner splashes toward his hide. Wildfowl spring into predawn darkness with noisy wingbeats and startled quackings, while over toward the refuge, speckle-bellies laugh, 'Klee! Klee! Klee!' returning from a night in the stubble fields.

"The east pales, gradually assuming overtones of old rose shot with silver, and overhead, the exciting and nostalgic whispering of wings. In the distance there is the mutter of an outboard, the thump of shotguns.

193

A cock pheasant crows derisively from the sanctuary of his cattails. Suddenly and magically, over Joice Island way, the sun climbs, like a ripe tomato, out of pickleweed; outward-bound sprig head for Grizzly Bay. The southern Pacific's Cascade whistles for Pierce Crossing. Another day has come to the Suisun."

For a few sweet years, this was Mira Monte. Some would remember African and North American big game trophies, collected by the proprietor, adorning the walls. Others would remember hunting and fishing films screened during the hour preceding dinner. Those interludes were complimented by smoked kokanee from Sandpoint, Idaho, or caviar on thin, toasted rye bread with chopped hardboiled egg, onion and lemon juice, accompanied by the finest of beverages.

But when a siren called them to a repast seldom served in a duck club, still others would remember it for the host's tossed salad with secret dressing, while an attendant passed San Francisco's celebrated sourdough bread, toasted with a hint of garlic. Or the Celery Victor, or fresh crab legs, followed by the entree—breast of sprig served so rare, some sent it back to the kitchen to recover.

For those who approved, they would note the sprig had been broiled on a hot, dry, salted range-top—six minutes to a side—skin-side down to start. Wild Spanish rice, accompanied by Napa Valley Cabernet Sauvignon, sanctified California's game bird supreme.

Demitasse and cognac were served in the clubroom, and for those so afflicted, antiacids or similar aids for gastric disturbances were readily available. No wonder guests often enthused, "Only way to go!"

When Uncle Bill took possession of Mira Monte, one of the first and best moves he made was to engage services of Doc Ward's former gamekeeper at Van Sickle Island Club, Albert Griffis—better known as "Buckshot."

Unquestionably one of life's most unforgettable characters, Buckshot was the only one (by his own admission) to knock honkers out of the sky with bricks, or pull striped bass out of head-gates with a pair of pliers. "Gospel trufe!" he would declare piously, his right hand upraised.

Built like a cedar stump, with the look of eagles, this extraordinary man could and did take hundred-pound sacks of wheat over his shoulder and trot off across swamp in the manner of a Chinese coolie.

Buckshot had been drawn irresistibly, all his life, to modes of employment involving fisticuffs or explosives, or both.

During Prohibition he "rode shotgun" for a prominent San Francisco bootlegger, developing a reputation that caused highjackers to

194

leave him strictly alone. Similarly, he had been a hard guard at San Quentin prison. After a few Hoosegow bailouts, one for wrecking several joints in the delta steel town of Pittsburgh, Uncle Bill served notice on Buckshot to shape up or walk. Mostly because of his affection for his boss, to Albert Griffis' credit, he never went on a public bender again.

Much given to canards, Buckshot delighted his audiences with a natural hillbilly accent and uninhibited gestures. His impersonation of an illiterate Negro preacher embarking on a sermon was legendary. Whenever possible, he liked to elaborate on exploits involving the manly art of fisticuffs. These were not just products of his imagination, and when word got around that his sledgehammer fists were about as lethal as his marksmanship, Mira Monte was never thereafter molested by poachers.

So it was quite natural when L. Evert Landon, who succeeded "Uncle Mark" as chief executive officer at Nalley's, asked Buckshot if poachers bothered him, he replied:

"No, Mr. Landon, ah bothers *them!*"

One lazy summer's day, when the two of us were alone, the marsh hushed save for drone of a bomber from nearby Travis Field and rumble of a distant Southern Pacific freight, Buckshot related an encounter he once had with a poacher:

"Ah heerd; this shootin' goin' on over by 'Three-Strap,' so ah got mah gun and drove over thar in the 'Cadillac' (Buck's nickname for one of the club's two ancient Jeeps) and ah see this ole boy standin' in the middle of our tules.

"Now, in such situations, Mr. Richeson, they ain't no use gittin' mad, so ah walks up and ah sez, real sociable-like, 'Say, brother,' ah sez, 'ain't you lost?'

"An he sez, 'no,' he didn't allow as how he was.

"So ah sez, 'Didn't you see them 'No Shootin'' signs over yonder where you clumb the dike?'

"Well, sir, Mr. Richeson, that sort o' riled him up and he sez, 'Goddam it, that's just the goddam trouble! I goes off and fights the goddam war in Korea and when I gets back and hankers for a little duck shootin', you rich bastards got it all nailed down.'

"'Wal, naow, brother,' I sez, easy-like, 'we got ourn, you gotta git yourn.'

"About that time an ole sprig comes sashayin' along, and he sees it, too, so I sez, 'Brother, ah wouldn't shoot that duck ef ah was you.' but damned ef he don't haul off and shoot it!

"Naow, Mr. Richeson, you knows and God knows ah'm a peaceable

195

man, but ah sez, 'Brother, you put that damn shootin'-iron o' yourn down and ah'll put mine down and we'll settle this rat here and naow!

"Well, sir, we mashed the tules down for quite a spell 'til ah gits an openin' and ketches him with a good solid right to the Adam's apple, and down he goes. While he's floppin' like a chicken with its head wrung, ah picks up his gas-pipe and snaps the stock off. Then, when he gits up, ah hands him the two pieces and ah says, 'Naow, brother, you git and don't you come back!' and he got!

"Then, when he's safe out of the slough in his tule-splitter, he shakes his fist and he yells, 'You big s.o.b.! I'll see you in hell!'

"'Naow, Mr. Richeson, there ain't nothin' more sartin than that, so ah yells back, 'Ah'll be thar, brother! Ah'll be expectin' you!'"

Late one summer's night after the war, when a hot, east wind was bending tules, Mira Monte burned to the ground.

First intimation the Griffis' had of impending disaster was when they were awakened by the crash of the heavy chandelier in the clubroom, sending a wall of flame funnelling down the hallway to quickly engulf the entire structure. Buckshot and his lady were lucky to get out with naught but their nightclothes. Fanned by the vengeful wind, fire quickly reduced the charming old club and all contents to ashes as they watched helplessly.

The aging retriever, King, mortally afraid of fire, vanished into the night and was never seen or heard of again.

Even apart from the sentimental side, loss was considerable with much of it, such as club records dating back many years, irreplaceable. Uncle Bill wept.

But not for long. Shortly, a houseboat designed for navy airmen in the South Pacific was acquired and installed precisely where the old clubhouse once stood. A two-story affair, superimposed on a redwood hull, it was complete with galley, walk-in refrigerator, dining, sleeping and recreational areas, crew and officers' quarters. A clubroom was installed on the second deck facing east. Birch-paneled and handsome, it had a fireplace, poker tables, bar and outside balcony where, in the off-season, Buckshot was wont to put his feet on the railing and survey "his" domain.

He was so situated one day when an outboard came charging down Suisun Slough wide open. The man steering yelled to his pal in the bow, "Look at that rich s.o.b. up there! He's got it made!"

Buckshot heard every word, and it pleased him.

Just then their motor died and the boat began drifting with the ebb, the man in the stern yanking away on the starter rope without result.

Finally he cupped his hands and yelled, "Hey, mister. You got any gas?"

"No!" the big man with the voice like a foghorn bellowed. "Ah'm too rich for gas. Row, you sonsabitches, row!"

Buckshot's Dolly died in 1960 and that, coupled with Uncle Bill's terminal illness, caused him to retire and rent a shack near Fairfield where, in the first year of my own retirement, he received me. The countryside was springtime fresh and green, a meadowlark sang enchantingly from a weathered fence post. If Buckshot's heart was broken, as I was sure it was, there was no indication.

"Welcome! Welcome, Mr. Richeson!" he exclaimed as my station wagon drew up before the little dwelling that, like its occupant, had seen better days. "Welcome to mah little ole retirement home where you is welcome to stay 'til the devil comes for bofe of us!"

So saying, he showed me around. I took special note of the nail where hung his ubiquitous spare overalls and the outrageous jockey caps he was never without. He took special delight in showing me how doors on opposite walls facilitated housekeeping, declaring, "When the wind is right, ah jes' opens *bofe* doors and poof! Goodby dirt!"

Time came for my departure. I shook hands with the man with the ice blue eyes and the face that looked as if it had worn out *two* bodies, both of us aware we would never see each other again. When Preston Levis, Buckshot's ". . . most beautiful friend" died, he lost whatever remaining incentive he had to go on living and, as so often happens, he didn't.

It is speculative, to say the least, if he kept that appointment with the poacher.

During his last years at his beloved Mira Monte, Uncle Bill shot a single blind because it was nearest the clubhouse and because he shot better when he was alone. Time after time, I could watch from Three-Strap, nearest his beautifully-brushed Mallard blind (he was a stickler for concealment), while he whistled to a couple of wary sprig just out of range.

The final act was invariably the same. The foxy late-season ducks, eventually convinced the coast was clear, dropped in and even before gunfire sounds reached my ears, one would be falling and then the other, from the top of his flare. A stylish double, perfectly executed by a master shot!

Uncle Bill made doubles look easy. He was one of the two or three best shots I ever saw. And why not? Trained from boyhood by a father who earned his living shooting for the market, he became an uncanny

197

judge of distance and as quick as chain lightning. He apprenticed on great numbers and varieties of game at a time when there were few restrictions and fewer "No Trespassing" signs.

In the old days, of 25-bird limits, he once wrote:

"I was on my way back to the clubhouse by 7:30 this morning after an hour and a half in the blind . . . thirty shots . . . and picked up 22 sprig and two widgeon, including eight doubles. Had to shoot three cripples over, so it was really 24 ducks with 27 shots."

A lifetime devotee of the double-barreled gun, his first was an L. C. Smith, followed by a Parker, and his last a beautiful custom-built Winchester Model 21, all straight-stocked in the best English manner. He was the first to admit that, everything else being equal, nothing took the place of experience in the development of an expert shotgunner.

And Uncle Bill sure popped a lot of caps!

Christmas Eve, 1962, Uncle Bill cashed in his checks. As Bret Harte once said: "He drifted away into the shadowy river that flows forever to the unknown sea."

For a time, the trustee leased the old club to a group from the city, but after Mrs. Cole's death it was sold to a moxy gent. He retained for himself the part where he found the *most* empty cartridges, dividing and disposing of the rest—including club quarters—to another group for the equivalent of what he had paid for *all* of it!

That was the kind of a deal Uncle Bill would have approved, and of which he was entirely capable.

That December evening, when the end of it all was near, I put the sun to bed as I had so often in halcyon days of another time. The death of another year impended as I contemplated the scene, fully aware I should never see it again.

Blackbirds, oblivious to my daydreams, gossiped in a craggy tree and Venus sparkled above the ageless hills of California, the fires of sundown paling before onrushing night. It was the hour of enchantment. A bittern bestirred himself from his own meditations, the muskrat sallied forth on his nocturnal questings, fashioning arrows of quicksilver that are born of twilight, and, high above, skeins of waterfowl headed for rice fields.

One by one lights in the distant clubhouse winked on, a dog barked, and somewhere beyond the reeds, a mallard hen called sleepily to her mate. The star of evening burned ever brighter now, white-hot from fires of an unseen sun. Night comes swiftly to a melancholy land.

The Black Brant at Home
by T. S. Van Dyke

This was written in 1891. Today most black brant winter in Baja. The brant hunting of San Diego is now gone. In Washington, Oregon, and northern California there are still a few bays that brant stop at.

The true black brant is the most gamy and fine flavored of American waterfowl. It breeds in the far northern part of the Pacific Coast in immense numbers and is rarely found on the Atlantic Coast. Even on the coast of California it is known only in a few places. What is there generally called the "black brant" is the common gray brant, or white-fronted goose, called the "black brant" to distinguish it from the snow goose or "white brant." On the nine hundred miles of the California coast there are but four points where black brant deign to stop. A few visit Humboldt Bay and sometimes a few tarry at Tomales Bay. From there they skip everything until they reach the bay of San Diego and Mission Bay, some three miles above it, and some of the bays of Lower California, especially San Quentin.

This bird passes all the favorite resorts of waterfowl in California and is unknown to the great majority of its sportsmen, and though millions pass San Francisco on their way south and back they are almost unknown in its markets. It migrates almost entirely at night, and during the day is hardly ever seen on the wing except when flying out to the beds of kelp in the ocean and returning. And this it does only at certain stages of the tide, spending the rest of the time floating on the water far away from shore, or waddling over the mud flats at low tide. It never goes inland and will not even cross a small point of land jutting into salt water if it can be easily avoided. The sand spit that forms the harbor of San Diego it crosses in a few narrow places to avoid several miles of detour, but once in the bay it circles around every point of land. The few birds that go out of the channel move not a wing over the shore, but go a long way around to pass over water.

But a few years ago San Diego Bay was gay with life as we rowed across it to the mouth of Spanish Bight, which was then a favorite "fly way" of this bird. Pelicans, both white and gray, flapped heavily by the boat, singly and in flocks, now descending in a spiral line head first into the water, then sitting a moment on the surface to swallow the captured fish, then rising again in air to repeat the performance. Large white gulls, with lazy wing, wheeled around the boat; large gray ones, with still slower wing, lounged about in the air; small white ones bustled all around and smaller gray ones displayed still more energy. With outstretched neck and laboring wing the merganser toiled through the air or drifted on the flowing tide; divers of all sizes rose and sank on the smooth face of the bay; little terns, swiftly descending from on high, went under it with a splash; fish ducks and butterballs skimmed the surface with whistling wing, while teal, canvasbacks, mallards and other ducks dotted the water far and near. But among them all you would see no black brant, for they are very aristocratic and associate not

200

with the common herd of waterfowl. Away down the bay you could see thousands of dark points on the bright sheen of the water, some looming above it in a faint mirage, black above and white beneath, but nearly all motionless and different from any other waterfowl. From their direction may come a confused noise like the babel of distant frogs, but no one not acquainted with the sound could imagine from what manner of bird or beast it came. But it would be quite useless to go after them. One must wait until they begin to fly and then be well hidden somewhere along their course; and fly they will not until the ebb tide is well under way.

The black brant has now become so wary in San Diego Bay that he can rarely be secured without a floating battery, in which you must lie upon your back below the level of the water. But this affords little view of the flight of the birds, which is one of the most interesting features of the hunting. A blind on one of the points projecting into the bay, made by surrounding a hole in the sand with a fringe of brush and seaweed, used to be enough and was far more pleasant.

All is quiet as we set our decoys on the water near the shore and ensconce ourselves in the blind on the edge of Spanish Bight. Not long do we have to wait. At the turning of the tide the spell is broken. First come the curlew in flocks of fifty or sixty, winging their way along the shore with buff-colored breasts and brown backs shining alternately in the sun as they pitch and twist in their flight. Over the water their clear notes ring, as with long curved bills outstretched they come directly toward us. With smaller bodies and short straight bills other shore birds flit by us, all unsuspicious of danger. Plover with tender whistle spin by but a few yards away, and bunches of little gray snipe of many kinds whisk so near us that we can see their little black eyes.

But let them all go and keep your eyes upon the low ridge of sand half a mile or more to the west that forms the end of the bight, where the breakers dash up against the blue sky beyond, showing that it is both narrow and low. Even as you gaze upon it a long dark line rises out of the horizon beyond it. Rising and widening again, the line comes swiftly on. Gradually it changes into a string of black beads stretched along the western blue. Soon appears a flickering motion on the side of each dark bead, and quickly this develops into the rapid motion of dusky wings. Nearly two hundred strong the line comes swiftly on, the birds that compose it growing larger and darker by the instant; yet they ride the still, warm air as lightly as a flight of arrows. Though a little larger than mallard ducks their flight is less labored and the motion of their wings is as if quivering with speed instead of beating the air with vigorous work. As they come nearer white begins to light up the

201

duskiness of their flight, and in the revolving maze of white and black they grow larger by the instant. When within some two hundred yards of us the birds all set their wings and glide smoothly downward, almost grazing the water some twenty yards beyond our decoys and displaying a broad skirt of snowy white below the swarthy breast and a white collar around a long jet-black neck. In solid and even array the flock sweeps past our decoys with a guttural "wa-ook, wa-ook, wa-ook" from a score or more of throats. There is a trace of suspicion in the note; but keep perfectly still. They are too far to shoot and they may return. On they go for fifty yards, when they lengthen out and rise in a long string, with black backs and wings shining as they turn upward.

Upward and onward for over two hundred yards they go, when the line swings with a precision that would charm a drill sergeant. Then around it comes, headed at first directly toward us. Then the ends of the line fold backward and in a wedge-shaped mass it bears off a little. For a single moment each dark wing fans the air with rapid stroke, then as quickly each one is set in a rigid curve, and, as if sliding down an invisible incline of ice, down rush the birds toward the decoys. In another moment the soft hiss of their wings becomes louder and harsher as the birds near the decoys and turn their pinions full against the air to check themselves. But just as we think they are about to alight a hoarse "wa-ook" bursts from a dozen throats and in a twinkling the orderly array of descending black turns into a rising confusion of white and black as with rapid beat of strong wings the whole flock wheels skyward and outward.

But wary as these birds are, all is not yet lost for the quick shot. As the first barrel spouts its fire over the water the heavy wiff, wiff, wiff, wiff of the wings of the hindmost bird suddenly ceases, its long black neck suddenly wilts, and down through the soft sunlight it sinks in a shining whirl of white and black. But before the smooth surface breaks to receive it another one wilts at the report of another barrel, and goes like a plummet below. As a third barrel rings over the water another brant halts in its course, sinks with laboring wing nearly to the water, twists sideways with a jerk and sheds a feather or two as a fourth barrel rolls its thunder across the bight; then seaward it stretches out its ebony neck, and skimming low along the water fades away in a rapid alternation of white and black.

Before the last flock is yet out of sight another dark line rises over the sand spit where the distant surf is grumbling. The brant we first saw in the bay were but a small portion of all that frequent it. Most of them are out at sea during the flow of the tide, feeding on the beds of kelp, and now at the ebb they are beginning to return. Now rising, now lowering, but swift and straight, in a long wedge-shaped column, the black ranks come on. Down the centre of the bight they fly, until within some four hundred yards of the blind, when the head of the column turns a little, and directly toward the decoys the whole mass bends its way. Soon the air sings beneath their stiffening wings, then comes the sharp, rushing sound as the birds set them to alight, then the splash of water as the lower ones settle among the decoys. As we rise in the blind the whole mass is turned into a flapping huddle of terrified confusion, a laboring turmoil of black and white, with a wild and clamorous "wa-ook, wa-ook, wa-ook" clanging from a hundred white-collared throats. Four barrels in quick succession bellow from the blind, and three brant sink with sullen splash into the water. Two more lag behind their fast-retreating comrades, one gradually rising and overtaking them, the other settling lower and lower, until, cleaving a long furrow in the smooth surface of the bay, it floats dead in the water nearly a half mile away.

Beyond where the curlew are flitting along the wet shore and the gull is winding his airy way, beyond where the snipe are whisking over the blue waters and the ever-hungry pelican with heavy plunge is shivering the smooth mirror beneath, our eyes are again fixed in deep expectation. What countless hordes of these dark beauties, the very nobility of waterfowl, have streamed over that sand spit in the dim ages gone! And how long shall it be before the whole winter shall pass away with never a dark-dotted line rising into the blue sky beyond it? Alas! Not long.

But a soft winnowing of the air behind us disturbs our reflections and reminds us that it is not from the sea alone that these birds come. But too late the discovery, for quick as the shying off of the swiftest duck is the wheeling of this active little goose. "Wa-ook, wa-ook, wa-ook," resounds from the air above amid the wiff, wiff, wiff of sheering pinions, and before the guns can be turned upon them the brant are out of reach. Vainly the fire streams toward them; not a twitch is visible in the black ranks; not a dusky feather parts its hold.

And now the armies of brant are gathering in earnest, for the tide is half out and the time for the grand march has come. Thus far we have seen only the skirmish line. But now they are coming in battalions. From the western horizon line after line rises into view, and from the bay itself long black streams begin to skim over the water. Some are in long lines point foremost, some in wedge-shaped masses, others in crescent lines, others in converging strings. Vainly you try to find the motive for all this activity. The brant are not feeding, nor are they on the way to feed. This particular stage of the tide seems no better adapted to wing exercise than any other stage, and yet nearly every brant in the land is in motion and nothing but shot can keep one still. Yet amid all this excitement they relax no caution, and unless all is quiet in the blind it is vain to expect a close shot. And, strangely enough, the majority of the flocks aim for the decoys and if not disturbed will settle among them. Though all the brant now want to fly and seem to have taken a strange aversion to the water, no sooner do they see the decoys sitting there than down they glide toward them—the best possible illustration of the adage, "One fool makes many."

And so flock after flock sets its wings and goes hissing with speed down the air to the decoys in perfect array and swiftly as a swooping hawk, until the first broadside is poured into the swarthy line and the second into the throbbing whirl of white and black into which the orderly ranks are instantly changed.

None of the winged myriads from the north can defy the hunter's fire like this dark wanderer from home. Sometimes two or three birds go splashing below as a full broadside opens upon a flock, but more often only one comes down, while another perhaps careens a little and lags behind for a few moments, then rights himself and overtakes his comrades or settles slowly into the far distant water. Here comes a flock so glossy, as the sun shines from their beating wings and white skirts, that they seem within easy reach; yet at the roar of the guns the line merely lengthens, swerves and rises, and not even a feather comes whiffling down. Here comes another flock so close that we can see the dark vests and snowy underclothes pictured in the smooth water between them and us. In abiding confidence we open a full battery upon them, yet the only result is a whirl of white and black, a clamor of hoarse throats and increased expedition in the line. The gun must have more powder to kill them quickly.

And so it goes on for an hour or more, with brant to the right and brant to the left looming up on the horizon, with swift wings bearing them rapidly toward the decoys, until the soft s-s-s-s-s-s of sailing wings is changed to the wiff, wiff, wiff of terror, and the bead-like string, so orderly and so swift, into a bewildered huddle of white and black. So thick and fast they come that one can hardly notice the dense flocks of curlew that fan the air half way between us and the decoys, the bunches of snipe and plover that shoot by in volleys and the sandpipers and dowitchers that alight on the shore nearby.

Geese of the North Wind
by Frank Dufresne

After decades in Alaska, Dufresne re-settled in Washington. This 1959 article was written about a unique population of lesser snow geese that choose to winter far to the north of the rest of their tribe. These birds winter between the Frazer River Delta of British Columbia and the Skagit region of Washington.

It was a morning of downpour and violence. A December gale, spawned in the crashing seas of the North Pacific, roared in on Washington State, blasting the weather side of Whidbey Island, yowling over its top and hammering down on the Skagit tideflats. As Moberg, George and I rowed our skiffload of decoys out through the chop to the margin of the salt marsh, raindrops rattled off our slickers like shotgun pellets.

Ralph Moberg, the man who talks with the geese, reached out a wet hand to stroke the curly coat of his Chesapeake retriever. "They'll fly today, old Lady," he told her. His voice whisked away with the wind as he motioned me to trail oars while he pushed back his earflaps to listen. Through the billowing murk came the first far-off clamor of waterfowl moving in the dawn. The calls came faintly at first, swelling when the wind swung our way and as quickly fading in a reverse current of turbulence. But in the short interval I head the lusty squawk of mallards organizing for a raid on Moberg's grainfields, the thin piping of widgeons and the mewing of hungry gulls. There had been another sound, wild and blood-stirring, a reedy babel from thousands of birds that sent tingles up and down a man's spine; a weird, highly pitched chorus unlike that of any other waterfowl, yet more exciting. It was the unmistakable cry of the snow geese.

We strung our white decoys along the edge of the foaming tide wash, then dragged our mud-colored skiff behind a waterlogged stump. Moberg fed some shells into his magnum pump, screwed up his face like a man about to have a back tooth extracted, and sent out a shrill yell followed by an unearthly outburst. It was like a saxophone note blasted until it split the reed, then soaring into ululations like nothing I'd ever heard coming out of a human larynx. He did it again to prove his tonsils hadn't been ruptured by the efforts, then turned my way to explain. "That's snow-goose talk. It means 'Come on down, boys, I've found it.'"

For a while there was no evidence that the white geese believed, or had even heard, the glad tidings. Dark clouds that sprayed moisture like hurled sponges continued to barrel across the Skagit Flats. We searched the light breaks between them but saw only flights of scurrying teal and sheets of sandpeeps rising as one bird to flash wings and land again on the mud bars. After a spell of waiting, my rain-blurred eyes picked up a flock of whitish birds bearing down upon us. The Chesapeake Lady saw them too, but didn't even wag her tail. She'd retrieved too many snow geese to be fooled by foraging seagulls. Besides, she'd found something of her own to study. Some bird specks high in the stormy sky, so far away as to appear like snowflakes tumbling in the overcast.

The Lady whined, and it was the signal for her master to wrench another string of anguished yelps out of his windpipe. I started to say, "They'll never hear you in this hurricane," when Moberg cut in, "Hark!"

There it was again, a great soprano blending of voices welling for a moment in the wet breezes, then dying away. Moberg yanked his face out of joint as he once more invited the distant birds to light down for breakfast, and when the answer came he interpreted, "They'll be along."

The female retriever rose on brown legs that trembled, and peered anxiously through the upended roots of the stump as the white flecks grew larger. Nearer they came—five hundred, a thousand, maybe more, veering right and left to buck the sodden gusts, soaring like kites in the sudden updrafts. The leaders were close enough for me to distinguish their shiny white plumage from the gray of the goslings.

We gripped our guns and shoved thumbs against the safety catches. Moberg started a count-down: "Ten, nine, eight—" That was as far as he'd got when the flock applied airbrakes. It was like shaking out a white tablecloth as bird after bird banked sharply against the weather, formed a funnel and came pouring down out of the driving mist to spread across the tideflats just beyond shotgun range.

The Chesapeake Lady poked me with her nose and cocked her head at Moberg, plainly asking, "What the—?" And Moberg all but strangled himself trying, with but one larynx, to imitate a whole flock of snow geese. It was a supreme try and not all wasted. Out of the multitudes of white birds two soot-colored juveniles detached themselves with cries of pleasure and flew straight down our gun barrels. We were still eying the main flock when the scrawny youngsters landed in the middle of our spread, gabbling happily at our paper decoys. Moberg waited a moment, then sent an alarm call clanging off his tonsils. There was a thunderclap of black-tipped wings as the vast raft of sitting snows took off. None came close enough to shoot.

"Had to flush 'em out," Moberg explained. "Once a big bunch like that sits down on a safe spot, they'll pull in every other flock that comes along. Now we'll start all over again with a fresh batch."

For the better part of an hour it didn't look as if there would be a second chance. The wavies were wary and wise, and no strangers to the pitfalls of the Skagit. It had been the winter home of the clan for centuries. Some of the old flock veterans had been visiting these Puget Sound marshes for twenty years or more. They knew every stranded log, every driftwood snag, every tule clump that might be hiding a gunner.

From the undulating white raft riding the waves far out in the bay, small groups lifted off like tag ends ripped free by the winds and blown our way. Each band seemed to be led by a pure-white old gander with X-ray vision as it drifted past us, just beyond reach, and settled down on the soggy green fields a half mile away. I don't think George or I would have fired a shot all day if it hadn't been for Moberg's freak vocal cords.

A group of five winged our way, high, wide and safe from all evil until Moberg twisted the corner of his mouth up against his left ear and made with the shrieks. Instantly the geese responded with a medley of confiding cackles. Three gray-feathered young of the year split away from the two white adults, came in forty yards up and pulled the strings on their parachutes. We reached beyond them with our loads of No. 4 shot to bring down the old geese first, then dropped gun muzzles to finish up on the grays. We were a fraction too slow.

The Chesapeake Lady watched the trio whip off to freedom, then turned quickly to follow the hit birds as they came tumbling end over end. One splashed out front, but the other suddenly recovered its balance and sailed a quarter mile out before it skidded onto the water. The boat rocked as the Chesapeake Lady jumped overboard. With no more than a quick sniff at the near goose floating pink feet up, she churned off like a sea lion in pursuit of the wounded bird.

I thought Moberg was going to give her an assist when he picked up the oars. But he rowed only far enough to retrieve the dead bird, then pulled back to the shelter of the stump. Much later the Chesapeake Lady came paddling into view, pushing a payload, clambered over the gunwale and deposited a still live goose at Moberg's feet. Pausing only long enough to shake sea water all over the three of us, she tensed herself for another plunge over the side.

"Hold it," said Moberg, and reached around to hold up the dead bird to her view. The lady poked it with snuffling nose, rolled brown eyes up to her master to say she understood, then once more took up her vigil where she could peek out over the bay. She didn't have long to wait.

The sky had brightened and the white wings of flying geese glittered like crystals when occasional shafts of sunlight stabbed through the clouds. The wavies were moving out now in great numbers, mostly in high flights to open fields, where they circled long and watchfully to make sure some hunter wouldn't poke his head out of a drainage ditch and try a moon shot. If all was clear, the circle gradually tightened, dropped down a notch for another sweep, and finally let go all holds and came spiraling down to earth like falling snow. Enough smallish flocks came within hearing of Moberg's magic tonsils to give us all the tries we wanted, but other spreads of decoys around the shoreline drew not a single customer.

"They're plenty smart," observed Moberg. "Hunting pressure is real heavy these days, but there are just as many snows as ever."

He explained that the Skagit Flats are as far south as this particular flock ever flies to spend its winters, and that the numbers vary from 15,000 to 28,000, depending on what kind of weather breaks they've had on the breeding grounds. This winter they were running high, he figured: a good 25,000 birds, which was only a small percentage of total wavy numbers.

Close to half a million of these lesser snow geese had bypassed Puget Sound to push down into California and Mexico. And there had been mixed flights of snows and blues from Hudson Bay to the Louisiana and Texas coasts. Still farther east, a heavier species, the greater snow goose, had produced its broods in Greenland and migrated down the Atlantic shoreline to Maryland and North Carolina. And the Ross' goose, rarest and smallest of the white geese, had been found nesting near Perry River in the Canadian Arctic. There was only one real mystery left to unravel in snow-goose life history, and it concerned these birds right here on the Skagit. Where did they spend their summers?

"Government men are aiming to find out," said Moberg. "They've been out here on the Skagit shooting cannons at the geese, with nylon nets for bullets. They've been clamping aluminum bands on their legs, and turning them loose for hunters to kill and report dates and locations." Moberg eyed a pair of snows winging by and decided they weren't worth tuning up for. "They've come up with an even better scheme for tracing white-goose migration routes," he said, "and you don't have to kill the goose. They've been dunking the snows in a pot of dye, and they come out as green as St. Patrick's Day."

In the light of available clues, red might have been a more appropriate color. At least one Russian bird band has been found on a snow goose shot on our west coast. During the spring breakup in Bering Sea I have several times observed sky-filling flights of white wavies swinging left toward East Cape, Siberia. Migrations back to Alaska in September have been even heavier. Because it would be good propaganda for them to claim that Siberia is raising waterfowl for capitalistic gunners, Russian naturalists should not be slow in telling the world if they see any of these green geese from Washington State, or flamingo-pink wavies that have been dyed in California.

But wherever the snows fly to lay their five to seven eggs and hatch their yellow downy young, it is almost sure to be far inside the polar circle. Not without good reason have these long-distance fliers been called "geese of the north wind," because as deep into the Arctic as explorers have been winter-locked, they have been cheered in the springtime by the lacework flights and shrill cries of snow geese passing overhead.

Moberg said he was a youngster of 13 when he first discovered that he could talk the big white birds almost into his lap. Before that he'd learned to quack a mallard within pot-shooting range, to whistle down a bull sprig and honk like a Canada goose. Of course, a lot of hunters could do the same with mechanical calls, and that's why Moberg decided to specialize on wavies. Nobody had ever succeeded in manufacturing a call that could duplicate the full scope of their tongue: the piercing squeals, the ringing yipes like a briered dog, the organ-toned grunts, the split-reed screeches of an old gander laying down the law to his flock.

Even after he'd mastered the art, young Ralph Moberg figured it was only a passing gift he'd be bound to lose when his voice changed. But it hasn't worked out that way. He can still peel off the high notes, still give out with the fractured-tonsil breakaway that is the real key to his success. Snow-goose talking has been almost a career with him. He's a celebrity not only in Mount Vernon, where he lives, but also with gunners who come from all over to shoot on his tidelands and hear him talk the white geese into his pocket.

Moberg and George had shot limits, and I was a bird behind when a single white wavy came beating past, mile-high and going places in a hurry. "Bring that one down to magnum reach," I challenged, "and I'll finish the job."

Moberg opened up formally with his routine "Greetings to all snow geese" hail call. The speck in the clouds kept right on traveling. "It didn't hear me," he muttered. "I'll have to switch on the loudspeaker."

His lips moved from beneath his nose to a spot under his left ear and shaped themselves into a trumpet. There was a moment of loaded silence, then an ear-shattering potpourri of hog screams, frightened guinea hens and coyotes howling at the moon. The lone goose stopped as if it had smacked into a stone wall, did an outside loop and started planing our way. I couldn't help it. I yelled, "Wow!" But neither Moberg nor George heard me. They were looking the other way, and no wonder!

It looked as if every snow goose on the Skagit was lifting off the green fields behind us. At first there was no direction in the eruption, but only the fluttering white wings of thousands upon thousands rising and forming a shimmery curtain against the dark spruces. Beyond the birds there was a salvo of shotgun reports, barely audible through the din of clanging tongues but enough to start the drift our way. Moberg kept calling until it wasn't any use to summon more geese. We had them all around us like confetti in a ticker-tape parade, settling and splashing between us and our decoys, blocking out the afternoon sun.

I straightened up for a better look at the incredible spectacle. There was a sudden, thunderous roar as they blasted off the water and rolled out across the bay in a great cloud to settle down again. It was a couple of minutes before either of us could speak.

"Well," said Moberg finally, "I guess I called down that snow goose you wanted."

He had, all right. Only I'd forgotten to shoot.

Goose Shooting in
the Sacramento Valley
by "Parson"

    As with the canvasback accounts, most goose shooting was histori-
cally described as taking place east of the Mississippi. But very likely
no place in North America had more geese in concentrations than did
the Sacramento Valley one hundred years ago. This account was
written in 1891.

C ommencing life in my youth in a game country and having an indulgent father, who early placed in my hands a good gun, I soon learned to despise all other boyish pursuits and pastimes in comparison with roaming the prairies of Illinois and the wooded hills of Wisconsin with gun and dog. The passion for shooting has therefore never deserted me, and today, in middle life, the tule marshes or stubble field, the mountain stream or brushy point, where lurk the trout or deer, the tangled gulch or canyon resounding with the call of the jaunty California quail, or the boggy ground lining the banks of some slow-moving stream, where squat and hide the English snipe, have many times more charm and fascination for me than the crowded routes of some fashionable seaside resort or the roar and bustle of a city's street.

After years spent in the most favored localities of those States which form on their edges the basin for the Father of Waters; having shot successfully over large portions of Dakota, Minnesota, Wisconsin, Illinois, Missouri and Arkansas; having killed deer and bear in the pine woods of the Northern Peninsula of Michigan and the cane brakes of Eastern Arkansas; having seen the prairie grouse disappear from Illinois and grow scarce on the great uplands of Minnesota and the Dakotas; having whiled away many an autumnal day on the lagoons of the lower Mississippi and the marshes of Central Wisconsin, luring with decoy and seductive caller to their fate mallard and teal, I find myself at last in the Golden State, with different surroundings it is true, but with the same old passion for gun and dog.

I well remember the impressions created upon my sporting instincts when, on a day some three years since, I made my first entrance into the beautiful Sacramento Valley.

The horizon all around, save just ahead, was set with snowy peaks— to the right the Sierras, to the left the more rugged Coast range, while at intervals as the train swung round a curve, hanging low down like a fleecy summer cloud more than a hundred miles away, great Shasta lifted his hoary head. But what set every nerve in my body tingling with excitement was the geese. The majority of the passengers paid no attention whatever to this, to them, common spectacle, but during that whole day's ride geese in countless numbers were never out of sight of our train.

I thought that I had seen geese and brant in Dakota, but, like Uncle Toby's reminiscences, they were "nothing to this." Snow geese, in white and glistening ranks on the edges of the green grain; gray geese, wavering up and down in slowly-moving flocks against the horizon; deliberate geese, only getting up as the train was just upon them; frightened geese, rising on nervous pinions from some sedgy pool by

213

the roadbed. Geese, geese, geese! While here and there over the green fields moved men and boys mounted and armed with Winchesters actually herding the geese off of the sprouting grain, as a rancher informed me while complacently spitting out through the window.

"Good many geese 'long here," I remarked to him as we whirled along.

"Yes, *tolerable*," he replied, "but *scarcer* than they were!"

"Plenty enough for me, however," I remarked to myself. But it was not until the following fall that I made my first acquaintance with the goose of the Sacramento Valley over the rib of my Parker.

The absorbing nature of my calling, among a new people and amidst new surroundings, prevented an early interview, and that spring I witnessed their countless flocks streaming northward overhead during the day, and listened to their unceasing clangor at night, with the mental determination that on their return southward I would know 'em better.

In the meantime, however, I was not idle. In June following I was initiated into dove shooting, which, while furnishing poor sport as compared with nobler game, still served as a pastime not to be despised—jumping doves in the grain fields and flight shooting on the passes requiring considerable dexterity in the handling of a shotgun.

The latter part of September found me waiting for the geese, with a goodly store of cartridges loaded with numbers 4 and 5 shot. I know that this will seem like the rankest heresy to the advocates of large shot, but I long ago discarded both big guns and big shot in decoy shooting at geese, being entirely satisfied with the performance of a light ten gauge and the smaller pellets.

I had discovered on inquiry that little real scientific goose shooting was indulged in along the Sacramento Valley, partly because of the abundance of the birds and partly because plenty could be obtained ordinarily by employing the simple principles of driving on the birds with a fast horse and light wagon; shooting them from hedges and ditches, when on a foggy morning they passed, flying low, from field to field; or else approaching the birds circuitously behind the shelter of a steer or cow trained for the purpose.

I had made my own preparations, however, to shoot this game in the way that I had been most successful in their pursuit years ago on the stubbles of Dakota. Having placed my order early with an Eastern firm for a mixed flock of profile decoys, I spent several mornings after the first flight began in locating the birds and in finding where the geese "used" in the neighboring grain fields. I located several feeding places, as a reward for my patience, where the geese came into the stubbles from the plains or sand bars of the river early in the morning and toward evening of each day.

It was, then, with no slight degree of satisfaction, that on the morning of the fourth day, while the stars were still shining, I put my horse into a light road wagon, into the rear of which were packed a lunch, a dozen and a half decoys and some hay. I had on the day before, with the aid of a light spade and a few barley sacks for the removal of earth, dug two shallow pits something like a mile apart, in which I proposed to take the morning and the evening flight. Very soon my little wagon was bowling over the hard ground, and with a fresh easterly wind in my face I left the town behind.

Crossing several fields I drew near a low-lying swale, distant from the river a half mile, and on which the wheat that year had grown rank and tall. With the not unusual prodigality and carelessness of the California rancher the wheat here had not been well gleaned with the header, and not a little remained in patches here and there uncut or "lodged." And here had been the geese for a number of mornings, as was plain to the most casual observer of "sign."

Hastily hitching the horse in a grove of live oaks and gathering up my gun and a part of the decoys, I indulged in a sharp run for my blind—hastened thereto by a clangor heralding the approach of the first flock. They espied me as I breasted a slight rise and sheered off, leaving me to seek my hiding place, which was a shallow pit carefully dug in the centre of a patch of partially-cut stubble, and from which every particle of loose dirt had been removed. Putting an empty barley sack in the bottom of the hole and disposing of my profile decoys, the majority with heads lowered as though unconcernedly feeding, I squatted down in the pit with my eyes on a level with the top of the headed grain.

The disposition of decoys, as all old sportsmen know, has much to do with success, more especially when dealing with as wary a bird as the goose. Profiles are particularly difficult to set out alluringly, but I had tolerably well learned the art and had my little flock of nine gracefully disposed at different angles, all feeding, save two, who, posted on a little rise, served as sentinels.

Repressing a strong desire to smoke I scanned the horizon eagerly, the deepening flush in the east giving evidence that Old Sol would soon put in an appearance. I had not long to wait. From the hidden river a short distance away, where a long bar lay exposed, came the clamorous sounds of a flock of snow geese—the commonest variety, perhaps, in California. They are beautiful birds, being of pure white, shading in some specimens to a delicate écru upon the breast, the feathers of the last joint of the wing being raven black.

I had shot many of these birds in Dakota and had found them the most vociferous of the goose family, their flight being characterized by a constant and (if close at hand) almost deafening gabble. Unlike the Canada goose, rare in California in my experience, they are rather poor as a table bird, their flesh, though gamy, being dry and very dark. They are tough birds, too, and although decoying more readily than other varieties they will at the same time carry off much shot. I have seen the blood follow the impact of the shot upon their white breasts frequently, only to pick up my game many yards away from the firing point. Following the noisy outburst of sounds from the bar a white cloud of birds rose above the line of the high river bank, outlining themselves clear and distinct against the gray surface of the distant Coast range. There must have been a hundred of them, and more, for it is a rare thing for these birds to move unless in large flocks. They were headed down stream, and the long line of birds—not as yet striking their flight—wavered up and down as though undecided as to their course.

Though a fair "honker," I cannot successfully imitate the constantly varying note of the snow goose, and I knew that if they were not determined on the field where I lay, or failed to catch sight of their downy brethren (I had three white decoys set out), they were gone geese for me.

But fate had destined that I should dip into that flock, and as the leader veered a little eastward toward the wind the balance of the flock swung well around him in the teeth of the breeze. That settled the business, for now they had seen the decoys, and with a renewed burst of cries, as though rejoicing over a prospective reunion, they came straight toward me, setting their wings as they came. By this time I was well down in my blind, watching through the close-growing stalks of grain the approaching game, with my right forefinger nervously toying with the trigger.

On they came, and I knew I must take my shot pretty soon, since it has been a rare thing in my experience to have birds actually come into and alight among profiles. The deception, on close approach, is too glaring for that and is generally detected in time to sheer off, but not until—if the decoys are well placed—the concealed gunner gets a fair shot. In this case the birds came near enough to drop their legs preparatory to alighting—whether they would have alighted or not will never be known. This was a good enough opportunity for me, and raising just above the stubble I poured right and left into the struggling mass, and as the birds rose wildly in the air—strangely silent now—I quickly transferred a shell from my mouth to the gun, and knocked down another with a broken wing. Three dead birds lay among the decoys, while two, including the one last shot, waddled awkwardly off,

216

dragging and tripping over their broken wings. Quickly securing and killing the wounded, and setting out those that showed the least blood by the aid of forked sticks, I re-entered my pit and yielded to the temptation to light my pipe.

While bending over hands which sheltered the glowing match, "whif, wif, wif," right over my head, and there go a flock of seven gray geese, the large and irregular spots upon their breasts plainly showing. To drop match and pipe and make a wild grab for the gun was the work of a second—but a second too late. However, those geese do not propose leaving the field, and though plainly unattracted by the decoys, over which they had passed, they turn and in a wide circle commence their inspection. These birds, very different from the last, are silent, save for a "peer wekes" now and then from the leader. The circle grows a little narrower, and now I see I must risk a shot, else they will alight a hundred yards from me. As the leader swings into the wind's eye to the westward of me, a full seventy-five yards away, I cover him, move well ahead and draw the trigger of the left barrel, which is heavily choked. Ah! see him climb and tower. That means a head shot, and even as you gaze he comes down tail first with a thump upon the ground.

Once more I crouched down in my burrow, and by the time my watch indicated 8 o'clock I added five more to my score; also a trumpeter swan which drifted by me, a lone bird.

The evening shooting was not as good, the location being not as well chosen and my luck was very indifferent. There were birds in plenty, and they came toward me, but from some inexplicable cause most of them located me and veered off. Nevertheless the rising moon that night found me trotting merrily homeward with nearly a score of birds jolting among the decoys in the wagon box, the result of some thirty odd empty shells.

217

Wild Goose Shooting
in the Northwest
by Major Charles S. Moody

Major Charles Moody was another early western writer on outdoor
subjects who shot over a wide area of the West beginning in the 1880's.
This 1922 article calls attention to the fact that the bountiful years had
passed.

I arrived in the Sacramento Valley, California, early enough to learn from observation what was meant by the term "goose herder," though the occupation soon afterward became obsolete. At that time, the Sacramento marshes were, at certain seasons, covered with Canada, white-fronted, Hutchins, and snow geese, and black brant, besides innumerable varieties of wild ducks. Their ravages on the growing grain crops compelled the farmer, in self-defense, to employ herders armed with firearms to drive them away from the fields.

At early morning the birds rose from the marshes and descended upon the growing grain in perfect clouds, formed a line and devastated the grain as they marched. It was difficult to frighten them away, for when the herder fired into one flock, then sought an adjacent field in pursuit of another, the first circled a few times and again alighted in the same or some other nearby spot. This contrived to keep the "goose herder" on the jump.

The voyage from Sacramento to San Francisco took an entire day, for the steamer stopped every few miles to take on a cargo of dead geese. By the time we had reached Oakland the upper decks would be piled high with geese, worth twenty-five cents each on the San Francisco markets. The reader may form some idea of the vast numbers of these birds when it is understood that this was a daily occurrence for several river steamers.

Like conditions prevailed in a slightly modified degree when we reached the Willamette and Columbia river valleys in Oregon. These rivers do not have the extensive marshes of the lower Sacramento, hence there were not so many geese, but at the same time enough to require the services of a "herder."

We turned north into eastern Washington and found many of the Canadas nesting in the tule swamps of Spokane, Stevens, Adams, and Lincoln counties. These were but a fraction of the thousands we had seen in California and Oregon. It was not until 1899, when I made a trip through the lower Yukon, that I learned where the geese really made their summer homes. Very few of these, however, were Canada geese, they having halted further south to nest. The nests of Hutchins, white-fronted, cackling, snow, together with the different brants, were so numerous that at times it was difficult to avoid treading on them as one walked.

Wild goose shooting anywhere west of the Rocky Mountains forty years ago was anything but sport; it was hard work to be paid for at so much per diem. If a sportsman wanted a day's goose shooting the farmer was only too willing to supply him with a gun, ammunition, and a horse.

In after years, more especially after the gold rush into the Klondike, and the consequent destruction of their nests, geese became less numerous, "herders" were no longer required, and legislative bodies enacted protective measures for migratory birds.

At the present time, in any place other than the Sacramento Valley, the Willamette and Columbia River valleys, and the Snake River country in eastern Washington, geese are becoming rather scarce. In the lake region of Washington, Idaho, and Montana, where geese were formerly quite numerous, to-day they are few. The marshes in many instances have been drained, depriving the birds of their nesting sites; the constant bombardment during the open season has frightened the few left until they are extremely wary. The wild goose is endowed with good horse sense and is abundantly able to look out for himself. It requires a considerable degree of stalking skill to get within range of a flock of these intelligent birds.

Aside from California and Oregon, where the shooting is largely owned by clubs, the best goose shooting I know is in eastern Washington along the "rim rock" of the Snake and Columbia Rivers. Fairly good shooting is to be had in Idaho, but nothing compared to that in Washington. In the Canadian provinces just north of the United States there are still thousands of geese and if the American can make his peace with the conservative Canuck he may find plenty of good shooting around Calgary and Edmonton.

In the autumn the Canadian geese come to the Snake and Columbia rivers in their fall migration in great numbers. Western rivers flow through deep canyons whose walls rise with considerable abruptness to the level plateau that borders them. These plateaus are cultivated right up to the canyon's rim. The geese spend the night on some isolated island or sand bar along the river and repair to the grain fields early in the morning. This exodus begins before daybreak and continues for three or four hours, during which time the geese pour up out of the river bottom in clouds.

When the bands first arrive from the north they may be found moving over the grain fields at all hours of the day, but they soon learn to limit their movements to the early morning and the late twilight. Shooting is done over decoys, from a blind, that is a pit digged on the brink of the canyon. This pit is occupied by two men shooting from either end and is covered with straw or dry sage brush. The decoys are either sheet iron profiles or live birds.

A sophisticated old gander, the Nestor and guide of his flock, will pay but little attention to an imitation goose, no matter how cunningly it may be contrived. Many times I have seen a flock of geese surmount the canyon rim and steer straight for our decoys, led by some wise old admiral, who, when he detected the fraud, gave a honk of derision and "steered for the open sea." One querulous live goose staked out to a picket pin is worth a cartload of sheet iron "boosters."

The most satisfactory gun is a ten-gauge double. Pump and automatic guns are unreliable. On windy days when the sand blows the mechanism of a pump or automatic gun is liable to clog at the crucial moment and leave the arm useless in your hands.

A reliable retriever, preferably a stout Chesapeake, is a necessity. The shooter should never leave the blind to fetch in a wounded bird during the flight. Five minutes spent in the open chasing a wounded goose will serve to warn every fellow goose in ten miles and they will cordially avoid the spot.

Not all the geese leave the river at one time. Straggling bands remain along the sand bars resting and preening their feathers. I have had fairly good success shooting such from behind the bulwark of some staid old farm horse warranted to stand anything less explosive than a charge of TNT. This style of hunting requires all the patience and perseverance accorded such a virtue by our Masonic brethren.

I have spent hours coaxing an old equine out on a sand bar, keeping religiously in his wake, to get nearly within range and have the "lookout" yell something to the flock, and away they would go. There is nothing for it under these conditions but to smile sweetly and try it again. Two shots are all you get from behind a horse, and it is well to make them count. It is a waste of time and ammunition to shoot into the flock in the hope of bagging several geese; more often you bag nothing. Personally, I pick out one goose and just as he rises let him have it.

I have a very vivid and painful recollection of trying to float on a lower end of Goose Island in the Snake River. I had tried it unsuccessfully in a row boat before. This day I secured two logs, nailed cleats across them, gathered plenty of sage with which to cover myself, pushed the raft off into current, lay down and pulled the sage over me. The scheme bore all the earmarks of a glittering success.

The raft floated calmly down the stream, the tiny wavelets slopping over me in a most enjoyable and chilly manner. Gradually, I drew near to where the geese were sitting, one vidette posted on a sand dune looking up stream, another sentry doing similar duty down stream.

As I neared the island the picket called the attention of the general to that suspicious-looking craft coming down stream. His remarks indicated very clearly that he had no confidence in the thing. The old gander looked my craft over, agreed with his sentry, and when I was some three hundred yard distant, flapped his wings, issued an order to his followers to move—and moved.

I never saw a more harmonious convention. There was not a dissenting vote. Every goose and goosess rose and flapped away, leaving me to work my unwieldy craft ashore and trudge three miles back through the sand to where I had left my boat.

The grass suit, theoretically the finest thing ever, has not been a success on my back. I have sat on a sand bank dressed in one of the things until I nearly took root and turned into a muskrat house, without a goose getting closer than half a mile. By some sort of avian intuition they seemed to know the thing concealed a "joker."

Goose shooting on the lakes of northern Idaho and eastern Washington partakes largely of chance. There are a goodly number of geese, but there is also a goodly amount of water—and the geese take advantage of the latter. I really believe, though, there is more genuine sport in shooting geese on Lake Pend Oreille, where you may go and not get a shot, than there is in shooting on the "rim rock" of the Snake, where you are reasonably sure of getting several. It is such elusive sport.

The hunter sallies forth at dawn, filled with hope, expectancy, and a ham sandwich, hunts all day, returns at night, his hope all leaked out, his expectancy ungratified, his ham sandwich long since transformed into caloric energy, his system clamoring for more substantial aliment—but 'nary a goose. He fares forth another day and luck, chance, accident, or simply effort brings a goose within range. Mayhap two or three stroll along at the psychological moment; the hunter staggers in at night, his face wreathed in smiles, bearing his load, the envy of every Nimrod less fortunate than he.

There are several ways of getting geese on open water, all of them more or less unsuccessful. The blind and live decoys is the most productive of game. The blind must be dug near the shore, where it promptly fills with water and thus serves the double purpose of a blind and a bath tub. It is one of the most pleasurable experiences on earth to crouch all day in two feet of water several degrees nearer the freezing point than necessity requires, a northeast wind filled with flying snow cooling your super-heated brain, and wait for a flock of geese, that persist, with fiendish perversity, in circling every part of the shore except that where you are located.

If a flock does invade your vicinity what an unholy joy pervades your system as you arise in your might and pour a load of BBs into that old lead gander and watch him double up! When he begins to drop, your desire is to hand him the other barrel just for good measure, but if you are a wise gunner you will reserve it for some agitated honker with his feathers all aflutter in his haste to get away from that immediate neighborhood.

Hunters go after geese on the Kootenai River marshes on snowshoes. Exactly. That's what I said—snowshoes. Inasmuch as the procedure is somewhat unique it requires a little explanation. The marshes of the Kootenai, and other western rivers as well, are the product of the industry in past ages of the beavers. There are wide, shallow lagoons reaching back from the river, overflowed in spring. The receding freshet leaves them with ten inches of water and ten feet of soft mud, and the geese are wise enough to remain out on this mud.

For years the wily birds laughed at the efforts to reach them. Then along came some bright Yankee and had an inspiration. He donned an ordinary pair of web snowshoes, walked out there one night, and held a surprise party.

This method of shooting is not without its drawbacks. It requires a high degree of skill to navigate a pair of snowshoes over soft mud. It possesses the added disadvantage that the feeding geese hollow out "pot holes" in the mud; and as the hunter has no light, he comes in contact with certain of these. After a man has stepped into a "pot hole" and spent the next ten minutes trying to get his feet under him he is in no shape to attend a full dress ball. Likewise the geese have gone visiting.

After all, any red blooded man can extract a great deal of joy out of prowling around over a marsh at night firing at the flash of white wings as the birds take flight.

There are many ways of stalking a Canada goose, but there is always enough of the element of chance about all of them to make the sport enjoyable. The Canada goose, like the white-tailed deer, has the instinct of self-preservation highly developed, and the man who can outwit him at his own game may without egotism call himself a hunter.

Salt Marshes and Estuaries
by Herbert L. Minshall

In recent years, such as this 1980 book chapter by Minshall, most California waterfowling is addressed in the past tense. Overlooking this sad fact, Minshall's accounts of early day San Diego Bay hunting is excellent.

I n the early twenties the shallow bays, estuaries and salt marshes along the coast of California, and Baja California to the south, still comprised thousands of acres of what was in effect a wilderness, visited by waterfowl hunters and fishermen but undisturbed by the vast majority of people who lived in the adjacent cities and towns. Those who did penetrate the winding channels, the flat tidal basins and the acres of rippling cord grass, pickleweed and tules were few in number, and although they took fish, clams and waterfowl, this minor depletion did little to upset the ecological balance there. Market hunting of ducks, geese and shorebirds had been outlawed many years before in California, and duck and goose hunters were already limited in the number of birds they could take and restricted to specified seasons, although bag limits were far more generous than in recent years. In Baja California, except for those around the gun club at La Grulla near Punta Banda, the waterfowl were practically undisturbed.

In the fall and winter months millions of birds congregated on the bays and marshes. At low tide long lines of black brant left their resting places at sea and wavered in over the strands and beaches to feed on the exposed mud flats from Tomales Bay, north of San Francisco, to San Quintín Bay in Mexico. Clouds of pintails, widgeon and teal at times filled the sky over the larger bays and lagoons, looking like billowing smoke in the distance. The open waters of bays and estuaries were often blanketed by huge rafts of resting redhead, canvasback and scaup, while several dozen different species of shorebird covered the shallow flats as the tide began to ebb, each kind occupying a slightly different ecological niche depending on food preference and the length and shape of its bill.

Because of these concentrations of waterfowl on the tidelands, the small lakes and ponds near the coast also had flocks dropping in constantly as they traded back and forth between lakes, ponds and salt marshes. Our family chicken farm was on one line of flight—within a mile of a marsh on San Diego Bay. As a young child I was forbidden to go down to the tule-choked pond below our farm buildings in the fall, for the blasting of shotguns could frequently be heard echoing off the hillsides in the early mornings, and we knew that hunters were there.

Once I went out to a car parked on the road near our house just after two hunters had climbed back up the slope from the pond. They laid out their birds in a long row on the ground and let me inspect them. In retrospect I can guess how they must have looked—drake mallards with glossy emerald heads, bright orange bills and rosy-brown breasts; exquisite little greenwing teal like feathered jewels; gadwall, pintail and widgeon in their bright patterned plumage. There were probably fifty birds, two limits of twenty-five each for two hours' shooting on one little stock pond.

Ever since that day I have been obsessed with the beauty of waterfowl, both in close-up detail and in flight, and I have hunted them, sketched them, painted them and thrilled to the sight and sound of their passage overhead all of my life. I can think of nothing in Nature to compare to the mellow, resonant calling of geese high in the sky—wavering lines of snow geese traveling south by moonlight, with their clamor drifting down like wind chimes and organ music. Few sights can equal, at least to a duck hunter, the color and excitement of mallards or pintails dropping down over a spread of decoys in the bright world of Autumn.

Around 1921, after we had moved to the city and lived on the mesa overlooking Mission Valley, my preoccupation with waterfowl became solidly reinforced. I had ridden my bicycle down to the foot of Mission Valley and the edge of the broad marshland that stretched away to the main body of Mission Bay. A narrow set of wheel tracks ran out to a huddle of shacks in the distance. I followed them and discovered Ad Pearson and Duckville. For a small boy with my particular interests no circumstance could have been more rewarding.

Duckville was a collection of battered, weatherbeaten wooden shacks used by duck hunters in season, and Pearson, known as "The Mayor of Duckville," was the caretaker and watchman paid a small wage to look after their property. But Ad Pearson was far more than that, as I soon found out. A man well into his seventies when I first met him, he was lean and tough, with leathery skin and exceptionally keen eyesight. He loved to talk, and since he had little to do in the summer and I was an eager and appreciative audience, he spun yarns to me by the hour. Although I discovered years later that much of what he had said was sheer fabrication, he had a lively imagination and I listened enthralled to his stories.

He told me that "Ad" was short for a much longer Cheyenne Indian name that I cannot recall exactly—"Adapoosa" or some such—and that it meant "Big Ears." According to him, his parents had been crossing the plains in a wagon train in the 1850's when he was a small child, and he had wandered away from the wagons and been captured by the Indians. He had been accepted into the tribe and raised by them, and he told me stories of buffalo hunting, raiding parties and the capture of enemy ponies. He even claimed that he had once killed a grizzly with just a hunting knife. Whether he had read these things in the romantic novels of the Nineteenth Century, I cannot say.

Despite his tales of the wild frontier and life with the Cheyenne, and

226

in spite of his rugged and rough-hewn exterior, Ad Pearson was a gentle, sensitive man and a highly accomplished self-taught artist and craftsman. In his little workshop he painted beautiful and extremely accurate pictures of ducks and geese, the first such work I had ever seen, and since I liked to draw and paint and intended to be an artist when I grew up, his work made an enormous and long-lasting impression on me. His panoramic mural painting of waterfowl graced the wall of Stanley Andrews' sporting goods store in downtown San Diego for many years. When I started to paint waterfowl in oils myself some years later, Mr. Andrews hung some of my pictures below Ad Pearson's on the same wall, to my great pride and pleasure.

I doubt if Pearson ever sold any of his paintings, but he also produced beautiful and functional wooden decoys which were in considerable demand, and would undoubtedly be extremely valuable today. He took particular pains with canvasback decoys, partly because they were highly effective from a distance with their white backs, but also because he admired canvasbacks so much, simply as beautiful objects. I agree. It seemed to me then, and still does today, that there are few things more majestic, more perfect in form and color, than a drake canvasback alert on the water. The finely-tapered black bill and rich chestnut head, set with jewel-like red-orange eyes and merging into the fluid S-curve of the neck; the glossy black breast and V-shaped black tail coverts contrasting starkly with the almost luminous white back etched with tiny, delicate gray lines, combine to present an uncommonly elegant effect. Although no wooden decoy can match completely the living bird, when carved by a master craftsman and painted by a painstaking artist, such objects can be authentic works of art and a joy to use in the field.

Beautiful as canvasbacks are when seen close up on land or on the water, they are even more thrilling to see on the wing. They are powerful, fast fliers, and when a flock suddenly dives from high above the marsh, the effect is heart-stopping. They fly close together, often in wedge-shaped formations which they maintain in the most intricate maneuvers. They dive almost straight down, reaching speeds of more than one hundred miles an hour, and the wind of their passage vibrating the big flight feathers of their drawn-in wings makes a sound like an express train rushing over a trestle. Just as it appears they will fly into the ground they level out and go rocketing off in a blur of movement, rocking from side to side so that their white backs flash and blink in the sunlight.

Unfortunately, because of the disappearance of both suitable breeding grounds and winter habitat on the coastal marshes, canvasbacks are becoming rare everywhere, and particularly on the marshes of California. They are shy and suspicious birds, and need undisturbed open water to prosper. Droughts on the Canadian prairies tend to deplete their numbers more severely than many species, as the puddles and potholes on which they nest dry up before the young can fly, unlike lakes and marshes on which water can be maintained.

In the early decades of the century on the Mission Bay marshes around Duckville, the commonest ducks, and the ones most frequently killed by the hunters, were widgeon, pintail and teal. These are all species that feed by tipping up in shallow water or grazing on exposed vegetation at low tide, unlike canvasbacks, which prefer to dive for their food. The latter were more plentiful on San Diego Bay, where they rafted by the thousands. Black brant, the compact little maritime geese found only on salt water, were also hunted extensively there. A handsome black and white bird only slightly larger than a mallard, the brant is one of the least wary of waterfowl, and its habit of flying in dense flocks and decoying readily to anything that even remotely resembled friends and relatives made it vulnerable to gunners on the marshes of both bays.

Fairly large populations of black brant wintered along the coast of California until quite recent times, but in 1980 were rapidly disappearing. There was still plenty of the eel grass upon which they fed, and they had been lightly hunted. Their depletion was due to a quite different problem. The birds bred on the Arctic coasts of Alaska and Siberia. Alaskan natives had always hunted them on the tundra during the nesting season. Federal law permitted so-called traditional subsistence patterns to continue by the indigenous people without seasons or bag limits, but now they had shotguns and plenty of ammunition, and Eskimos were driving out from town in pickup trucks and filling them. The destruction of nesting pairs and eggs would soon make black brant a vanishing species unless strict regulation could be undertaken by Federal and State agencies.

Ad Pearson made brant decoys with far less care than other kinds, just knocking out oblong shapes with little knobs for heads, and painting them black and white. He was scornful of the birds, and said you could lay out his crude decoys on the ground and sit in the middle of them in a kitchen chair dressed in a Santa Claus suit, and they would still fly right over your head begging to be shot. But with pintails and widgeon you needed the best and most life-like decoys you could get, set out in a natural pattern, and even then the birds would sense something wrong unless a breeze was moving the blocks about on the water. Consequently, and probably less from need than his great joy in the work, he made duck decoys in exquisite detail.

I was much too young to hunt at Duckville by myself, and had no friends or relatives who were hunters and would invite me along, but I hung around like an undergrown baseball addict at spring training, listening to Ad Pearson and longing for manhood. I absorbed marsh lore like a sponge, and could identify all the different species, even on the wing, long before I ever went hunting. In this I am reminded of a cousin's young grandson of about the same age whom I took sailing recently in the vicinity of the Naval Air Station on San Diego Bay. He could instantly identify and describe in technical detail every airplane we saw in the air, even at great distances, but couldn't distinguish a tern from a sea gull, since he had never lived on the coast but had spent his childhood near an inland air base. The years just before puberty seemed to include a marvelous receptiveness for observation and retention.

Hunting on the marsh at Duckville was for grown men—it was difficult and even dangerous. The land was cut by dozens of small canals and channels winding around like a labyrinth, producing islands and making travel on foot almost impossible. Some of the waterways were almost, but never quite, narrow enough to jump across. Others were as much as two hundred feet wide, but all of them shared a common characteristic: they were floored with almost bottomless black muck in which a tall man could sink over the tops of his hip boots. Although I never heard of it happening at Duckville, I know of two cases where men have been trapped in soft mud and drowned—one in the shallow end of San Diego Bay, and the other on the edge of the Salton Sea in California's Imperial Valley. Ad Pearson told me that some of his hunters had had narrow escapes and had been trapped on the marsh overnight by falling tides or boats going adrift.

The tide was the key to this hunting, in fact to all hunting done in the tidal zone. At low water the channels were unusable by boat, and could not be crossed or followed safely on foot. Skiffs were used both for transportation and for dry platforms from which to shoot. After carefully placing their decoys, the hunters dug out small indentations just skiff-size in the banks at suitable locations near open water, ran the boats in and scattered weeds over them for camouflage, but of course had to watch the tide level carefully and leave before the water got too low to float the boat.

Another problem was recovering the ducks. Dogs could not be used successfully because of the soft mud, so the boat had to be shoved out promptly when ducks were down in the water, or the current would carry them away. Every effort was made to drop them on dry land. But despite all the problems, the hunting must have been spectacular, for there were thousands of ducks on the marshes and the bag limit was still twenty-five. Unfortunately for me, by the time I was old enough to own a shotgun and use it years later, Duckville and Ad Pearson were both gone and hunting was no longer permitted on Mission Bay.

I recently read an account of gunning on San Diego Bay in the 1880's. The hunters rowed across the open water from San Diego to the reedy and uninhabited shore of what is now the city of Coronado, concealed their skiff in the weeds, and filled their game bags from the huge flocks that constantly traded up and down the shore over the marsh growth that then lined the bay. Geese, brant, ducks and shorebirds of many species thrived on the vegetation and marine life there, and were practically unmolested by man even though market hunting was practiced on a limited scale until after the turn of the century.

By 1928, when I began to hunt on San Diego Bay, the marshlands were rapidly disappearing. A few mud flats remained around the northern curve of the harbor, while in the southern end of the bay, once containing acres of cord grass and brackish delta around the mouth of the Otay River, the marsh had been converted into a series of salt evaporation ponds, separated by a network of earthen dikes. The western shore still had a broad fringe of shallow flats and marsh growth along the Silver Strand almost to Coronado, a distance of over five miles, while several hundred acres remained at the mouth of the Sweetwater River halfway up the eastern shore. There were thousands of shorebirds feeding on the flats at low tide, and great flocks of ducks and brant fed on the eel grass and sea lettuce and gathered on the open waters of the bay.

In 1980, of the hundreds of acres of wetlands which had, in prehistoric times, nourished the waters of San Diego Bay and the adjacent ocean, only remnants at the mouth of the Sweetwater and a tiny patch at the south end of the strand remained, the latter designated the San Diego South Bay Marine Biology Study area. All the rest of the marshy shore that used to stretch along the Silver Strand behind the wind-sculptured dunes had been transformed—filled, graded and occupied by luxurious marina homes, a State Beach picnic park, a Navy Housing tract and the Naval Amphibious Base. The prolific tidal flats were gone, and with them the numerous flocks of curlew, willet, avocet and waterfowl that had darkened the sky a century before, and had been still abundant in my own lifetime.

In the summer of 1928 I had at last turned sixteen, received permission to own a duck gun and obtained a driver's license so that I could

230

use the family automobile on Saturdays. For five dollars I purchased from a friend a second-hand twelve-gauge shotgun, an old single-barreled, single-shot weapon that had seen better days but appeared to be mechanically sound. The seller threw in a khaki shell vest with loops to hold my shells. A box of these cost eighty-five cents for twenty-five cartridges, so they were never recklessly squandered.

My new gun consisted simply of a barrel, a stock and a trigger mechanism with a firing pin, cocking hammer and safety catch, with no provision for absorbing recoil. When fired it kicked like a mule, and the first time I loosed off a round at a rabbit in the valley below our house, I went reeling backward and almost fell down. Being of extremely light build at sixteen, I found it necessary to lean forward with my shoulder before pulling the trigger, as though trying to push open a swinging door with my arms full. At first these physical preparations seriously hampered my aim and reaction time, allowing the game to vanish before I could shoot, but eventually the strange, hunched firing position became automatic. I learned to plant the gun butt firmly against my shoulder, lean into it and pull the trigger, snatch another shell out of my fancy shell vest, reload and fire again, all in a time period as brief as those shooting double-barreled shotguns could manage.

Most duck hunters in my area went to the back country reservoirs to do their shooting, but there one had to buy a permit and rent a boat. The total outlay including gasoline and shells could run up into several dollars, placing such expeditions substantially beyond my financial reach. I did go hunting on the lakes a few times over the years, usually with friends, but I felt more at home on the saltwater marshes along the coast, and the hunting there was free.

My first ventures after I got my shotgun were to the south end of San Diego Bay, and if I report them in considerable detail it is because such activities are completely impossible in the changed world of today, whereas one can still hunt ducks on the lakes under conditions little changed from those of a half century ago, except for the greatly reduced numbers of birds. The salt ponds on the bay are still there and much the same, but hunting on them has been prohibited for many years. The Western Salt Company that operates them has been especially vigilant in keeping out trespassers, for their premises are used as breeding areas by Caspian terns in substantial numbers during the spring and early summer, and many shorebirds feed on the brine shrimp in the shallow lagoons, resources that are becoming rare in the region.

In 1928 the ponds were unposted, and hunters were tolerated if not welcomed. Shooting from shore there was uncomplicated but something less than highly rewarding. One simply walked out on the dikes until he felt that a strategic location had been reached, then hunkered down in the mud and pickleweed behind the dike and facing the open water of the bay, and waited for a suitable target to fly within range. There was no feed in the ponds, but in strong winds and at low tide when the water receded from the mud flats they offered sheltered resting places for waterfowl, and some of the less cautious species like bluebills, shovelers and buffleheads flew low across the dikes to land on the ponds. This kind of hunting was highly frustrating, for no matter where one elected to make his stand and regardless of how well he concealed himself, the birds invariably crossed just out of shotgun range on either side. If he moved, they flew over the place he had just left.

It was frustrating on another score, too. Waterfowl in those years rafted up by the thousands out on the open bay in plain sight. When shooting began on the lakes a few miles inland, literally clouds of ducks used to fill the sky and stream over the mesas and the bay shore, to take refuge on the open water. But even though this pageant of waterfowl was beautiful to behold in the sunrise, only a disappointingly small number of stragglers flew over the dikes and ponds.

I was frequently accompanied on later trips to the South Bay by Louis Blankenburg and his cousin, George Carter, who had inherited double-barreled shotguns from their elders, and were fledgling hunters as eager as I was. Our bags of ducks were usually meager, maybe two or three apiece, and seldom the most desirable of species. From time to time we were granted glimpses of waterfowling on a far higher and more fruitful plane, as veteran hunters in beautifully-crafted duckboats sculled silently in up the channel from the bay with their decks covered with limits of canvasback and pintail. I regarded these intrepid men with the same admiration and awe as today's youngsters might feel upon seeing astronauts striding by in their space suits, ready to take off for the moon.

These hunters had long, double-ended wooden sneak boats, decked over fore and aft and with small cockpits amidships. The cockpit coamings had canvas weatherclothes that could be raised in case of rough water. They drew only a few inches of water, and when the hunter lay down with his legs under the forward decking and worked his sculling oar back and forth gently and directly astern, the profile presented from head-on was hardly noticeable by a duck on the water, and certainly not alarming. The hunters could work their way down wind toward a raft of resting birds and be well within gun range before they were discovered. When the birds flew, the hunters raised up and fired Browning automatic shotguns, chambered for three-inch mag-

232

num shells. Boom—boom—boom—boom—boom. They could get off five rounds in less than three seconds and their aim was deadly. We would see a cloud of ducks rise in the distance, break up and circle around in smaller flocks while we waited with bated breath, shrinking down as small as possible behind our dike, hoping a few might swing in over the ponds. Occasionally they did, but our skill at wingshooting was so minimal and our chances so few that we owed more to luck than ability when a bird actually fell.

Early in my career as a duck shooter it became obvious to me that what we needed was a set of decoys, so that even if the birds didn't actually land in a pond, they might be influenced to fly over us instead of elsewhere up and down the dike at random. I made a half dozen out of short lengths of four-by-six redwood, roughly pointed at the tail end and rounded forward, and with silly little knobs for heads. When they were painted they didn't look too bad at a distance, and they were augmented by a few proper decoys we had found adrift.

Our success picked up immediately. With our modest little spread of decoys behind the dike on the pond nearest to the open bay, and a rough blind of driftwood boards and pickleweed, we began to enjoy a fair amount of success on bluebills and buffleheads, and even picked up an occasional pintail or widgeon. Once a flock of snow geese actually began to circle our decoys while we huddled shivering and quaking in our blind, afraid to move a muscle. They swung far inland over the other ponds, then came directly toward us, low and with their wings set. When they were only a couple of hundred yards away, a gun suddenly barked from behind another dike, one goose came spinning down, and the rest flared frantically amid an uproar of honking and screaming, and were soon out of sight. It would be impossible to exaggerate our disappointment and fury, since we believed it had been our decoys that had attracted the geese in the first place.

Another pressing need had soon made itself apparent. Sometimes we dropped one or more ducks in the winding tidal channel and saw them moved inexorably by the current downstream toward the open bay. When it had become obvious that the floating birds would not drift ashore or within reach, we solemnly drew straws like the members of A. Conan Doyle's Suicide Club. The loser had to disrobe, get into the icy water and swim out for the drifting birds, retrieve them, then pull on his clothes over his wet, muddy skin and sit shivering in the cold air for an hour or so. As the winter advanced this process seemed increasingly unsatisfactory to us.

I determined to build a duckboat in the back yard, not the elegant kind the scullers used, but something more modest and within my

233

slender resources. I got some sugar pine and laid out a kind of skeleton shaped like a pumpkin seed, bending thin boards for the sides and intending to cover the frame with heavy canvas nailed only on top so the nail holes wouldn't puncture the underwater parts. My reasoning was superior to my skill with hammer and saw. The frame came out lopsided, and when I started to stretch canvas over it, I realized for the first time that the covering would be a mass of unsightly pleats and folds. Nevertheless, I refused to destroy the boat's watertight integrity by cutting and sewing, so the sleek lines I had visualized never emerged, and the result was untidy, lumpy and bulging in places.

I bought a pair of oars and oarlocks, painted the boat a dark, manure-like brown to look like a mudbank, and carried the flimsy, misshapen object on top of the family Studebaker down to the bay for a shakedown cruise. When I had set it into the water, I was astonished to see how small and fragile it looked. Nevertheless, I carefully climbed in and shoved off. Despite its appearance it proved to be reasonably stable, and I could row it along with fair speed, although there seemed to be no suitable place for my knees, and they soon became black and blue from being knocked by the oars. I used the boat for several years on the bay and collected many ducks with it. Although it was an ungainly and even disgusting object to look at, I can't remember that it ever leaked a drop.

Hunting on the south end of San Diego Bay was never easy nor rewarded with limits of waterfowl, at least for us, but I have often thought we learned valuable lessons from our excursions. Sitting in the mud on bleak, icy mornings, sometimes in the rain, waiting hour after hour for the ducks that never came, clearly did little to improve our marksmanship, but it was magnificent training in how to suffer with patience and dignity.

A Christmas Eve Swan Shoot
by J. C. Bliss

Both trumpeter and tundra swans were prized by waterfowlers in the West. There seemed to be an especially avid swan hunting group in Portland, Oregon during the late 1800s. They shot along the backwaters of the Columbia River. This article was written in 1892, describing a hunt in 1883.

Shooting swan by night may seem hardly the correct thing in the estimation of many, but we fowlers of the wild and "feathery" West do not scruple to occasionally obtain under cover of the night what we cannot always acquire by the light of day. And so, at a friend's suggestion, it came about that he and I decided to put in a night after swan before they left us, perhaps forever.

It was in the early eighties and in Oregon that this deed of darkness was perpetrated. It had not been a good year for duck; the home-bred fowl (wood duck and mallard) had been pretty well "shot out" before the winter rains set in, by which the water fowl of the great Northwest are so innumerably augmented. And as these rains were very late in coming that year, our shooting so far had been considerably below the average, hence our nocturnal visit to the sanctuary of the swan.

Six or seven miles from Portland, on the Oregon side of the mighty Columbia, runs an immense piece of bottom land, known locally as the Columbia slough; and dotted here and there, at frequent intervals, along this bottom are numerous ponds and lakes, every one of which, in turn and season, is well tenanted with wild fowl. To the lakes, growing in the greatest profusion the succulent wapitou (a bulbous root of acorn shape and to the fowl of Oregon what the wild celery is to those of the Chesapeake), come the swan and canvasback, and, indeed, almost every other kind of water fowl, although only the swan and deep-water fowl of the canvasback species are able to dig the bulb from its tenacious mud bed, two to four feet below the surface. The other fowl (widgeon principally) ride gracefully at anchor close by the spot where some hungry canvasback has recently disappeared, and when it comes to the surface with the hard-earned spoil it is frequently only to be pounced upon and robbed by the thieving horde of shallow-water pirates waiting, hungry and alert, on the surface.

Cygnus Americanus also contributes materially to the levying fowl around him. His head and neck will disappear, followed soon after by a rocking motion of the body, as he excavates with his powerful feet the mud holding the precious root below. Lots of little tidbits thus freed from the bottom rise to the surface, to be immediately seized by the numerous tribe that follows in his wake.

One evening in December, 1883 (the night before Christmas), a farmer friend of mine, owning a milk ranch on the Columbia slough, drove to my home in East Portland and invited me to "get my gun and about a dozen shells and go with him to 'Old Dave's' place on the slough, for a whack at the swans." I had been duck shooting that day already, but I never refuse a good offer to shoot wild fowl, so long as I can keep an eye open or have a leg to stand on. So getting back again

236

into my long rubber boots and donning a couple of flannel shirts, my shooting jacket and overcoat, and taking a .12 gauge and twenty-five shells loaded with No. 3 shot, I jumped into the cart and we were soon on our way to the river bottom.

The "Old Dave" referred to was then a wealthy man, but a man, nevertheless, whom I have heard attribute his start on the road to wealth to the first piece of real estate he purchased from the sale of wild fowl that fell to his gun when land was cheap and ducks were plentiful. The lake we were bound for was known as "Old Dave's," from his monopoly of its shooting at the period referred to.

Half an hour's drive brought us to a long muddy lane leading to the lake in question. Presently the pony clattered over the log bridge spanning the last slough, and pulling up in a fence corner we threw a blanket over his steaming loins, and left him to a heap of hay and his ruminations.

My friend (whom we will designate as P.) had a .16 bore and No. 1 shot; not a gauge most fowlers would advocate for use on swan, but one that did good service nevertheless.

We first walked down to the lake's end and inspected the boat. It seemed to me like a much weather-beaten and frail old craft for two men to put out in, and so I expressed myself; but P. laughed at the idea, assuring me that, even if we did swamp, the deepest place in the lake was less than three feet; whereon I parenthetically added, "Deep enough, with twelve inches of mud added, to get thoroughly wet in." However, after caulking some of the seams with contributions from our handkerchiefs, we put off and pulled quietly through the many necks and loops of the lake's chain into the lake proper.

Presently P. ceased rowing, and, listening an instant, remarked "D'ye hear 'em?" Yes, I heard them; from away over in the bend of the lake, toward the timber, came, clear and distinct, the resonant call of *Cygnus Americanus*. "Now," said P., "tell you what we'll do. We'll pull ashore here, and I'll run and take a stand just this side the cottonwoods, while you scare 'em out. And, see here"—he added, emphatically, just before stepping from the boat—"if you hear me shoot have everything ready to pull out the moment I get back; for the hired man at Sunderland's will be down with a gun, sure, when he hears the shooting. Don't scare 'em out till I whistle," and he disappeared in the night.

It was now about ten o'clock; a peculiar night, not dark exactly, though no moon was visible, although she must have been riding high somewhere behind the fleecy, quick traveling clouds. Away across the lake could be heard the calling, flapping and splashing of the fowl we sought. A little breeze was stirring—the only element of the night that caused P. to steer for the cottonwoods, his instinct, born of that breeze, telling him, almost to a certainty, how the birds, upon being disturbed, would fly. The only other sound noticeable was the barking of some dogs from where a solitary light twinkled on the distant hill.

Ten minutes perhaps had passed, when a long, low whistle came from the vicinity of the dark line of cottonwoods. Now, how to raise the birds? I clapped and then called as loudly as I dared, when all sounds on the waters immediately ceased, but not a bird moved. There was but one other way I knew of to lift them from the shore, a very subtle and effective method, though not advisable as a rule—simply to strike a light. The lucifer burned within the hollow of my hands, and then at its instant of extreme lightness I exposed it. A moment's quiet supervened that in its intensity was almost oppressive; then there came a clanking roar from away out in the lake, and the swan were a-wing. A few moments later and the heavy beat of their many wings fell faintly on my ears as they filed complainingly out into the night. A few moments more and seemingly out from under the dark-blue line of the cotton-woods leaped in quick succession two flashes of flame, followed an instant later by two startling reports; then "thump, thump" as two heavy bodies struck the yielding earth, telling that the little .16 bore had not spoken in vain.

I held the boat's stern right ashore, and presently I could detect the rapid swish-wish of P.'s corduroys as he hurried over the sward; then his heavy breathing became perceptible, until at last his tall figure suddenly appeared at the lakeside, and, swinging two heavy swan off his shoulder into the boat, he gasped, "Pull out," and jumped in. Not knowing—and he being too winded to explain—whether he was pursued or not, I bent to the oars and pulled as vigorously as I considered the frail old craft would stand, and was soon beyond gunshot. I expected every moment to see some outraged individual open fire on us from the bank, but we were not molested. Presently, arriving at a small patch of tuleys about the middle of the lake, we decided to tie up there for the night; so pressing an oar into the mud we made fast, and placing the two swan in the water as decoys, we let them float whither they would, having nothing to set them up or secure them with.

An hour or more must have elapsed when we heard the beautiful call of approaching swan away off in the night. P., nothing daunted, lifted up his voice, and their answering calls came nearer and nearer. "If they come over," whispered P., "you take the leaders and I'll look after the rest." At judicious intervals P. would call, and I could not help but admire his clear, flute-like voice as it went echoing through the night.

238

Presently P. seized an oar and, with a whispered "Look out," commenced to rock the water violently over the boat's side, "calling" vigorously the while. Passing my thumb between the hammers and strikers to be reassured of their position, I prepared myself. As P. ceased his call and commotion there came clear and distinct from the heavens above us the purring-like whistle of the deluded fowl. "Let 'em circle, let 'em circle," whispered P., "they'll come right down to the decoys if we let 'em." We could now hear the beat of their wings, and as they passed a lighter patch in the clouds overhead I counted five of the noble birds.

Another well-timed call or two from P., a cordial response, and their line was broken, and three, with wings steadily set, slanted down to the decoys, now some distance away from the boat. Two seemed hardly satisfied yet and took another turn around to my left, when, feeling that the supreme moment had arrived, I pulled on the first and as quickly as possible swung on the second, which, with a wing snapped close to the body, whirled round and round like a windmill and struck the water with terrific force within a dozen yards of the boat. Hastily reloading, I stopped my first bird as it flapped noisily along the surface of the water, and P. winged a third from away out over the decoys. In our haste to recover the game the oar in the mud was snapped at the blade, but with the remaining one as a paddle and a couple of timely shots P.'s cripple was secured, the other two gathered, and we returned to our station.

The two decoys had seemingly stranded, so we left them where they were. Only their bodies were visible, their heads and necks under water; but at night they were just as attractive as any other mute decoy would be, however shapely and good looking.

Deciding that no swan would come in again for a while, we lighted our pipes and made ourselves comfortable. The renewed barking of the dogs away on the hill, and the occasional hurried beat of wings as some smaller fowl hurried by, were the only sounds which broke the stillness. After the warmth and excitement had abated somewhat it seemed to get awfully cold. We buttoned our coats around us, but were soon so cold that our pipes shook between our teeth.

One of the three swan was lying in the boat at my feet and a touch of warmth therefrom seemed to penetrate my boot. Leaning forward I pulled the heavy fowl toward me, and observed that both its wings were broken. Grasping the bird by the neck I slung its body over my back; it seemed to lie there admirably. Then taking a wing in each hand I drew them under my arms and crossed them over my breast. Then giving the beautiful, boa-like neck a twist around my own I laid my gun

239

across my knees, folded my arms over the wings and complacently awaited the result of my experiment. Soon a subtle warmth pervaded my whole body and I was deliciously comfortable. P. requested me to "take off the ghost-like apparition." I suggested that he try the idea himself, and then, as far as appearances went, we should at least be equal. I was perfectly satisfied with mine. He tried it, and although "his wings" were a trifle untractable, being unbroken, he finally "fixed" them, and ten minutes after he was snoring soundly.

It must now have been early morning—Christmas morning. The fleecy clouds of earlier night had become heavier and darker, and the moon at her highest altitude was barely distinguishable at all and shed little or no light on the darkling waters that flip-flapped restlessly against the sides of the gently-rocking boat. The warmth of my downy quilt, supplemented by the slow-dying heat of the swan's body, induced sleepiness, and, in a moment of unconsciousness, I fell asleep. How long, I know not, but my dreams were angelic. Sleep had transported me into other realms, where the air seemed filled with soft musical sounds and seraphic forms floated lightly about me. Suddenly my own garb of snowy whiteness fell from me and I seemed to be rushing back to the "cold" earth with terrible velocity, fetching up in the boat (at that agonizing instant when annihilation seemed certain) with a start and shiver that waked me most effectually. Snow was falling in large, downy flakes, and around and above us the air was indeed alive with forms as nearly angelic in their beauty, whiteness and purity as deign to visit us here below.

Presently, from away to my right, came a clear, bugle-like call, and I knew that a magnificent bird was afloat somewhere in the air above me.

Almost like an echo to the call came another from the far left, and yet more distant bugles sounded softly over the lake. Fate had played us one of her kindest pranks, and more by good luck by anything else we had located in the best spot of all for sport under the existing conditions.

We were evidently upon their feeding grounds, and I was beginning to conjure up in imagination the pile of game we might have down and around us when morning dawned, if we only played our cards right. Reaching forward I was endeavoring to waken my sleeping companion with as little noise as possible, when a swan suddenly appeared off to my left. I could hear the beat of its wings and dimly discern its form, as it headed straight for the boat. Dropping on one knee I prepared to receive him. As I raised the gun to shoot I became conscious also of another bird approaching rapidly from behind, but sticking to the first, which I felt sure was the noble trumpeter, I pulled; then, without waiting an instant to see the result of my shot, I swung around on the other, now presenting a beautiful side shot. As I touched the trigger a body went rushing past my head and behind me, with a screech that was positively maniacal, and so close as to actually touch me with its wing. A sharp collision, a tilt of the boat, and men, guns, swan and all were pitched unceremoniously into the chilly water. I knew how it all happened, for I saw enough of it to know. Excruciatingly uncomfortable as the cold ducking was, I could not help laughing at P.'s gasping and rude awakening from what perhaps but an instant before had been the sweetness of sleep and pleasantest of dreams.

Whether he thought we had been struck by a typhoon or a whirlwind I could never satisfactorily learn; in fact, he told me afterward, confidentially, that he imagined he was "home, and that the house was on fire." As we stood there waist deep on water, clutching our craft, consisting now of but a side, stern piece and bottom, I explained, as well as my chattering teeth would permit, the cause of the catastrophe, and requested P. to hold on to the boat while I fished up the guns. But owing to the deepness and tenacity of the mud I could not do this alone, so we two sorry-looking specimens tilted the boat until her keel was formed by the angle of one side and the bottom, then baling the remains of her out as well as we could with my cap (for P.'s had disappeared), I manipulated her from the stern while P. stood clinging affectionately to an oar he had thrust in the mud. Steering cautiously about the "scene of the wreck," I soon felt a gun with my foot, and reaching down, until my nose was almost under water, I recovered and placed it in the boat. It was my own, but P.'s was stepped on a minute later and recovered. Then I cruised around and picked up our dead swan and the so forcibly ejected side of the skiff. Upon the latter I "laid out" the dead, and there, in the middle, looming up larger than any of the rest, and with an awful gaping wound extending across the breast from wing to wing, lay my beautiful trumpeter, the cause of our cruel collapse. With both wings broken close to its body, it had fallen from high in air an inert mass, and its heavy body had struck with resistless force the inside upper edge of the boat's side, dashing it from its fastenings; and as swan and timber went by the board on the port side, we were as unceremoniously tumbled out on the other.

Each now taking hold we waded ashore at the nearest point; then, having no further use for our craft, we cast her adrift, and shouldering our game started for the pony and cart.

Oh, how cold it was during those few minutes it occupied us to reach the farm house. Soon we reached P.'s home. Just as we dashed in the early milkman was in the act of raising a cup of hot coffee to his lips, but it never reached there; for, whether through astonishment or not, he replaced it on the table, while he contemplated our appearance with open-mouthed surprise. I meanwhile thoughtfully seized his cup and shared its hot, fragrant contents with my unfortunate comrade.

Calling California Ducks
by R. P. Holland

Holland was the famed editor of FIELD & STREAM from 1924 until 1941. This 1913 article was among the first he ever wrote. He was an easterner, and rarely crossed the Mississippi during most of his life. This California account is based on one of his few times in the West.

The first thing I heard on arriving in the State where the sun shines on both sides of the fence for three hundred and sixty-six days in each year was that unless a fellow was a member of a gun club, or was lucky enough to be invited by a member of some club to join him on a hunt, it was impossible to get anything like good duck shooting. And this in a country where there are more ducks, or at least as many ducks, as any other place in the world. The more I inquired the more hopeless it began to appear. All the ponds and lakes were either owned outright by the clubs or controlled by leases. These clubs varied in size from a two-acre pond up to clubs containing thousands of acres.

Get on any of the interurban cars in Los Angeles and as you are swept out through the country you will pass innumerable sloughs and ponds, and on nearly all of them you will see ducks of many different varieties. These ducks scarcely look up as the car rushes by, and you think to yourself how tame they are and what a wonderful country to hunt in. But as you look again you will notice that all these ponds and sloughs are fenced and on every third or fourth post is a little sign. That there is reading on this little square of canvas is plainly seen, and the conductor tells you that it is a gun club, and that if you were close enough to read the sign you would be informed of how many different things the law can do to you if you step across this fence.

Like all questions, there are two sides to this gun-club argument. To which side a man belongs is generally determined by which side of the fence he is on. All outsiders are called road-hunters by the club members, for the reason that on shoot days in the clubs when the ducks are driven from one club to another or out to the ocean, you will find all the roads running by these clubs well supplied with hunters who give the ducks a parting volley as they pass out. One of these road hunters told me that he had been invited once to shoot with a club-member and that it was simply slaughter. The ducks are fed twice a week in most of the bigger clubs, and shot twice a week. This man told me that in front of each blind about twenty yards was a table on which the ducks were fed. This table was made just flush with the water, and when the grain was placed on it the birds could climb out of the water, up on the boards to eat.

Naturally, when the ducks came in, they would come straight to these tables, looking for food, and instead would be bowled over by Mr. Clubman, who was sitting comfortably waiting for just the very thing. My friend told me that this club prided itself on the fact that its by-laws prohibited the use of decoys as unsportsmanlike. I believe that the last legislature of California prohibits the "baiting" of wildfowl in gun clubs, and if this is the case I will warrant that these same club-members

244

will feel that it is sportsmanlike to use decoys. Many scientists claim that birds and beasts can not reason, that whatever they do out of the ordinary is due to instinct. Whether it is reason or instinct, it is wonderful to watch these club ducks loaf around, within ten feet of the club fence, as though there was no such thing as a shotgun. But again should he wish to cross that fence to an adjoining club, you will find that he goes a good hundred yards up before he chances it.

Should you talk very long to a club-member, he will tell you that the road hunter is usually a rascal of some sort or other who hangs around the fence in the hope of getting a cripple, in the meantime shooting at everything that passes over, no matter how high, thereby ruining the shooting of the club-members. Most of these clubs shoot on the same days of the week, namely, Tuesdays and Saturdays. The other five days the ducks are left at peace. For this reason alone I claim the clubs are a good thing, for without them in a country as thickly settled as this part of California a duck would know no rest. Also, much of this club land would be drained and made to produce crops, were it not that it is set aside for the ducks and the sport of shooting them.

One of the largest clubs in that section is supposed to contain 3,700 acres of land and water. Of this amount perhaps 1,000 acres are water. A great deal of the land is very valuable as celery land, and were it not for the club-members, it would undoubtedly all be drained for this purpose. I was told that the initiation fee in this club was $20,000.00, and that the annual dues were $1,000.00 per member. As there are forty members this gives them $40,000.00 a year for running expenses; and my informant told me there had never been a year that they did not have to make a re-assessment. In the year 1912 the expenses ran to $70,000.00; so, you see, this gun-club business is not exactly a poor man's game. This one properly controls five miles of ocean frontage.

My friend the duck-hunter had told me in his last letter that if all went well he would be out to take a good old hunt with me in California, and I was trying my best to get things fixed up before I should receive a letter saying what train he would be on. I knew that as an old-timer he would not enjoy standing out in a road taking long shots at high ducks as they passed over. Neither did I have the necessary to buy a club of my own. The only thing to do was to find some salt-water bay and try to decoy some of the club ducks when they passed over, going to the ocean. The clubs are not allowed to fence off any navigable water, therefore bays and rivers are all that are left for the decoy hunter.

Newport Bay seemed to me to be the best place I could find, although the natives told me that no one had ever had any success there in shooting over decoys. When the ducks pass out over the bay to go to the

245

ocean, they are too high and will not notice the stools. Still, what more could I do? To all appearances this place was ideal. The salt marsh extended for six or seven miles back into the country, and beyond this was a gun club in which there were thousands of ducks. On days when they shot in the club all of these ducks passed out over the bay to rest on the ocean until the big noise was over. I had all the confidence in the world in my old friend the duck-hunter and his ability to call some few of those ducks to our decoys. At least, I would bring him up here and let him try it once, and if we couldn't kill any we would join the ranks of the road-hunters, or hire one of the many motor-boats rented to shooters who satisfy the lust for blood by slipping up on a bunch of unsuspecting ruddies or coots and potting them as they try to leave the water.

The duck-hunter arrived in good time, and I laid the plans before him and told him that in my heart I was afraid of results. His reply that unless they were different from any other ducks he had ever seen we would get some of them did not ease my mind to any great extent. There was no use in our going until Tuesday, when I was told they would shoot in the club. So on Monday night we fixed everything in readiness, and long before the first sign of day had lightened the east we were chugging up the bay in a little motor-boat. It was just beginning to get light when our engineer told us that he could go no farther with the motor, and that we would have to get into the skiff which we had towed with us.

While we were still rowing through the shallow water toward the club, we heard the first shot fired, and literally thousands of ducks raised into the air and began circling, while others cut straight out over our heads for the ocean. "Fair enough," said the duck-hunter. "We have their line of flight now, so let's get over to this north bank as quickly as possible and get our decoys out."

Over we went, and while he set the decoys to suit himself, which in past years I had found always suited the ducks, I busied myself with the blind. But, say, you fellows who have cut willows by the wagon-load and pulled slough grass by the armful in order to hide yourself from the ducks should have seen the material I had to work with. The day before I had spoken to Joe, our boatman, about a blind, and he had told me to leave it all to him and he would have the material in the boat, so that I would not have to bother with it in the morning. His word was as good as his bond, for there in the bottom of the boat lay six big palm leaves, with the ends all sharpened to stick in the ground. They were dry and just the color of the dead grass behind us. Such a blind! I never saw a better one; two leaves in front, two behind, and one for each end and your blind was completed.

With blind all built and decoys set, we were ready for the ducks; that is, I was all ready—the duck-hunter was not. He was out at the edge of the water soaking his duck call, to take the rattle out of it, he said. No, indeed, not one of the boughten kind, but a homemade affair, made from a piece of hard maple, grown right on his farm back on the old Missouri River. As he raised up from the water and put the call to his mouth to try it out, I noticed a bunch of bald-crowns weave and dip as the sound of the call reached them, and my heart was glad, for I had confidence in this man and his duck call. In years gone by I had seen him perform wonders with it and the sound of it once more brought back old memories of hunts where the ducks actually acted as though they wanted to get into the blind with us, so anxious were they to find the call.

"All set," said the duck-hunter. "Let's see what that old mallard thinks about it." And with that he commenced to call, first the long mallard call, sharp and very loud, and as the duck approached he kept up the same call, lowering it as the bird drew nearer; then, all at once, he changed the music into the clucking feed-call of the mallard hen. This was too much for our green-headed friend high in the air, and with set wings he swung out over the open water in front of us, circled, and started straight back for the decoys. As he slid in over the outer edge of the decoys, the duck-call by my side ceased its noise and everything was quiet except the whispering quack of the old drake as he sailed over the decoys, looking at each one carefully to see where the caller was located. "Take him," said my friend, and before I stopped to think that he was my guest it was too late, and the first California duck had fallen to the wiles of that Missouri duck-call.

"Fair enough again," said my friend. "If they all fall to it as easy as he did, I don't think we will have much trouble getting a mess for to-morrow's dinner." Another volley was fired in the club grounds, and fifty or more bald-crowns jumped from the grass just the other side of the club fence and started for the ocean. "Here come the next victims," and he fairly crowded the words out of his mouth with the duck-call. It was the same old long mallard call as before, and it seemed to be making an impression on the widgeons, for as they passed over us fully two hundred yards high you could plainly hear them whistling in answer to the call. Still they did not lower their flight, but held straight on for the ocean.

When about three hundred yards down the bay from us a little squad of five or six was seen to leave the bunch and start back up the bay. It was then the call was again changed to the feeding call with an occasional rasping quack of the widgeon. Straight they came; their minds had been made up before they had made the turn. All of them whistling, it seemed as though they were racing to be the first one there. Were they surprised when the first shot rang out? I owned the second shot and I know only that it went at least three feet under the duck I had intended it for. Can a widgeon get away fast? The duck-hunter says they can outclimb any duck on the getaway, and whatever he says about ducks is law.

We were not so lucky with the next flock or two of bald-crowns that came out of the club, and had to be content with watching them wing their way on to the ocean. "Here comes a bunch of blue-wings," and the duck-hunter commenced to talk teal talk as fast as he could. Everything seemed to be going nicely, when of a sudden he stopped calling.

"What are they?" he exclaimed. "They are not blue-wings."

"Cinnamons," I replied. "The same talk will do the work, with maybe a little variation of spoonbill occasionally."

"New ones to me," he answered, and the music was continued. The interval that had elapsed was time enough for the little rascals to think it over and they had decided that while it sounded pretty good, all was not well. With a circle or two they slid into the water about a hundred yards out from the decoys. And there they sat, perfectly motionless, with heads held high, looking straight at the decoys.

Now was an opportunity for real work with the duck call. It was evident that they wanted to come, still you could see that they were more or less frightened, perhaps by the calling having stopped so suddenly and then starting again. One false note would send them skyward, for they were all attention and on their toes ready for a jump. First he tried several little blue-wing calls, then a clear spoonbill call, followed by the contented chuckle of the feeding shoveler. Apparently these little red-breasted teal hadn't moved a muscle; none of the calls seemed to have the least effect on them.

The whole list was tried over several times with an occasional high-pitched green-wing call. I had about given up all hope of ever pulling the wool over the eyes of these wise little fellows, when I felt a jab in the side, and, looking out through the peephole in the blind, I saw that they were swimming in. For twenty-five yards they swam straight for us; then, with a short little quack, one of the hens jumped into the air. In a second they were all up and coming straight for us. Had it not been for the shotguns they would have passed the decoys and lit almost at our feet, so anxious were they to find the owner of that coaxing voice.

Could anyone ask for better shooting than this? The next bunch of bald-crowns that passed over gave up two of their members to the combined influence of the call and the decoys. As they left the flock and swung over the decoys we decided to let them light, with the hope that maybe the flock would wheel and come back. But not so; on to the ocean they went, leaving two of their number sitting perfectly at ease among our decoys. "Now watch them beat it," said the duck-hunter, and with that he let out a regular Comanche yell and at the same time tossed his cap high in the air. Did it scare them? You know what I said a while ago about a bald-crown climbing. Well, those two were among the foremost athletes in the bald-crown family. They seemed to spring fully ten yards into the air before they ever began to fly, and I think they were easily from twenty-five to thirty yards high when the shot reached them, and we were doing our best to get them as quickly as possible.

We next tried our luck on a little bunch of blue-bills we had seen light way out in the middle of the bay. If we could only make them hear we could probably swim them over, although it was a long way. Did you ever hear a blue-bill's call? It is a cross between the quack of a duck and the "caw" of a crow with a guttural roll mixed in. My friend could do it better than a blue-bill could himself, and he was doing his best to attract their attention. We had noticed a motor coming up the bay, and it was evident that they also had seen the blue-bills, for they had altered their course and were now headed straight for them. While I have always contended that this motor-boat shooting was unfair to the game, I must admit that with the exception of the poor little ruddies the Pacific coast ducks have the business down to a fine point. When the boat was still a good hundred and fifty yards away from them up came the blue-bills and straight for us they headed. As they neared us we could see that there were eight of them, four hens and four drakes. Right over the decoys they swept.

"Rough the drakes first," I heard whispered in my ear, and the drakes were surely roughed.

Back behind us was a sort of marsh before the hills began, which was covered by the high tides twice each day. When we had set the decoys in the morning this had been free from water, but now the tide had raised until we were all but run out of our blind, and behind us the water was knee deep. The shooting had about ceased in the club, and it looked as though we might as well pull out for home. The duck-hunter had waded out behind the blind to try and find a wing-tipped widgeon hen he had lost earlier in the day, when I looked up and saw a nice little bunch of sprigs coming out of the club. Calling to him, I ducked into the blind to await developments. Immediately he opened up on them with the long mallard call and the rasping, squeaky quack of the sprig thrown in. Did they answer it? You should have seen them sweep down toward the water. Now was the time when I must do myself proud. In the blind alone and here came eighteen or twenty big sprigs right at me.

But were they coming right at me? Believe it or not, they were paying no attention to the decoys, but had sailed out over the grass behind me and were planning to light as near as possible to where the duck-hunter crouched in the weeds. And when he raised up and went after them with that old pump he did better than I would have done, and I also got one when they passed out over me. Funny how you can hear some fellows argue that a duck-call is a detriment instead of help in decoying ducks, fellows that have hunted a great deal, too, and know the game. All I can say for them is that they are mistaken, and I hope that each and every one of them will some day have the opportunity of hunting with a man who knows how to call.

Duck Shooting
in Southern California
by Bruce Douglas

Written in 1893, this article is documentation of what waterfowling in California once was.

C ount H.'s shooting-trap stood at the door as we came out from luncheon. It was only a matter of a dozen miles or so to the ranch, and as we had no wish to arrive there before four o'clock, we could afford to take our time, and let the tough little mustang make his own pace. There had been no rain to speak of since April, and we were then in November, with a hot sun and a blue sky over our heads, and a road several inches deep in sand to pull through. This fact didn't seem to bother Jack (the mustang) in the least, however, and he jogged along contentedly at a five-mile an hour gait. I smoked, of course, but, *mirabile dictu!* his Excellency, although an Austrian and a sportsman, was not a devotee of tobacco.

"Are you asleep, Harrie?"

"No, only dreaming, Jaro. Why?"

"Oh, nothing. Only I haven't heard a sound from you for twenty minutes, at least. I didn't know but that pipe had sent you off to Elysium."

"Souls don't sleep, do they, Jaro? and as for Elysium, it's a state hardly in correspondence with this road, even though a fellow has a pipe and good tobacco."

"Are you going to pull up here at the gunsmith's?"

"Yes; he has some shells for me."

We were in Santa Ana. Our road had been through a long avenue of eucalyptus and pepper trees and over a level country smiling with glowing orange groves, and radiant with vineyards heavy with purple and creamy clusters of ripened grapes.

Santa Ana was trying hard to be a city, but had not as yet succeeded.

From Santa Ana on, the road grew rougher till within about two miles of the ranch, when we turned off to the left, and drove about a mile across an alkali plain to the laguna. There was a chance of finding a few duck here, and possibly some plover in the newly sown grain fields. I had thrown a couple of shells into my gun, when as we came around a clump of dwarf willows there was a low whistle from the Count, and from the freshly plowed field on our right up got a bunch of gray wings, which, taking a circle, offered me a very long snap shot.

I let 'em have both barrels in quick succession, almost before the Count had brought Jack to a standstill, and was rather surprised than otherwise to see several distant bunches of feathers come to earth. Tipperary (the Count's Gordon setter) leaped the irrigating ditch and shortly came back with a couple of fine plover in his mouth. We sent him back again and again, until he had retrieved in all five birds.

"I'll drive you round the edge of the laguna, Harrie, and we'll send 'Tip' on ahead; there may be an occasional duck, but I don't think it's

252

worth while to get out, because it's half-past three now and we ought to be at the ranch by four so as to get over to the marsh by five. The ducks will be coming in by that time, and we must be on the ground first and well hidden in the tulas, or else good-bye to our luck for to-day."

I picked off a few single birds here, a brace of red-heads, a green winged teal, and three mallard, and then passed my gun to the Count and took the reins as his face began to twitch with excitement as I dropped the mallard.

Jaro did even better, for as we rounded the last curve of the laguna, there was a loud splashing in the water, and a flock of geese followed by at least a dozen canvas-back, got up within easy range. Jaro gave it to them right and left, paying no heed to the geese but playing havoc with the duck, four coming down to his two barrels. The rest of the flock swung round in a wide circle and came back, as they sometimes will, over the spot they had left. This gave Jaro time to reload, and as they swept by with a rush of wings he brought down three more, which made our bag so far foot up five plover, a brace of red-head, three mallard, one teal and seven fine canvas-back.

Not a bad half hour's work, and we felt amply compensated for the couple of miles or so we had taken out of our course to the laguna.

A route was now chosen directly across country for the ranch. In doing this we met the difficulties of driving over alfalfa patches literally honeycombed with ground-squirrel burrows, and usually divided by irrigating ditches, which once or twice Jack made very decided objections to wading.

But we at last struck the road leading into the ranch, and in less than five minutes afterward drew rein before the low frame house.

Tipperary had already begun his usual row with the farm dogs, and at the noise Glynes (the man kept there by the Count to work the ranch) came out to greet us and take charge of the pony and trap.

As quickly as possible we pulled on our rubber wading boots, and taking the trail which led through the cornfield and alfalfa patches, in a half hours' time we arrived at the edge of the marsh just as the sun was dropping out of sight away over to the westward behind rocky Catalina.

At the first pool we came to, and before we even reached the slough, Jaro plucked me by the arm, while from the other side a big flock of geese rose above the tula with a roar of wings and a startled honking and sailed off. We both blazed away but they had flown out of range, and only a few white feathers came floating down as recompense for the powder wasted.

The ball had been opened, however, a trifle sooner than we anticipated, and from all sides sounded a frightened quacking and loud splashing of the water, as the duck that had already come in and settled down on their nightly feeding ground in the wild celery rose at the report of our guns. A number came down again if anything quicker than they got up, and presently several brace of duck, mallard, teal and widgeon were sought out by Tip's unerring nose and brought to bag. We now moved ahead very cautiously, as the quacking of the undisturbed duck still feeding on the succulent celery could be plainly heard.

In this country, at this season, duck, and in fact most varieties of water fowl are very abundant. The entire coast line, ranging from San Pedro on the north to San Diego on the south, is indented with an almost uninterrupted line of inlets, or, as they are called here, lagunas and sloughs, which are simply long or short arms of the sea stretching away inland.

Many grain fields lie within easy access of the marshes, and afford excellent feeding grounds throughout the day; while, at sunset, the birds fly back to the sloughs, where they pass the night resting and feeding on the wild celery which grows in great abundance wherever there is water.

This latter vegetable gives to the flesh a peculiar and delicious flavor, and even the tough old widgeon loses much of his fishy and oily taste, and is vastly improved, after enjoying for any length of time a diet of this kind.

The sun had left us and the wind from the sea came sharp and cold in our faces, the Count called Tipperary "to heel," and carefully watching each step, as there was every possibility of one of us stepping into some slough in the dusk, we separated to take up our stations at the arms of two large sloughs which last experience had proved to be favorite feeding grounds, and which commanded strategic positions.

The ducks were beginning to come in rapidly, they were flying high, but we could hear the sound of their wings like the whizzing of balls above us, and their shadowy bodies were dimly visible in the gloaming of the fast approaching night.

It must be quick work if we would have anything to show, as barely more than thirty minutes of shooting light were left. They were coming from the south and would reach the Count's stand first, and on getting his fire, would probably sheer over in my direction. The Count called out: "When it's time to stop, I'll give the signal by three blasts on an empty brass shell, then you take a course about three points southeast of the pole star and we'll meet about here."

"All right, Jaro, only don't go too far inland without me, because I'm not up in astronomical bearings as you are, and I'll be hanged, as often

254

as I've been down here, if this marsh, after the sun leaves it, isn't always a trifle worse to me than ever before. I've no particular fancy for spending the night on a tula hummock in this temperature."

But where are the duck? Not a call, not a wing, not a sound of any kind.

On the western horizon still lingered a few streaks of brilliant vermilion against the back-ground of rich gray fast merging into pale transparent blue; and a single glittering star seemed to rest on the frowning summit of Catalina, which was mantled in soft black tones.

But all this, while suggesting poetical fancies and producing a charming picture, was not what "my soul craved," and I turned from it with disappointment and pulled my pipe from my pocket for solace. How long the time seemed. My ears and eyes were strained to a pitch of nervous tension that fairly made them ache with expectancy. Every minute that passed seemed of an hour's length, and yet, while the time seemed to drag, I was nervously anxious lest the night should fall and render shooting out of the question. My position, crouched in the tulas on a hummock surrounded by four or five feet of water, was the reverse of comfortable. My hands were like icicles as they clasped the cold steel barrels, and yet I hardly dared moved, not knowing what instant the ducks might come.

Altogether, what was in reality only about fifteen minutes, seemed the longest hour I had ever passed. I had almost given up hope, and had recklessly risen to my feet to stretch my legs, when two reports in quick succession rang out from the direction of the Count's stand. I think they were the most cheering sounds that have come to my ears. In an instant, hope, anticipation and glorious expectancy glowed like magic, and with the sudden reaction I dropped my pipe, and almost tumbled off the hummock in saving it from the water. The gun went to my shoulder, as to my ears came the welcome rush of wings, and as I glanced quickly up and southward, I saw a disintegrated mass of black forms coming at what seemed lightning speed directly toward me.

I let them have right and left, and then foolishly jumped from the hummock to retrieve my birds. In doing this I lost the next flock, which saw me and wheeled before getting within range. Then came two more reports from the Count's gun; so, grabbing up a couple of birds near to hand, I leaped back to my quarters in the tulas, just in time to greet the next arrivals, and dropped three.

The shooting now became of the fast and furious order, the echo of Jaro's gun being caught up and continued by the report of mine. After thirty minutes, in which time I had shot at least twenty rounds and heated the light barrels of the twelve-gauge, the third finger of my right

255

hand and my gun shoulder began to feel the effect of such sharp work. What at the outset had been sport had become almost an *embarras de riches*. Everything outside of a certainty I let go by me. And, really, the murk had grown so dense that any object a dozen yards away blended as a confused mass with the atmosphere.

So, I was not sorry to hear the three faint calls made by the Count blowing on the rim of an empty brass shell, and after some difficulty in locating from the surrounding nebulæ the pole star, I jumped with stiff joints from the hummock and, following the Count's directions as to bearings, soon came up with him about where we had separated.

"Good sport, eh Harrie? We'll let Tip pick up what birds he can find and leave the rest till morning, as, honestly, I'm both tired and cold."

The dog had retrieved most of the birds that had fallen to his master's gun and Jaro was literally loaded down. We moved on to a comparatively dry spot, and, sitting on a hummock, waited in the cold starlight for the well-trained animal to bring in the slain.

At last we grew tired, and Tip was pretty well fagged himself. So, stringing the birds by the neck, and cutting a stout sapling, we tied them to it, and each taking an end, "packed" them over the mile and a half of hard tramping to the ranch.

There were thirty-seven and a half brace to the two guns, that we fetched in; with probably half as many again still in the marsh. Widgeon, red head, and black head predominated, but with enough mallard, teal, and canvas-back to well pay us for our work. Glynes was delighted with our success and bustled about cleaning the guns, and providing for our comfort.

I was very tired and glad to turn in, and when Jaro's repeater struck three o'clock in the morning, and he reached over and shook me, with "Come, Harrie! it's time to be stirring," it seemed to my half-awakened senses that I had hardly slept an hour.

Glynes was ready with a bite of food, and in the gray of the early dawn we faced again the cold wind from the sea, and took up our positions of the night before. We now waited for the ducks to leave the sloughs for the grain fields.

Our morning's work was a repetition of the past night's, with this satisfactory difference—we had plenty of light, and our shooting was more removed from the pot-hunter type. I don't remember now the exact number of birds bagged, but there were more than we cared to pack with us to the ranch.

Away off to the westward lay Catalina, sparkling in the flood of golden sunlight, like a huge topaz on the bosom of the blue Pacific. To the northward and the eastward towered old "Baldy" and Wilson's peak, wearing their spotless mantles of the first snow of the season. The rich perfume of the vineyards and orange orchards came to us on the soft breeze.

We bowled merrily through the avenue of eucalyptus, and almost before I was aware of it, Jack pulled up short in front of the hotel. As the boys came out to take in the traps and birds, and half a dozen pretty girls rushed up to us with a dozen questions asked in many charming ways, Jaro turned to me as he stood for a moment on the broad piazza, with, "Not a bad twenty-four hours, was it, Harrie?"

And as I looked around me at the glowing landscape, at the form, the color, the life before me, and thought for one fleeting second of the happiness I had known in this land, the answer came straight from my heart, "No, Jaro; not bad, old fellow. How could it be, and still be California?"

Duck-Driving at Sweetwater Lake
by Ernest McGaffey

S.C.

This account, written in the early 1920s, documents a once very popular method of duck hunting in southern California.

To the old, dyed-in-the-wool duck-shooter, the sport of wild-fowling is usually associated with shooting over decoys, either from blinds or from a battery. Other modes of pursuit are pass shooting, and jumping ducks from a small boat or wading in rubber hip-boots where the water is shallow enough in sloughs or around the edges of the smaller lakes. But in far western waters a new wrinkle has been added to this program in the shape of duck-driving. Driven grouse are shot in immense numbers on the English and Scottish moors, and the butts, or places of concealment, are so skillfully distributed that the birds are not too difficult to bring within range.

My own duck-shooting experiences have covered many years and a wide range of country. They have included Massachusetts and New Hampshire ponds, with black duck (dusky mallard) shooting, Louisiana and Arkansas swamps for mallards and teal, Minnesota and Wisconsin lakes for canvas-back and red-heads, the Mississippi Valley in Iowa, Illinois and Indiana for mallards, pintail, blue-bill, wood-ducks, ring-bill, and many other varieties of ducks, British Columbia for golden-eye, scoters, harlequin ducks, buffle-heads, mallards, and widgeon, and lastly in Southern California, where almost every known species of ducks comes in during the shooting season.

It was here that I had my first dip in the mysteries of the duck drive. They do it here on a grand scale, and they get results. Every man who has shot ducks has occasionally slipped up slowly on ducks feeding in a narrow cove and induced them to fly back to the main waters of a lake in such a way as to afford him a shot, but here the scheme is scientifically handled by twenty or thirty shooters lined up abreast.

At Sweetwater Lake, near the City of San Diego, and reached from there in about half an hour over velvet-smooth boulevarded highways, fine shooting is had in this particular line, and it was there we headed for one bracing November morning. Duck drives at Sweetwater are quite a society event at times, the Army and Navy officers being sometimes specially invited to be the guests of the day. Twenty-gauge guns are mostly used, with an occasional sixteen. Boats are expected to go up the lake in fairly regular order at something like regular distances apart. As the ducks rise and come back they scatter and fly high and the use of the small-gauge guns means picking your bird and giving him the center of the charge. It was the most difficult of all the duck-shooting I have ever known, for the shots were made when the birds were in full swing and flying very high.

Sitting behind a blind and calling in mallards, or shooting blue-bills, red-heads, or canvas-backs as they come swinging in and slowing up to decoys is dead easy as compared to this style of shooting. Fifty, sixty, and seventy yards are the average ranges, and with the ducks coming lickety-split overhead, it takes the acme of skill and experience to get your birds. Not many birds are killed at seventy yards, it is true, but some are, and you never get those thirty and thirty-five yard shots with the ducks spreading out their wings and dropping their legs as they do when settling to decoys.

The Sweetwater is without any timber on its banks, a few straggling trees some distance away being all that is visible. There is some growth of tules sufficient for blinds at a few points along the shore, but shooting over decoys is an apparently uncertain proposition for these waters. By driving only two days in each week, the birds are not in the least burned out by over-shooting, and many thousands of them come and go without having been molested in the slightest.

The Federal Migratory Bird Act has unquestionably increased very substantially the number of ducks all along the Pacific Coast and bettered the shooting immensely. The system of wild-fowl refuges is another phase of latter-day sportsmanship which is bearing good fruit and which might well be further advanced west of the Rocky Mountains.

I used a sixteen gauge gun in the drive, but I believe the twenty gauges will do better work at the longer ranges. They seem to shoot wickeder, for I certainly saw some sky-scrapers brought down by them. We started at 8 A. M. There was no necessity for the before day setting out of decoys, and the waiting for that first sleepy, red-eyed wink along the eastern horizon. It was a new lesson in duckology, for me, a pitting of craft and marksmanship against duck sense.

The boats moved slowly up the lake after we had stepped in and taken our places, and we ranged up much as a bunch of horses gather for a running race. Ahead of us were several ducks. Pin-tails, or sprigs as they call them here, widgeons, canvas-backs, red-heads, spoon-bills, green and cinnamon teal, blue-bills, and ruddy ducks—locally termed wire-tails, were there, but I did not see any mallards. Groups of ducks, single birds, pairs, flocks, rafts of ducks, bushels, gobs, hundreds and thousands of ducks. It was certainly a great day for the duck tribes.

As the line of boats came stealthily along, certain clusters of the fowl, after swimming rapidly ahead, took wing with the water dripping from their plumage, and flew quite to the farther end of the lake, dropping down into the main body of the ducks at that point. Occasionally daring little bands or a stray pair turned back and ran the gauntlet of the boats, but were not fired at, the time for the opening of the fusillade being reserved until the big droves at the upper end took wing. As the boats narrowed the distance between them and this dense mass of wild-fowl, there was a gradual uprising of pinions, and then a splattering, scurrying shuffle of webbed feet, the sky was full of ducks, and the flight was on. "All ready," shouted the Captain.

Ducks to the right, to the left, and overhead bore down on us. Mostly overhead. Long shots and difficult. They were all coming past in a wild swing for the lower end of the lake. The patter of shots which greeted them was like the popping of fire-crackers in a barrel. Big ducks and little ducks dropped to the water, and hundreds of inoffensive air-pockets were riddled by some of the less expert gunners. I had been cautioned before-hand to "hold ahead a mile," and what with the uncanny clearness of the atmosphere, making a duck seem like he was from twenty to forty yards nearer than he really was, and the hasty motion of the birds, I found the advice invaluable.

My first forty shells brought me in eleven birds, which my companion said was "doing fine." With my next twenty-five shots, fired on the return drive, I got an even dozen, with three ruddy ducks at one shot to help my average. I had begun to hold two or three townships ahead of the fastest flyers and getting better results.

I forget who it was that suggested that the way to get them regularly was to "shoot at them Tuesday evening if you were going out for the Wednesday morning drive," but that, I think, was rather an exaggeration. I can safely recommend yards and yards and yards of "lead" on a green-wing teal going over at seventy yards on the way back to get something it forgot.

Ducks will fly back and submit most cheerfully to be shot at, when by flying away from the lake and circling they could keep entirely out of range. Why do they take these chances? Because they cannot seem to keep entirely away from the shore-line, but hug it when going up and down the lake. At Sweetwater, because of the absence of vegetation and the habit of wounded ducks to seek the land, scarcely a wounded bird is ever lost.

My bag of twenty-three birds included seventeen big ducks and six ruddies. Canvas-back, red-head, widgeon, and pin-tail figured among the larger birds. A few full limits were made, some wonderful shots were made with the twenty gauge guns, and some phenomenal missing by the "tender-feet" was observed.

After the drive was over, the Sweetwater was as quiet as a church. The shores were carefully combed for cripples, and by two o'clock the boats were all hauled up and deserted.

Out on the shining surface of the lake myriads of ducks swam or floated amicably about, possibly exchanging notes on narrow escapes of the morning. The tules stood straight as arrows, dark-green against the adjoining shore. Blackbirds flew past overhead, and water-hens and grebes paddled about close to the lake's edge.

Anyone here during the season can get full information about the drives and how to join them by inquiring at the offices of The Automobile Club of Southern California in San Diego, or by calling at the Chamber of Commerce there, or getting in touch with any of the shooters in the City. To those who have had the shooting along the New England and the Virginian Coasts, over decoys or from batteries, to those who have had the mallard shooting over live wild decoys in the Mississippi Valley ducking grounds, to those who have shot canvasback and red-heads in the Minnesota lake regions, here is a new sensation, and one worth experiencing.

If you are one of that select class who "kill 'em every time," come out and see how easily you can miss 'em sometimes in this elusive ozone that hangs above the California lakes and gives you a chance to take a post-graduate course in duck-shooting.

When the Graywings Come
by T. S. Van Dyke

S.C.

This 1904 article is largely reflections on Van Dyke's long experience
hunting in California dating back to the War Between the States. His
suggestion of using a rifle for geese as being more sporting was
influenced by the sheer number of geese in California in the 1800s. His
mention of early Spanish settlers riding on horseback into flocks and
whipping down birds is almost hard to comprehend today.

Few know that there is still a place in a civilized part of our Union where the wild goose is so plenty as to be deemed a nuisance. Yet such is the case in California, where this fine bird raids the grain fields in winter in such vast throngs that bands of mounted men, riding about and shooting just to scare them, have long been an important feature on many of the great ranches. So great are the numbers and so difficult to reduce with any number of guns that, though everywhere standing high in the esteem of sportsmen, they are treated like the hare and the bear—left without any protection from the law, that is so strict on other game.

Like the bear, the goose knows quite well how to protect itself. The impression that it is a fool arises from comparing it with its tame cousin. No one who has spent a day in the attempt to verify the comparison ever made it again. The wildest creatures in captivity are generally those that, like the quail and grouse family, have little fear of man until he comes within a few yards. But the sandhill crane, the whooping crane, the turkey and the deer family, that have little use for man at any distance, quickly becomes so tame as to eat out of his hand. In the latter class is the goose. But so long as it is wild and free it is the hardest to bag of any bird found in equal numbers, with the exception of the sandhill and whooping cranes. By fair means it is often impossible, while the foulest often fail to amuse those who hunt for the bag alone.

The charm of game is like the charm of beauty—indefinable. If reducible to line and rule it would evaporate. Thousands prefer the little bob-white or woodcock to the superior avoirdupois of the pin-nated grouse, but none can say why, just as it is with thousands who hunt the deer, but would not leave their business a day to bag the larger elk or moose. So no one can say why the silvery honk of the Canada goose sends such a strange thrill through every nerve as it falls from the autumn sky; why the white cloud of the snow goose wakes such queer sensations as it floats across the dark blue vest of chaparral that robes the distant hills; or why the wild, tumbling descent of the white-fronted goose to the surface of the lagoon stirs such tumult in his blood. He can only say that they are game, which is but another way of saying that they are beautiful—which they are in all their aërial movements.

And why should one wish to kill them?

For the strongest of reasons—because their ways of baffling your greatest care are so many that you find you are the fool instead of the goose. The fact that they are not so quick as many other birds is of little aid when the great problem is how to get close enough to make sure of one, even with the rifle.

The common method of shooting geese from a pit in the ground so deep that it is impossible for the birds to see a man, with tamed cripples staked on the greensward around it that retain just enough of their old nature to call their comrades to destruction, is almost indispensable to successful market shooting. So is killing trout with dynamite in places. And the two bear such a painful resemblance that no sportsman cares to hunt in that way more than once. Not much better are the painted decoys with which the stupidest kind of murder may often be committed when a good line of flight lies over rolling hills, aglow with the bright green grass of winter, and with no bushes near by, or anything else behind which a man can hide. The fact that such means should be resorted to, and expensive outfits maintained to keep the decoys and carry them to the field, in a land where geese remind one of the palmy days of the passenger pigeon in the old Western States, indicates that there is something serious about bagging this big wanderer from the North. Such is the fact, and he who would bag even one by fair means must be a master of patience and caution.

For nearly thirty years there has rarely been a time when any amount of snake locomotion would be of much use, for the goose long since lost confidence in rushes, bushes, weeds, fences or rock-piles behind which a man can sneak. In like manner the goose long since learned to suspect that embodiment of innocence, the gentle ox, and can often tell quite well whether an ox has too many legs or when two of them are too large or lack the right shape. The days when the native riders of the old Spanish blood could make a sudden whirl with a swift mustang, and dash down wind into a flock so suddenly that before they could rise against the wind, as is their fashion, the rider could strike one with a whip or reach one with a club thrown into the flock, have long since passed away. The same is true of driving into a flock with a light wagon and a pair of sure-footed mustangs in runaway speed, in time to catch one, or even two, with a shotgun before they could get out of reach after rising against the wind—a wild and exciting sport in which you were almost as liable to get pitched out of the bouncing, careening wagon as to make the coveted double shot.

Though it is many a year since I have tried it, I presume there is little use now-a-days in lying flat on the ground, face downward, with the gun underneath, and not moving even an eyelid, until you can hear the wings just over you. This was once very effective, if you were quick enough in jumping to a shooting position. Lying the same way in a cut or little gully in the ground used to be still better. But neither is reliable now.

Not very much is gained in trying to reach the goose with huge guns or heavy shot. If you cannot in some way lure it within range of an ordinary gun your bag will not be very heavy, no matter what you may use. Nor do you gain much by increasing the size of the shot above that required by the ordinary gun. At one hundred yards or over BB shot will likely be more effective than No. 4 shot, but you are not likely to bag a single goose with either. Nothing has ever surprised the tyro more than the way a heavy charge of buckshot will find its way through a big flock inside of a hundred yards without bringing a feather, or the way you can hear some shot strike—on the wings generally—without making one of the flock even waver. If they cannot be brought within reach of No. 3 or 4 shot there will be little game bagged with the shotgun, and it will be still better if they can be got within reach of No. 6 in a twelve gauge. A light load of shot and an extra heavy one of powder will then do more all-round work than a more murderous-looking arsenal.

One who wants a large bag of geese today will do best by hiring the pit and decoys of the market shooter as well as his attendance. Hardly any sportsman keeps such an outfit, and hence there is scarcely any way of getting a good bag with the shotgun in most parts of the Pacific Coast except at night. This, even by moonlight, is not half as simple as it sounds, but it is far better sport than shooting from the pit with live decoys; and, as it is not forbidden by law, and is less destructive in results, it is quite as respectable. There are places where the geese still fly low enough by day for fair shooting from a common blind without decoys. But they are so rare that it will seldom repay one the trouble to look them up.

The main resource for enduring sport is the rifle, and as far back as 1880, when geese thronged the flowery plains, dotted the smooth waters of the lagoons, and made every quarter of the sky ring with their wild notes, I laid aside the shotgun as too easy, and relied entirely on the rifle.

But not for shooting on the wing. The "champion wing shot with the rifle," who used to challenge the world so often because he could pulverize glass balls at no distance and with no cross motion, would have had a grand surprise in finding that the goose that looked so large and so slow was really farther, smaller, and swifter than he imagined. It is always too far for snap shooting, and before you can catch your sights against the sky and throw them the right distance ahead of the bird, it is sheering in a way that rapidly increases the distance while deranging all calculations about its forward motion. Occasional hits give great satisfaction, but as it takes most of one's wits to get even within shotgun range, good flying shots with the rifle are necessarily rare.

One not used to the rifle begins by firing into the middle of a flock. The way the ball can skip through what seems a solid mass without touching a bird is one of the strange things about shooting. Although one may have had similar experience with the shotgun, he has to try it again with the rifle many a time before he will learn that he must shoot at a single bird. Never did nature furnish more attractive targets in such great numbers and on such a lovely rifle range as on the sunlit green of California's winter. Breeding far beyond where Klamath spreads its leagues of marshy shores beyond the orbit of the white man, the geese streamed down upon the broad plains and rolling slopes of California as soon as the first rains of autumn changed the sad summer hues to smiling green. Before the sheen of maturity crept over the scarlet berries of the heteromeles or the gold of the lucerne began to glow along the hills; before even the burr-clover lifted its green above the brown carpet of last winter's grass, or the fern-like leaves of the alfileria covered the somber red of the sunburned slopes, the "honk" of the Canada goose fell from the darkening sky. So wildly sweet, so penetrating, yet so soft, it drew the eye at once to where in long, majestic lines the wild goose swept along as if earth and sky were his. And it seemed as if they were. The light green shoots of barley and wheat, responding to the first touch of moisture, vanished on many an acre where in long, curling spirals, thousands of geese sailed softly down out of the upper sky. Like some other creatures they appreciated what costs money and labor—of others—and left the rich grasses on which their fathers had fattened to tell the new settler that he was welcome to their land. And few things were more amusing than the frantic endeavors of that same settler to protect his crops and secure a game dinner at the same stroke. It did not need a very large field to give the geese time to secure quite a bite before the granger could get within dangerous distance; and then a mile or so to the other side of the field was nothing to a goose, but considerable to the irate farmer who saw his grain disappearing along with his hopes of dinner. A little of this taught him that the surest way to get bread was to abandon all hope of meat, dash about on horseback, and fire merely to scare the geese. As his fields expanded, so did the geese; more riders became necessary, and so "goose cavalry" became an established branch of the service on some of the great grain farms of California.

In this work the Canada goose was assisted by its little brother—Hutchin's goose—in smaller numbers, and in even larger numbers by its cousins, the white-fronted goose, commonly called gray or black brant, and the snow goose, commonly called white brant, to distinguish him from the white-fronted goose. From the cold and rainy North all these descended in numbers untold upon the sunny slopes of the southern coast. Wherever the valleys or plains were open enough, and where the hills were low and bare of brush, but covered with the silvery green of the springing wild oats, or preparing to unfold a wealth of poppies and violets, all these geese could be seen every day in winter until the soft pink of the purslane began to pale beneath the brighter red of the painted cup and the heavy indigo of the larkspur to overwhelm the tender hues of the blue-eyes. All they needed was room enough to satisfy a love for the wild and free, and even as late as 1885 they had enough. There was no fairer sight than a hundred or more Canada geese standing in solemn gray upon a sunny knoll, with black necks and heads like the tops of so many ten-pins, with white collars gleaming in the sun, and so closely massed it would seem as if a small ball could score at least one. Yet it was easy to see not one such flock but hundreds, with one glance over the greening land. And among them many a patch of white reflected the warm sun where the snow geese, in still larger flocks, were feeding on the rich grass, mingled with many a one of lighter gray where the white-fronted goose associated only with itself. And all this time the clamorous call of more snow geese rang to the sunlit earth with the clangorous cackle of more white-fronted geese and the ever welcome "honk" of the Canada, with flock after flock rising from earth to sky, and as many more descending in all sorts of lines to earth.

About the middle of the morning most of the geese sought the smooth face of some large pond, and the best shooting with the shotgun used to be on the lines of flight they took in going and returning. But this was far out on the land, and near the water was generally the last place to attempt a bag. For the action of geese alighting in water is very different from their action in alighting on land. In all the range of nature I know no more charming sight, yet nothing is more marvelous than the number of people who have never seen it even among those who have hunted a great deal. The Canada goose sometimes alights in water for his morning sunbath in much the same style as he settles downward to the plain; but the snow goose rarely does so, and the white-fronted never within my observation. A long, curling line, as if the birds were descending an invisible flight of winding stairs, with every wing stiffly set and every white-collared throat silent as the grave, generally marks the descent of the Canada. It is rarely less than several hundred feet where the birds come from a distance, and when coming in over table-lands to a lagoon in a valley, is often a thousand feet or more. Often it is in a long, slowly lowering line or wedge, but in all cases it is marked by vast dignity and generally with impressive silence, until bird after bird, with gentle splash, settles into the water, when every throat is hushed.

Coming from afar in a big white cloud, the snow geese before reaching the edge of the pond mass suddenly up in a long column inclined some forty degrees from the vertical. Every black-tipped wing is thrown outward and downward and rigidly set, with the axis of the body about corresponding to the axis of the whole column. Anything like sailing is thus impossible, and the whole descent is a slow settling, or drifting downward, almost as gentle as the fall of a gossamer skein on the still air of Indian summer.

Both these geese may thus enter the pond low, but the white-fronted goose swings over it high in air as if he enjoyed the play. He is reasonably silent about it as he floats a thousand feet or more above the water, where he lines up for the great plunge. Then the edge of the line breaks, and as if struck suddenly rigid by the thunderbolt, yet with every throat tuned to concert pitch in a wild medley, the birds pitch, dive, tumble and gyrate sidewise, upside down, rolling over in air in every imaginable way, a cataract of whirling life, down to within a few feet of the water. There the grand go-as-you-please march suddenly ends, the wild clamor of every throat is stilled, each goose rights itself in a twinkling, drifts into an orderly line, and floats a few yards along the surface of the water, then drops its feet, raises its neck and head, and throwing back its wings slides into the water as gently as the reflection of the fleecy clouds it left above.

Every lover of the rifle knows at once what such conditions imply— plenty of shots that call for the very highest skill. When this can be enjoyed on a landscape that in the East would set the spring poets crazy, yet one over which the sportsman can travel almost anywhere in a buggy or saddle without meeting swamps or any of the ordinary discomforts of wild-fowl shooting, fun with the rifle comes near reaching its climax. But the very charm of the rifle is that plenty of targets does not always mean plenty of game, and never was the contrast so striking as here. You were never farther from the possibility of committing mere stupid murder than you were here when you could see a million geese in a day, and sometimes almost at once. Your shots are all too long to permit of anything but the greatest care in sighting. You have a small dull bull's eye at an unknown distance instead of the bright contrast you have on the target at a measured distance and always in the same light. The four inches that you may have learned to hit so well on the target at one hundred yards become painfully small when the dull gray of the goose on a green ground is used instead of the white against the black of the target. You soon find that open hunting sights, coarse enough for reasonable quickness on flying shots, are not fine enough for the many fine shots you are offered beyond a hundred yards. You need globe and peep sights also, and to know how to use them—or rather how not to use them—for the art of letting long-range sights alone when after game is one of the fine arts of shooting. When shooting at geese in water you may have distances ascertained beforehand by floats in the pond at which you have tested the rifle. Even then you are a long way from a sure thing; for not only is the mark small, but the effect of light on the water in creating aberration seems greater than on land. In shooting on land you can get no sighting shots, for geese never wait for any. Your first guess must be correct. But you can go on for another flock, which may not be very far, whereas, if on the pond, you must await a new arrival, for every shot clears an ordinary lagoon of all the geese.

With the conditions of to-day somewhat changed by increased settlement, such is the shooting on the Pacific Coast. Most people prefer the gun, and if the only object is a bag it is the best, provided you are properly fitted out. But wherever geese are plenty enough for that they are plenty enough for the finest of shooting with the rifle, and in the great Sacramento and San Joaquin valleys one can hardly fail to find fine sport almost any day in winter or early spring, with no one to object to making all the noise one wishes. Better legislation has helped matters too.

Oregon: East and West
by Lee Richardson

Although Richardson lived his adult life in Washington, he was a native Oregonian. He was well known throughout the state, and apparently hunted and fished everywhere, with everyone over several decades. He was a club shooter of the most exclusive type, but his accounts are interesting chapters in Pacific Coast bird hunting history.

There were a lot more wild ducks than people in Oregon at the twentieth century's turn, and a lot more places for them to alight. For early Portlanders who held waterfowling in high esteem it was a bonny time, especially shooting at Sauvie Island.

It was my good fortune to be present at two clubs there on several occasions, though never as a shooter as I was much too young for that. Yet memories persist, as they helped set the pattern for the life that was to follow.

In 1908, Uncle Bill Cole and Heine Metzger leased shooting rights for $150 from a dairyman named Schneider, who agreed to feed and watch the property for an additional $40. Most people worked Saturday mornings those days, so the little steamers *Iralda* and *America* sailed Saturday afternoons, calling at various clubs as far as Deer Island, returning following afternoons.

Arrival at the clubs was in stark contrast to some departures from Portland, where chauffer-driven Pierce Arrows or Pope-Hartfords might be seen dockside. Downriver, at each club, however, a 12x2 timber was placed ashore, making it mandatory for hunters to literally "walk the plank" to club quarters.

Sleeping accommodations could be equally elemental. At Schneider's, Uncle Bill and Heine found primitive woodshed conditions infinitely preferable to the house which, on occasion, was also the abode of poultry and some livestock.

Heine and Uncle Bill would trudge about a mile to their blinds, mostly through mud and water and frequently in rain, after an early breakfast. Often they would be back by ten o'clock with limits of fifty ducks each—mostly mallards, with a sprinkling of sprig, widgeon, teal and gadwall, all shallow water birds as the ponds weren't deep enough to attract divers.

Thirty-five German carp, brought to Oregon from a San Francisco holding pond in May of 1880, had multiplied into a bronze invasion horde by this time, mucking up the shooting ponds to the disenchantment of waterfowlers. When wading to his blind in the pre-dawn darkness, it was not uncommon for the unwary to step on a recumbent twenty-pound carp. The carp's sudden departure usually deposited hunter in the water, to his discomfiture and his companions' amusement.

Once a year, authorities allowed these clubs to kill all they could, with the understanding that all birds would be donated to hospitals, charitable institutions, etc. I remember Uncle Bill reminiscing of one such day:

"Schneider had helped me out to my blind with a case of shells.

272

When they were gone, I picked up 137 birds. I was too tired to chase cripples."

Honeyman Hardware in Portland sold low-base 12-gauge shotgun shells for $11.55 per case of 500, Uncle Bill told me. Smokeless powder was just beginning to replace the traditional black powder which, when fired, cast a pall causing one—on a windless day—to duck or squat to see if anything had fallen through the smoke.

While pump guns and automatics were becoming available, Uncle Bill was among those preferring side-by-side doubles, his being a 12-gauge Parker with Damascus barrels. He also preferred No. 6 soft shot to chilled, and if a bird was beyond 25 or 30 yards would let it go. Later, when the high-base loads became available, he shot nothing but 7½'s on ducks and fours or sixes on geese.

As he and Heine became more prosperous they joined a club of four who needed two more guns beyond the banking brothers named Schmeer, a tire company representative named Carl Cadwell, and another I can't recall. They had a comfortable scow on what then was called Willamette Slough (later changed to Multnomah Channel) with a kitchen on one end, dining area admidships, and bunks at the other end.

Carl was the club's unpredictable comedian. One day he returned, soaking wet, and committed the unforgivable of unloading his gun inside the barge. While his pump had a side button for emptying the magazine, he depressed the trigger and put six quick shots into the deck, close to astonished companions' feet. No one was hurt, but the membership drank more of Carl's "Cyrus Noble" than usual before dinner, went to bed early, and waited until sleep came. They then dragged Carl out and pitched him, bedclothes and all, into the slough.

Sauvies, as it was called when I was a boy, could produce enough material for an outdoor bookshelf, I'm sure. I was lucky to share even just a bit of its specialness.

Though I grew up in the Webfoot State, I was not familiar with vast hunting regions east of the Cascades and south of the Columbia until an attractive gent by the name of Pennell Hixon came into my life. He introduced me to some terrific shooting while I, in turn, directed him to some of my favorite fishing holes.

Penn came from a prominent Minneapolis family with timber holdings in eastern Oregon, a sawmill (Shevlin-Hixon) at Bend, and a chain of retail yards in the Middle West. He was accustomed to the better things in life, including polo ponies, private shooting and fishing clubs, and sports cruisers, to name a few. A loyal client of Abercrombie &

Fitch, Gokey and L. L. Bean, he possessed more outdoor equipment than some sporting goods stores. And though he was familiar with the aristocratic halls of Hotchkiss and Yale, as well as the boulevards of Broadway, he was most proud of a diploma attesting he had graduated with honors from "Oscar Quam's School of Duck-Calling."

Our first hunting trip to southern Oregon in 1938 was a new experience for me, though not to Hixon, who had not neglected rod or gun while apprenticing in the family business in Bend. Our first stop was *the* place to stay at that time before motels, the comfortable old Pilot Butte Inn, with a sweep of lawn down to Oregon's justly famous Deschutes. The great fireplace, deep leather chairs, and ready room service were of that age of quiet luxury and good manners. And though the Inn's dining room was more than acceptable, we chose the Pine Tavern, run by retired schoolteachers, Marne and Eleanor (Bechen), the latter subsequently opening her own House on the Metolius on that noted trout stream.

Next morning, before departure for the Syd Harris ranch, we went shopping, first to Magill's Drug. While the store's genial proprietor, Lloyd, would be joining us for the duck season opening, Penn, a hypochondriac, had to check out the pill inventory, ". . . just in case." Finally, we got out of Bend on the Klamath Falls highway, via Lapine, where Summer Lake road cuts southeast across high desert to Harris' place. The old ranchhouse's windbreak of stately poplars was golden in late autumn sun when we arrived to join hunters from previous years who had already checked into the sleeping cabin across the road.

We split up for assigned hunting sites after the usual ranch breakfast next morning. Lloyd Magill and Peyton Hawes, founder of Payless Drug, departed for the vast sheet of shallow water to the east, Summer Lake. Sandy Paul, Penn and I headed for Kittridge Ranch where a huge spring burst from the alkaline ground and a lake called Duchy was born.

Bunches of ducks and geese were flying everywhere, making traceries against a crimson dawn, skeins of waterfowl hurrying to their rendezvous with another day. The tableau's magnificence transfixed us and it came to me that good fellowship in such a setting is why some men go duck hunting. The rest is just a means to that end.

There was no dearth of ducks that morning and soon we were on our way back to Bend, where a quail hunt had been arranged for late afternoon. Bend would never be a stranger to me again!

Summer Lake was fun while it lasted, but as more and more people heard about it, the primitive aspects that had made it so attractive to me grew fewer as the mob grew larger. Finally, with World War II over and the Williams and Kittridge ranches declared public shooting grounds, we threw in the towel.

Our last shoot there still is too painfully vivid to block out. Besides being the opening of the migratory bird season, Oregon had seen fit to add the pheasant season and also to open deer hunting to both sexes. Cars poured through Picture Rock Pass in a never-ending stream, trailers cluttered roadsides, and tents and red hats blossomed in sagebrush. We stood in line to obtain hunting permits.

As the east began to flame next morning, we crawled under Kittridge's fence and headed for familiar posts in tall sage while headlights still lighted the pass. At 5:30—forty-three minutes before legal shooting time—a shot rang out far down the lake, and within ten minutes cannonading was general.

Dogs barked and men yelled; "Get the s.o.b., Jack, he's comin' your way!" Some birdbrain with a 10-gauge magnum shot at everything from magpies to mud hens on the theory that if he could see it, it must be in range. Gut-shot geese sailed off, stiff-winged, to fall in some inaccessible part of the marsh.

High up on Winter Ridge ("It's winter up here but summer down there." —Fremont, 1843) rifles cracked as bucks and does alike took it in the belly. About nine o'clock a skirmish line bore down on our positions, firing at anything that ran, swam or flew, everything from jackrabbits to killdeer.

"We don't have to put up with this!" Hixon exclaimed. "This place is ruined." And so it was, at least insofar as we were concerned. We never went back.

In the case of G.I. Ranch, the letters had nothing whatsoever to do with U.S. Army, but rather are the cattle brand of a prominent eastern Oregon ranch and timber family, the Gilchrists. And of the time I now write, they also signified a duck hunter's paradise.

A book could also be written about the "Club de G.I." and the people who passed through its portals or slept on its floors during the nine years of its existence. Of the stories that are legion, there is room here for only a few.

The G.I. Duck Club was born in 1941 when Lloyd Magill, the Bend druggist, posed a solution to John Pausch's problem of dealing with vandals on the 27,000 acres where he and his aging mother lived. The lonely place of mostly sagebrush and tumbleweeds had been providing good duck shooting (as distinguished from duck *hunting)* to Lloyd, Penn Hixon and other Bend sportsmen. But the lawless element from town also persisted in shooting locks off gates, breaking down fences, filling the "No Hunting" signs with birdshot, and shooting an occasional cow. As John appeared helpless to deal with that situation, Lloyd suggested he lease hunting rights to a group which would so advertise the arrangement and, if necessary, patrol the property.

Original membership included a Bend faction of Magill, Dutch Stover, Doug Ward, Lloyd Blakeley, Doc Skinner, Sandy Paul and Bob Schueller. The only other Oregonian was Peyton Hawes of Portland. From Seattle there were Penn Hixon and myself, along with Lawrence McLellan, who gave up his spot to Claude Bekins, the storage/van man, after WWII.

During the war, at least, most G.I. members continued to open the season at Summer Lake, with out-of-town gunners storing their first day's bag at Bend Dairy while they filled out possession limits next day at G.I.

My first visit there was on a grand Indian summer day, after dinner at Brothers, so we arrived just as a flock of sandhill cranes circled and landed on prairie near a body of water.

Pausch, a middle-aged man of medium build, and his mother occupied one sandblasted house next to a windmill and a barn that appeared on the verge of falling down. At some point in time, a dike had been built to impound springs, providing irrigation for a hayfield—the sole evidence of progress in a land devoted mostly to jackrabbits, coyotes, pack rats, and some of the biggest greenheads I've ever seen. A few wretched-looking cows bawled their discontent from within a patched-up corral while several untidy sheep chewed their cuds outside.

If ever there was a scene of utter neglect, this was it. But ducks and geese just loved it! And so, incidentally, did I.

Lolly McLellan had driven us down from Seattle on his first and last trip. The Bend boys—Magill, Schueller, Stover, Paul and Ward—were there with guests Jim Gilfillan, Don Williams and Judge Hamilton. Peyton Hawes had arrived from Portland, as had Hixon and his guest, Maj. H. C. Tobin.

This pushed sleeping accommodations in short supply and several of us—Sandy, Lolly and myself—shared the floor of what we shall refer to as the "guest cottage," residence of a pair of owls during daylight and race track for mice during darkness. The odd mouse provided a new sensation, scampering across our features with cold little feet as we lay in sleeping bags.

Back in sagebrush there was an outhouse to which a clothesline had been attached, connecting it with the back door. To a chain with pulley had been attached a "pet" coyote, and when anyone opened the door it was to the accompaniment of rattling chains and the yellow animal rushing off in the darkness. We never did learn who did this, but I suspected ranch hands, playing a practical joke on "them dudes."

We awakened to a frosty morning, the thermometer indicating 10°F, freshened up at the ranch house where there was a pump, a sink and a roller towel, and sat down to rolled oats, mutton chops, bacon, eggs, flapjacks and coffee.

Afterwards, for the benefit of first-timers, Sandy addressed us thusly:

"The hunting area isn't very big, maybe a couple of miles north and south and a half-mile wide. Eight guns minimum are required to keep the birds moving, the nearest resting water being Malheur Refuge, fifty or so miles southeast."

He suggested Penn, familiar with the layout, take Lolly and me to the dike.

"After Lee gets a feeling of the place, maybe he could walk around to South Pond and keep birds from bunching up there," Sandy suggested.

He advised that rotund Major Tobin, since he didn't care to walk far, shoot Stock Pond with Judge Hamilton.

"Lloyd and Peyton will cover Logan Water and the rest of us will jump-shoot the 'crick' from dam down and ford up. And one more thing," he concluded, "Let's figure to be back here by noon, at latest, for Hixon's tail-gate lunch!"

With wooden shell boxes for seats and Penn's bouncy little springer, Gypsy, we three left for the dike. As we passed the barn, a gadwall jumped from the watercress, followed by a jacksnipe. The sun now well up, ducks were trading back and forth between main bodies of water. A honker called melodiously from somewhere out on the prairie and five white swans flew by majestically.

"What a wonderful place!" I reflected, "and still just like it's always been. No blinds, no boats, no decoys, only Hixon and his duck call."

We were back before noon with limits of mallards, big buggers, and also canvasbacks, gadwall, widgeon, sprig and greenwing teal. The sunloving cinnamon teal that nested here were already gone. All hands were ecstatic over the shooting, especially Hixon with a double on speckle-bellies.

To partake of one of "Colonel" Hixon's tail-gate luncheons was to participate in the ultimate. What made this one even more memorable was that the setting was as bleak and ridiculous as the cuisine was extraordinary.

We made ourselves comfortable in camp chairs, and with stimulants from Scotland and Kentucky, while the feast was set and then disposed of. Penn brought out cheese from France, sourdough bread from San Francisco, ice-cold celery hearts and fresh tomatoes, plus the piece de resistance—a five rib roast of beef, rare as only prime beef should be, prepared faultlessly in the ovens of Pine Tavern. Chocolate truffles, frango mints and black coffee concluded a banquet only Hixon with his flair for the exotic, his familiarity with and zest for the uncommon, could have staged.

The magic of the moment moved me to borrow a toast from an absent comrade, Fred Karlen:

"Lift the cup, what memories to repeat. How time is slipping beneath our feet. Dead yesterdays and gone tomorrows. Why fret about them if today be sweet?"

During the war, we "northerners" were lucky to get down to the G.I. once a season; the boys from Bend maybe once a month. But at war's end, some barracks in Redmond that had been used by the Desert Corps were made surplus, and we acquired one. Assisted by several Seabees, we dismantled the structure, hauled it to the ranch and there reassembled it. The result was a "club house" complete with hospitality center, mess hall, kitchen and bunkhouse capable of accommodating twelve in reasonable discomfort, eighteen in a state of gastric distress, for which the only known cure was to become hors de combat before retiring. A few did.

We kept adding amenities. Hixon ordered a duck-boat from Minneapolis, and he and I got a dozen oversize Oscar Quam cork decoys. When Claude Bekins assumed Lolly's membership, we two purchased a duck-boat for our joint use. And during the 1946 off-season, with the assistance of Monte Bass from Seattle, we built blinds at Hixon Pond, North Arm, West Arm, and South Pond.

Finally, in late May of 1948, Penn at his own expense engaged services of Clyde B. Terrill Wildlife Consultants of Oshkosh, Wisconsin, to survey G.I. and recommend a program to attract more ducks. The G.I. naturally had abundant growth of two excellent duck forage plants, roundstem bulrush and sedge. To them were added:

At Baker's Pond and the 30-acre central ponds complex, including Hixon and South Ponds, West and North Arms, and Pot Hole—varying quantities of horned pond plant, sage pond plant tubers, deep water duck potatoes, wild celery, long-leaf pond plant and water weed.

At House Marsh, below the dam—giant burreed roots, horned pond and longleaf pond plants and water weed.

The water in the north, previously referred to as "Logan Water," was enlarged and renamed "Magill Lake."

To celebrate and commemorate the club's coming of age, I ordered a gross of Libbey Safedge tumblers from a division of my company with the names of the founders in color on one side and an exact replica of the 1936 federal duck stamp on the other—three Canada geese coasting in on cupped wings.

Once Bekins became a member, we frequently drove to G.I. together, occasionally with his young son, Wells, and always with a Labrador retriever as Claude once served as president of the Northwest Retriever Club and the national organization as well. Perhaps his most talented and well-mannered Lab was Nipper, a medium-sized bitch with Shed of Arden breeding. This is a happy little story of first-ever experiences for Claude and Nipper:

We were shooting West Arm for geese in late October of 1946, a new venture for Bekins and unsuccessful until almost mid-day when I spotted a long, low line of Canadas heading our way as we stretched our legs. The lead gander detected our dive for cover and, with a loud outcry, the flock veered, eventually settling out of sight on north arm of Hixon Pond.

Chances of Claude sneaking close enough for a shot were slim, we decided, unless I could drive them his way, once he was positioned in lakeshore rushes. When I made my move, sculling around a point of tules, the birds came in view. I headed directly for them upwind and as I neared, their long black necks went up. Then, with a tremendous clamor, the flock—all 46—became airborne.

As I had no idea of Claude's position or where the geese would go out, it was a thrill to see a big bird drop out of the center before any sound reached my ears. Then another went down. Claude had doubled on honkers, his first! When I saw his tall, spare frame rise from tules I waved my hat and received an answering salute.

Later at the boat landing he exclaimed how he had first busted the big leader stone dead and wing-tipped the second. Nipper, who had yet to retrieve anything as big, went for the cripple first, as she had been trained to do, and took an awful beating from the bird's good wing before getting a secure hold.

"I don't think she likes geese any more," Claude laughed.

"You'll never forget this day," I said in offering my congratulations, "but what are you going to do with that big one? It's probably older than John Pausch and just as tough."

Claude wasn't fully convinced until I pointed out knobby old feet and rusty cheek patches, reflected a moment then asked, "What's the matter with having it mounted?"

And that's how it ended. "Rudolph of the G.I.," his ancient feet forever anchored in the Seattle headquarters office of the board chairman of Bekins, commemorating an unforgettable morning at the Club de G.I.

My diary records another especially great morning—December 27, 1947—with Claude and Nipper at the G.I., as follows:

Claude gave the dogs a run in the cold dark, mixed rain and hail falling softly, we breakfasted and, as dawn lighted sagebrush hills of the ancient land, we ran the station wagon down to the dike. Hixon and Major Tobin followed, the latter grouchy after a sleepless night on bunk house boards. Again he had forgotten his air mattress, over-optimistic because 'Penn always has two of everything.'

We launched to cross to South Pond. Ducks were awing and dogs were eager, especially Nipper, balanced on the gunwhale of our deeply laden boat and shivering as she scanned overcast sky. Claude was put ashore with the dogs to make a cattail blind while I set out decoys—a dozen mallards, eight oversize Wildfowler canvasback and, off to one side, three honkers.

Ducks took to the air all over the marsh when shots sounded downlake, and I had just pulled the boat into tall reeds, about twenty yards from Claude, when he warned, "Mark north!" Three canvasbacks, streaking downwind, banked high over West Arm and, even as we watched, screamed down on our location. I stood and, swinging with the inside bird, touched off the right barrel and heard the shot charge rip home. As I went for the leader, out of the corner of my eye I saw the off-bird collapse. Three big cannies fell like stones and landed with an enormous splash.

We grinned at each other across tules as empty casings popped from chambers of our little Model 21's.

Shooting that followed was sporadic but nothing could diminish that moment in another great day at the G.I.

Judge Hamilton added several worthwhile anecdotes to the history of the club during pre-dinner libations, recalling, in one instance, when a member of his party was in hot pursuit of a crippled goose and not watching his step. As result, he sank to his armpits in infamous quagmire associated with South Pond. As he went down, so did his automatic shotgun, discharging as it went under, causing the muzzle to split in several places and peel back like an orange.

The judge's guest eventually extricated himself, cleaned up, changed clothes, and with aid of a hacksaw, removed the damaged part and went on shooting. But ever after he was known as "Rabbi Schultz."

On another day, the judge was shooting the stock pond with Major Tobin, an old soldier to be reckoned with in any relationship. The anecdote was so unusual I made special note of it:

"Suddenly a bunch of canvasbacks appeared over Table Mountain and dove, bulletlike, for the pond, as was their custom," he said. "We were standing maybe twenty paces apart, on goose manure-slick shoreline, and my one shot cut the leader in half at point-blank range. I was too petrified to cry out as the dismembered body hurtled straight for the major's head.

"An arm appeared suddenly," the judge continued, "picked what was left of the 'can' out of the air, like Willie Mays catching a fly ball, and in one fluid motion tossed the remains over the dike. Then the old bastard looked around, tobacco juice streaming down his chin, just as nonchalant if this sort of thing was an everyday occurrence!"

Another story was then forthcoming from Don Williams, a Brooks-Scanlan sawmill employee whose Model 97 Winchester "gas pipe" turned many a G.I. duck upside down and whose handsome yellow Lab, Duke, retrieved them with equal aplomb.

He described placing his father-in-law, basically a non-hunter, on a sure-thing flyway where the few birds moving—mostly singles and doubles—were right over his head, not telephone-pole high. When no shots were fired, Don checked to see if his in-law had suffered a heart attack or gone to sleep. His description of their conversation was too good not to set down in my diary:

"Hey!" Don said, "why the hell ain't you shootin' them ducks?"

"They're goin' too fast," father-in-law answered.

"Well, they ain't goin' to go no slower," Don says.

"Maybe not," was the rejoinder, "but I thought maybe they might start comin' a little thicker."

Came a day all of us feared, but knew in our hearts must happen. At our annual house-warming, John Pausch drew me aside with "Lee, may I speak to you in private?" I followed him out into the desert night, where he came right to the point.

"Mother is getting old, Lee, and so, as a matter of fact am I," he said, "for her sake I'd feel better if we lived closer to town. I've decided to sell the ranch and wanted to give you boys first refusal."

So "we boys" talked it over and decided to pass it up. As I recall, we agreed the price was right, the money was available, and even, aside from the hunting, it probably would have been a good investment.

A logger named Lundgren, who had done well during the war as had most in that line, recognized a good thing when he saw it and snapped it up, and that's how we let the G.I. get away from us.

Though our lease still had a year to run, Lundgren informed Lloyd Magill that, since ducks had no part in his plans for the ranch, he would like to refund us our money and get on with his program—a first-class cattle outfit as he envisioned it. Under the circumstances we had no option but to submit.

Thus passed into history one of my most delightful waterfowling circumstances with unforgettable companions.

Don't Blame the Oldtimer
by Frank B. Wire

Frank Wire was a talented individual. Today he is best remembered as a driving force in the Oregon State Game Commission during the 1930s. He also was noted for making bamboo fly rods. In this article, written in the early 1950s, he stressed the single vital component in wildlife management—habitat. And today we are feeling the painful reality of Wire's warnings.

The area was full of birds that spring of 1896. The big flight was on, and most of us market shooters were making good wages while it lasted. I had orders for all the jack-snipe I could deliver; so I loaded the horse rig with my entire stock of fine shot and headed for the meadow. It was ideal cover for snipe in those days. The water stood a couple of inches deep over a big expanse of short grass and weeds. When I waded out into it that morning, I hit the jack-snipe-pot.

In an hour I was down to my last shell. The birds were still *scaiping* all over the bog; so I drove a couple of miles to the little village of Halsey, Oregon, and bought every No. 8 shot shell in town. Then I went back and kept the barrels smoking until it was too late to see the feathered dodgers any more. When I picked up the last one, my bag for the day stood at 208 birds. Mace and Company of Portland bought the lot for $2.50 a dozen and asked for more.

Now, this wasn't a bad day's work, even fifty-five years ago. Of course, I was lucky because there wasn't another hunter anywhere on the marsh, I had it all to myself–thousands of birds. Most of the professional guns wanted no part of these corkscrew-flying jacks. They always claimed they couldn't make any money on anything smaller than green-heads. Maybe they were right. Water-fowl were my bread and butter too, back in the good old days of no limits and no closed season.

As if it were yesterday, I remember one good day on Columbia Slough. The shooting was so good that I had to keep dipping the barrels of my double in the water to cool them off. Brass shells loaded by hand with generous amounts of black powder generated heat like a blow-torch when you ran them through the scatter-gun as I did on that day.

Long before the first red streak in the east, I'd waded to the little pond which I knew the ducks had been using heavily. The stars were still out and it was nippy as I waded through the waters they had muddied with their dabbling. Ice tinkled under my boot soles, sending flock after flock thundering into the black sky. There were endless thousands roaring up ahead and swishing through the air above me. I knew it would be a real pay-day.

A lot of people would smile at the decoys I packed on my back that morning. They were crudely hacked cedar blocks daubed with black and white paint, but they worked. They brought in mallards and widgeons on set wings faster than I could pull triggers and reload. Mostly I was using the old market gunner's trick of taking three birds with each two-barrel salvo. It piled up game fast. It challenged a man's skill, too, but mainly it saved ammunition. I use it today whenever I get a chance.

You have to get some ducks to work on. You watch them come settling in over the decoys. You hold your fire until they are in short range and you see where two of them are going to cross. At the exact instant, you take this pair with your open barrel, then swing on a third duck with your choke. That's all there is to it. It was routine for us market lads fifty years ago. It would still work if it weren't for the few idiots you find on almost every marsh you hunt nowadays.

I mean the spoil-sports who start puncturing the clouds with bird-shot before the ducks are within range, robbing every every other man within a quarter of a mile of his shooting. In the early days we waited. We let the birds come in close–as they'd come in today if you'd let them. We didn't figure on crippling a half dozen ducks for every one we scratched down, which is about the score of these moronic moon-shooters of the present time. Take a tip from an old-timer: quit the fancy, barrel-stretching stuff. It sends millions of your ducks fluttering down to die a lingering death far beyond retrieving distance. It's a cruel, needless waste of a resource already whittled thin by a lot of adverse factors.

On that long-ago day on Columbia Slough I picked up 106 ducks and sold them for 50 cents a piece–all mallards. I passed up widgeons because they were worth only 35 cents each. Mallards were our meat. This being the case, you'd think it would have been the first species to show a decline. The facts show otherwise. As Exhibit A in my defense of the old-timer I submit that the mallard is now the most abundant species of duck in the country—the same bird that we shot almost to the virtual exclusion of all other kinds. How come? Boiled down for easy swallowing, the fact is that neither we old-time market shooters nor today's crop of gunners can be blamed for what's happened. The birds weren't shot down. They were brought down by circumstances beyond the control of any hunter.

How come, again? For one thing, America doesn't set the table for ducks that it did when I was a stripling. Take that Columbia Slough, for instance. I've had an eye on it for close to sixty years. The first time I saw it, the bordering ponds were almost solid with wapato when the hungry ducks flew down from the north. Dinner was ready and there was enough for all. Take a look at the place now. I can show you one of the ponds that has become a stinking, barren pot-hole filled with rooting carp. There's nothing to feed a duck any more, and there are no ducks. Are the old-timers to blame? Is it the fault of latter-day shooters? The answer is in the negative. The finger of guilt must be pointed elsewhere. I'll tell you where to point it.

The pheasant story is right along the same lines. Oregon, my home-state, had the first open season on ringnecks. We were years ahead of the Dakotas. Neither of those prairie states ever saw the day when it had greater concentrations. It started in 1880 and 1882 when Judge Denny, our American Consul to China, sent over several batches of live pheasants to his estate in Willamette Valley. By 1892 they had mounted to such terrific numbers that a shooting season was declared—six weeks with no bag limit. And yet there was no great rush of hunters. Circumstances didn't allow it. You couldn't drive out along cement highways as you can nowadays. Our roads were slow and muddy. The only way you could get out of town was to hire a horse rig. When the livery stable man rented four or five teams, the barn was empty. Lots of days I didn't see another hunter. All I saw was pheasants.

My two setters would hardly be on the ground a minute when each was frozen on a different bird. I'd walk maybe a hundred feet from my rig, make my shots and carry the long-tailed birds back to the wagon. We had four years of no-limit shooting before the state finally placed a daily bag of twenty on ringnecks. Meanwhile the exotics seemed to spreading and increasing. There were thousands of acres where scarcely a shot was fired at them. They kept on multiplying and reaching into new territory until something else happened. Not disease, but something fully as sinister and far-reaching in its deadly effect.

As more and more settlers moved in, the land naturally became more valuable. Farmers started to utilize it heavier. They began claiming every yard of it. They started burning the old worn fences which zigzagged the country and along which a wide margin of brush furnished ideal protection for pheasants. They began stringing woven wire. They drained the rich, wet bottomlands. They set torch to grass-grown swales. They plowed more and more land. They brought in the big combines for reaping, then began plowing and seeding within a few days. No longer were the stubbles permitted to stand for weeks while the pheasants fattened on the waste grain. Development, they called it. It was taking place in Oregon, and it was happening all over the country. It is still going on. Improved farming methods!

When Old Dobbin did the mowing, a hen pheasant had some chance to get out of the way of the cutting bar. But when mechanized mowers began racing across the hay-fields, they lopped off the heads of brooding hens at a cruel rate.

You can't blame the old-timer for this sort of thing. You hear about some of his big kills, and you maybe jump to the conclusion that he ruined things for you fellows of the present day. Hooey! Let me tell you this: our guns didn't kill one-tenth as much game as the hoe on a farmer's shoulder. It was his land, and he had a right to till it as he wished. Our weakness was in failing to see clearly what was happening right before our eyes. We fell down on our job mainly because we didn't wake up soon enough to prevent a lot of the damage. Because the thing crept upon us quietly and from a source that none of us suspected, we failed to bring the landowner into our planning soon enough. Heaven knows, we had plenty of chances to see what feed and security did for the birds. A striking case thrust itself upon me when a rancher friend asked me to help him shoot the geese off his place before they ate him out of house and home.

For once I wasn't thinking about the pay. Goose hunting didn't bring in near as much money as duck shooting. You got 50 cents for a mallard, and only 25 cents more for a goose weighing two or three times as much. Also, the honkers were harder to shoot. I'd say they were just as crafty sixty years ago as they are today.

On this trip I did all the shooting. The farmer went along just to make sure I didn't lay down on the job. He wanted those geese killed. I carried two gunny-sacks. In one I had thirty-five cardboard profile decoys. In the other was my secret weapon, a female goose that was as eager for the hunt as any dog. When she saw a bunch of wild ones coming, Susie would strut among the decoys, twist one eye to the sky and send out the most seductive honks you ever heard.

After picking up the downed geese, I'd put that old Judas female back in the sack to wait for another flock to show. She would always do her siren act better if you kept her bagged between flocks. When it was time for me to head back to town with my hired horse rig after a few hours of shooting, my share of the bag amounted to an even two dozen. The farmer had about the same.

The stubble where I shot was not hunted again that season. The place would have made a wonderful public shooting ground. But it's too late now. There's a railroad right in the middle of it, and a lot of freight cars near the spot where Susie did her calling.

Feed and cover and water are the magic keys to more game and better hunting. There are no substitutes, regardless of species. Our deer herds furnish the proof. The numbers have held up because our way of developing the country happens to provide them with more to eat and better places to hide. As a result, our deer herds are riding one of the highest crests in all history. Not much credit is due us. We logged the land of its evergreens, and browse came in.

Nobody berates the old-timer for killing off all the deer, because they are as plentiful as man can remember. Yet we market hunters of the early days gave the deer a stiff working-over. In the West it was common practice for us to take a string of pack-horses into the hills and bring them back loaded with jerky. We could haul more meat to town that way because every pound of jerky represented five pounds of fresh venison.

Once in Cow Creek Canyon two other fellows and myself knocked down eight bucks in that many minutes. We could have killed a hundred and still been within our legal rights, because it was several years before the state fixed the bag limit at five bucks. But eight was enough for this one trip. It gave us a load. After boning out the animals, we slashed the flesh into strips, salted them overnight and hung them on racks four feet above a smoldering fire of nonresinous wood like alder, willow and vine maple. Twenty-four hours of sunlight and warm smoke cured the jerky. My share was 80 pounds, and the standard price was 60 cents per pound.

We killed a lot of deer, but, as in the case of other kinds of hunting, we saw very few other hunters in the hills. Not many could spare the time and money to hire horse rigs. It wasn't like today, when everyone has a car to go racing from one spot to another.

You won't find any old-timer who is ashamed of what he took back in the good old days. Conditions were different. Wild game played a big part in the economy of the land then. We shot to live, and we put every pound of game meat to good use. The Indian had lived on it exclusively. We followed in his trail until we learned to grow our own meat. And we did not kill off all the game.

Remember those 208 jack-snipe I killed in a single day back in 1896? There are no snipe there today, none at all. If one happened to land on the spot, it would need a riveting hammer for a bill, because the land has been drained and is nothing but hard-baked clay. The jack-snipe weren't shot out. They were starved out.

Once in a while I drive along the Columbia River and look at some of the spots where the ducks swarmed fifty years ago. A four-lane highway roars with traffic. I pull out of line for a moment when I come to the marsh where I sacked up 106 mallards in that one morning of 1895. The only objects flying over the place today are airplanes. Most of it is covered with cement air-strips. There is a golf course nearby. The only duck that made news around there in recent years is the one that flew into a pilot's propeller and had its mangled body slung back through the windshield. Nobody wants ducks around there any more. They are actually a menace to human life.

All over Oregon, all over the rest of the country the story is pretty much the same. You can't blame the old-timer. The truth is that we have traded away a big chunk of our wildlife for town sites, football stadiums and more farms. We didn't shoot off the birds. We just robbed them of

288

their food caches and set the torch to their homes. Nature did the rest. She trimmed the wildlife to fit. She will provide more game when we set a better table and show her a decent place to house the increase.

Belatedly, but better late than never, most of the states are now working along these lines. They are staffed with competent technicians, and most of the head men are looking ahead. Largely with the help of Pittman-Robertson funds acquired through the special excise tax on ammunition, they are buying and leasing lands and fitting them for wildlife. These places are not inviolate refuges. There is no use in stockpiling game that cannot be utilized. Until something better comes along, the ideal management plan combines hunting and sanctuary. For one month of the year one-half of the unit is opened to public shooting. For the next eleven months it joins the other half as a sheltered area where the table groans with the right kinds of feed.

If enough states keep hammering away at this type of program, acquiring and building up new places for maximum feed and cover, then figure out a national scheme that will persuade the farmer to go along on a similar square deal for game on private lands—making it worth his while to do so—we could all have good hunting for a lot of years. I don't believe it can come any other way. It won't be easy.

But don't get side-tracked into the ridiculous notion that we early-day hunters are responsible for game shortages of today. The birds we killed were nothing as compared to those wiped out by the ax, the match and the shovel. Don't blame the old-timer!